Regency Cheshire

Regency Cheshire

Sue Wilkes

ROBERT HALE · LONDON

First published in Great Britain 2009

ISBN 978-0-7090-8530-0

Robert Hale Limited
Clerkenwell House
Clerkenwell Green
London EC1R 0HT

www.halebooks.com

A catalogue record for this book is available from the British Library

2 4 6 8 10 9 7 5 3 1

Typeset by e-type, Liverpool
Printed in Great Britain by the MPG Books Group, Bodmin and King's Lynn

For Nigel, Elizabeth and Gareth

Contents

Acknowledgements

Many people have helped to make this book a reality. Special thanks are due to Mr George Twigg for his kindly explanations regarding Cheshire open-pan salt-making. The staff of Cheshire Libraries, Cheshire Records Office, Cheshire and Chester Archives and Local Studies Service, and the Stockport Heritage Trust, have been unfailingly polite, patient and helpful with my research. Last, but not least, the biggest thank you of all is for my husband Nigel and children Elizabeth and Gareth, without whose help and support this book could not have been written.

List of Illustrations

1

An Age of Contrasts

The story of Cheshire in the late Georgian period reflects the stirring events then taking place in Britain and on the world stage. It was an era of extreme social tension.

England was in peril from Revolutionary France and its offspring, the seemingly invincible Napoleon. These were the days of Nelson's glorious naval victory at Trafalgar and Wellington's masterly defeat of Bonaparte at Waterloo. News of these great events came to Cheshire by the speedy Royal Mail coaches. The man at the country's helm was the Prince Regent (1762–1830), eldest son of King George III.

The Regency was a necessary consequence of the King's long and distressing illness. This much-loved monarch began his long reign in 1760. Worries surfaced about George III's mental state in the summer of 1788. His Majesty's behaviour became increasingly erratic; by October, it was obvious the King wasn't in a fit state to govern. Court business ground to a halt. The exact nature of the King's illness (now believed to be the hereditary disease porphyria) wasn't understood. Medical treatment was in its infancy; the King suffered greatly at the hands of his doctors.

As the winter progressed, the King's health gave grave cause for concern. On 2 January 1789, the *Chester Chronicle* carried some sombre news: 'We are truly sorry to inform our readers, that the hopes of his Majesty's recovery are now much fainter than ever. His general health is much impaired, and there are all the symptoms of a consumption actually commenced.'

The King's illness created a constitutional crisis which was exacerbated by political tensions. The heir to the throne was George, Prince of Wales, an ardent supporter of Charles James Fox and the Whig party (roughly equivalent to today's Liberal party). The Whigs believed the Prince should automatically become Regent because of the King's incapacity to govern. However, the Tory Prime Minister, William Pitt the Younger (1759–1806), guessed that as soon as the Prince became Regent, he would expel the Tories and put the Whigs in charge. So Pitt promoted the view that only Parliament could decide whether the Prince could be Regent or not. He introduced a Regency Bill which severely restricted the Prince's powers. The *Chronicle* reported the House of Lords' debate on 26 December on whether the: 'most amiable of Princes … nurtured in the principles of our constitution' should undertake 'the exercise of sovereign authority, during the indisposition of the King, and no longer' (2 January 1789).

The Bill became law on 12 February. But to the country's huge relief, and the dismay of the Prince and the Whigs, the King recovered later that month.

The shadow of insanity returned to haunt George III in the spring of 1801 and he became ill again three years later. The death in 1810 of his favourite daughter, Princess Amelia, greatly distressed the King. He lapsed into madness, and never recovered. Physical illness took another toll; the King gradually became blind and deaf. But he never lost the affection of his subjects, who felt immense sympathy for their monarch.

The Prince of Wales became Regent on 6 February 1811, when he took the oaths of office before the Privy Council. To everyone's surprise (and the Whigs' unmitigated disgust), the Regent decided to continue with a Tory government. He was now ruler of a great nation. It was a nation menaced by Bonaparte, the conqueror of Europe. And it was a nation with a yawning chasm between rich and poor.

At the top end of the social scale was the *beau monde* or *ton*. The Prince Regent was the head of the fashionable world. He cut a leading figure, not just because of his royal birth but also because of his increasing girth with age. The phrase 'conspicuous consumption' could have been invented for him. At one of his levées at Carlton House during his first year as Regent, the centrepiece of the 200-foot long supper table was a wandering stream filled with live fish. A feast created by the famous chef Carême, which was served to the Prince's guests at Brighton Pavilion in 1817, had over 100 different dishes on the menu. French food, fashions and furniture were all the rage during the Regency, in spite of the long war with France.

The Regent had a taste for homely Cheshire fare as well as French cuisine. Molly Coppock of Knutsford was famous for her tasty black puddings and the Prince enjoyed them so much, he ordered some to be sent down to London.

'Prinney', as one of his more waspish chroniclers dubbed the Prince Regent, lavished vast sums on his residences, mistresses, clothes, jewels and art. His extravagance alienated him from his subjects. He lived a life of idleness and dissipation. It must be said in the Prince's defence that he'd begged the King to let him serve his country in a military capacity like his brothers. But the King was adamant; the heir to the throne could not be risked. The Prince was made a colonel in the 10th Light Dragoons and wore its uniform proudly, but to his great chagrin he was barred from military action.

This was the age of the dandies, with their white starched cravats with high collars, and sombre black dress coats. Their leader was fashion dictator Beau Brummell. Brummell stood high in the Prince's graces until shortly after he became Regent, when the dandy famously commented loudly on the Prince's corpulence. Dandies like Brummell lost and won fortunes at the gentlemen's clubs like Watier's and White's. The most exclusive venue for ladies of high fashion was Almack's; even the Duke of Wellington had to obey its patronesses' strict rules on dress. Regency bucks who wanted a less refined night out frequented the equally glittering but disreputable world of the *demi-monde*, with its saucy courtesans such as Harriette Wilson and her sisters.

The Prince Regent was a great patron of the arts and literature. He filled his mansions with a vast collection of paintings and sculpture by the great masters. He also presided over a glittering explosion of home-grown literary talent: Jane Austen, Scott, Byron, Keats, Shelley, Coleridge and Wordsworth. The Romantic poets were the vanguard of new ways of thinking; the old certainties were being undermined.

There was a dark backdrop to this flowering of culture. Violence permeated every layer of society. The statute book was savage beyond expression. It was littered with capital crimes; children under the age of ten were hanged for petty theft. The game laws were harsh: poor men faced death or transportation for poaching a pheasant to feed their families. The 'quality', even MPs, fought duels (despite their illegality) over real or imagined slights to their honour. Ordinary folk emulated their 'betters' by brawling with fists, sticks or clubs at the drop of a hat, often with a wager on the outcome, and prize-fighting was a popular sport; it was the fashion for gentlemen to take their gently bred and elegantly dressed young lady friends to watch a 'mill'.

Gambling was socially acceptable at all levels of society and there was a national lottery. The *Macclesfield Courier* for 22 June 1822 advertised a lottery with £30,000 and £20,000 prizes, but the tickets, priced at £1 18s each, were way beyond the reach of ordinary families.

In Cheshire, the city of Chester, 'a great town inhabited by opulent families', took centre stage in everyday life.[1] The County Palatine institutions were still in place; Chester had its own Exchequer and Court of Sessions (a busy social occasion for fashionable families.) The county was proud of its links with the capital; the cream of its gentry was well known in exalted circles. George Cholmondeley, 1st Marquess of Cholmondeley, was Chamberlain of Cheshire and Lord Steward of the Prince's Household. The Prince Regent gave the bride away when the Marquess's daughter, Lady Charlotte, married Lt. Col. Hugh Seymour in 1818.

The social life of the upper classes was largely dictated by the London season. Members of Parliament and peers such as Earl Grosvenor of Eaton Hall (near Chester) were needed to take their seat in the House of Commons and House of Lords respectively. (Before and after the Reform Bill, MPs' seats were normally filled by noblemen and their sons, relations or friends.) Earls Grosvenor, Macclesfield and Cholmondeley often attended the Regent's levées or receptions for honoured guests.

When Parliament began sitting in January, Cheshire families like the Grosvenors and Cholmondeleys drifted back to their London houses ready for the beginning of the main London season in the spring. Keen fox-hunters delayed their return to the capital until the beginning of April, when sport had finished. Then a grand round of entertainments began: balls at Almack's, assemblies, parties and masquerades, and the wonders of the gardens at Vauxhall.

London became unbearably hot during the summer months, so in

June the *beau monde* retreated to their country seats, or visited friends around the country, while Parliament took its summer break. The 'little season' in September heralded a return to London, before the opening of the fox-hunting season a few weeks later sent aristocrats and gentry scurrying back to their country houses. The Grosvenors and their political opponents the Egertons at Oulton also rushed home in the run-up to vital city and county elections. Corruption was rife in politics at county and national level and elections were notorious for bribery on a massive scale.

Society was in turmoil. The French Revolution sparked a huge debate on the existing order in Britain; the very nature of society was questioned. One hugely influential voice was Thomas Paine, whose *Rights of Man* (1791) was a best-seller. Paine supported the ideals of the French Revolution; he argued for the abolition of rule by hereditary monarchy. Paine wanted universal male suffrage, and proposed a welfare state, among many other ideas. The *Rights of Man* was political dynamite; Paine's works were classed as seditious writings, and banned.

The spirit of reform took root. Radical societies sprang up in industrial towns such as Manchester and Stockport. Cheshire historian George Ormerod had no sympathy with the reformers, or the 'emissaries of treason' as he melodramatically labelled them. He claimed that 'seditious assemblies' took place under cover of darkness; private houses were broken into and weapons stolen.

But at Chester, which had a much smaller manufacturing population, chronicler Joseph Hemingway 'was not aware of a single inhabitant who was drawn into the vortex of disaffection'.

The conservatives launched a counterattack against the Radicals and their ideals. An effigy of Thomas Paine was set ablaze in Stockport marketplace in 1792; another was burnt at the Cross in Chester the following year.

The outbreak of war against Revolutionary France in 1793, and the horrors of the Terror, caused a change of heart among many Englishmen who had previously supported the Revolution. One long-lasting consequence was that any kicks against authority were regarded as the precursor to a bloody insurrection here. Reform became synonymous with Revolution. The authorities lost their heads over the prospect of the importation of the guillotine.

As well as facing a Continental war, Britain had its hands full with a bitter uprising at home. Catholic Irishmen were struggling for freedom and Cheshire men were among those sent to keep the peace. Sir Watkin Williams Wynn's cavalry regiment of Ancient Britons included many Chester lads. The regiment was first raised in 1794; it served in Ireland for over a year.

To pay for the ever-mounting costs of the French wars and the Irish rebellion, the country was asked to make a voluntary subscription of money as well as men. Chester raised the huge sum of £6214 12s 3d, and Congleton patriotically presented a gift of £100 to George III 'to enable him to carry on the war against the French Republic'.[2]

At the other end of the social scale, the working classes were feeling the pinch. The people groaned under the burden of taxes: paper, soap, tea and sugar were just a few of the everyday items taxed to help pay for the war. A new tax on dogs, introduced in April 1796, led to many humorous skits in the newspapers at the Prime Minister's expense. In December 1798 Pitt introduced a tax on incomes for the first time – a measure described as 'indiscriminate rapine' by one politician.[3]

While the Prince of Wales and his guests feasted on huge banquets and enjoyed all the delights of the London season, angry workers in north-west England took to the streets. Rocketing food prices led to explosive results in Cheshire: there were food riots in Stockport in 1795 and 1799. During 1800, wheat in Chester market reached an alarming 25s per bushel. The rise and fall in bread prices was a good barometer for civil unrest and the distress of 1812 led to an upsurge of Luddite activity.

Meanwhile, across the Channel, an ambitious young officer was making a name for himself. Napoleon Bonaparte (1769–1821) first achieved prominence at the siege of Toulon in 1793, when he forced the Allies to flee. This was just the beginning of an amazing military career which brought him fame and shocked the world. By the end of 1796 Napoleon had defeated three great Austrian armies and most of Italy lay at his feet.

As war raged on land and sea, these were worrying times for Cheshire families with loved ones facing the enemy. The progress of the war was reported in rival newspapers the *Chester Chronicle* and *Chester Courant*. The papers were anxiously scanned for news of the regiments and ships in which husbands, sons, fathers and brothers were serving.

The county shared England's pride in the thrilling victories of the day. Chester was brilliantly illuminated to mark Nelson's 'glorious action' of the Nile (*Courant*, 9 October 1798). The nation rejoiced again at news of the Peace of Amiens in October 1801. Celebrations were held at Stockport and Chester and a royal salute was fired from Chester Castle. The treaty was ratified in 1802, but peace was short-lived: hostilities were renewed the following year.

A Cheshire officer, George Wilbraham (1779–1852), met Bonaparte during the Peace, when Napoleon was First Consul of France. Wilbraham was a lieutenant in the King's Own Regiment; his father George owned Delamere Lodge at Cuddington. The young man was later imprisoned as a POW at Verdun and in Paris, returning home in 1806.

Nelson's epic victory at Trafalgar in 1805 meant Chester was beautifully lit up again. The castle artillery fired a royal salute and the volunteers fired joyful volleys of gunfire from around the city walls. It's said that, at Stockport, the church bells of St Mary's rang so long and enthusiastically that the church tower was permanently damaged.

The Treaty of Paris in the summer of 1814 brought hopes of a permanent peace. Napoleon was exiled to the island of Elba and the Congress of Vienna began to redraw the map of Europe. The people of Cheshire, believing war was over at last, paid tribute to its soldiers. Chester celebrated in style; the cathedral's bells rang out for the first time in sixty years. On 15 August 1814, Sir Stapleton Cotton (Lord Combermere) and another war hero, Lord Rowland Hill (of Hawkestone, Shropshire), were given the freedom of the city. Lord Combermere had distinguished himself in the Peninsular campaigns. The generals were carried through Chester in a decorated triumphal car pulled by four white horses; their drivers wore scarlet livery. The mayor and corporation, gorgeously clad in ceremonial robes, and bearing the sword and mace of the city, met the generals at the Bridge-gate. After being conducted to the ceremony at the Exchange through files of the 22nd Regiment, the brave soldiers were treated to a grand dinner at the Royal Hotel: 'for their noble exploits under the immortal Wellington'.

But peace was snatched away again in February 1815 with Napoleon's dramatic escape from Elba. His defeat by Wellington at Waterloo on 18 June 1815 finally brought an end to over two decades of almost continuous war. News of Wellington's historic victory reached

Chester at midnight on Tuesday 20 June. The horses, guard and coachman of the mail-coach which brought the longed-for tidings were festooned with ribbons and flags fluttered from the coach windows. Cheering crowds gathered around the post office. The news came too late for the *Courant*, which was published on Tuesdays. So the *Chronicle* was first with the scoop: 'FINAL DESTRUCTION OF THE FRENCH ARMY!' by the 'immortal Wellington' (23 June).

Napoleon was banished to the island of St Helena, where he remained until his death six years later. A military man with family links to Cheshire witnessed the end of Bonaparte's career. Major-General Sir Henry Edward Bunbury personally broke the news to Napoleon of his exile. (Although Bunbury didn't live in Cheshire, he owned the parish of Stoke on the Wirral; two of his ancestors lived in Stanney, and represented Chester as MPs.)

Waterloo had a massive human cost: over 11,600 British and Hanoverian troops died in this battle alone. Relief funds were set up to aid the widows and orphans of British soldiers killed at Waterloo and Macclesfield's townsfolk raised over £540. The battle was commemorated in an unusual fashion at Bollington by the construction of an ornamental tower, White Nancy, in about 1820.

Cheshire welcomed the hero of Waterloo, the Duke of Wellington himself, when he visited in December 1820. He'd come to stay with Lord Combermere, whose second son was being christened; the little boy was named after the illustrious commander. After his furlough at Combermere Abbey, Wellington was invited to a grand public dinner at the Exchange. The Duke then moved his billet to the Albion Hotel. He toured the castle and inspected the armoury before tucking into a sumptuous banquet with 150 guests, including Lord Combermere and other Cheshire notables.

Wellington went on to visit Nantwich, where the citizens did him proud. The Duke's carriage was mobbed by gentlemen desperate to shake his hand. The Crown Inn was: 'brilliantly illuminated with the word "Waterloo" formed with variegated lamps'. A triumphal arch of laurel wreaths was decorated with 'WELLINGTON' spelled out in lights; the Duke was said to be 'highly gratified'.[4]

The Napoleonic Wars had a huge impact on trade. The loss of foreign markets directly affected Cheshire textile workers. The silk towns of Macclesfield and Congleton in particular benefited from the lack of foreign competition: 'The superiority of the British Navy shut up our opponents in their own ports, and we commanded the commerce of the world at the cannon's mouth.'[5] But Napoleon's defeat and the ensuing peace brought new problems: unemployment, a trade slump, and dearer food. The gulf between the privileged world of the elite and the labouring poor yawned ever deeper.

The Corn Laws (first introduced in 1815), which had the effect of keeping the price of bread artificially high, were greatly resented by the lower classes. Poverty, hunger and unemployment proved efficient recruiting sergeants for reformers, as workers grew tired of waiting for the establishment to change its ways.

Duellist and Waterloo veteran Captain Gronow commented in his memoirs:

> When I call to mind the dangerous state of the country at that time, the very bad feeling of the people towards the upper classes, the want of employment in the manufacturing districts, and the great misery all over England from the high price of bread – when I recollect, at the same time, the total absence of any sort of police, and the small military force we possessed, I am astonished that some fatal catastrophe did not occur in the years immediately following the war.

Although Cheshire folk maintained a sturdy independence of opinion from the government line, this independence was underpinned by a strong backbone of patriotism. Despite the Prince Regent's unpopularity, there was great alarm in January 1817. After the opening of Parliament, the windows of the state carriage (in which the Prince Regent was travelling) were smashed by a flying missile. The citizens of Macclesfield sent a 'Loyal Address' to the Prince Regent in February after the 'late base and treasonable' attempt on his life. This address followed hard on the heels of two petitions against the Corn Laws from Macclesfield.[6]

The ruling classes felt under siege and civil liberties were sharply curtailed after the attack. The Habeus Corpus Act (which meant people couldn't be imprisoned without a trial) was briefly suspended, restored, then suspended again later that year. The Act wasn't reinstated until February 1818. Chester townsfolk expressed their dismay at the suspension of Habeus Corpus; there were petitions (and some counter-petitions) against the new legislation.

The 'spirit of insubordination' exploded into action in the north-west while the pages of Ormerod's monumental history of Cheshire were going to press. The Blanketeers' march in 1817 was swiftly mopped up by the authorities, even though it was intended to be a peaceful demonstration. In a backlash against the Radicals, nearly 150 patriotic gentlemen formed a King and Constitution Club in Chester later that year.

The government was determined to keep order, whatever the cost. The carnage of the French Revolution, like the spectre at the feast, was always at the back of the authorities' minds. They feared for their homes and lives. These fears were fuelled by incidents such as a mysterious fire, possibly started by arsonists, at Tabley House in the summer of 1819. Tabley's owner, Sir John Fleming Leicester, was Colonel of the Cheshire Yeomanry. The Cheshire Yeomanry and other volunteer regiments were in the front line whenever conflict broke out between the authorities and the working classes. Because of the fire, Sir John was unable to lead his men when they were sent to police a Radical meeting in Manchester on 16 August. The authorities' heavy-handed crackdown on this meeting became notorious as the Peterloo 'massacre'.

Newspaper coverage was largely unsympathetic to radical ideas and meetings. One widespread but patronising viewpoint expressed at the time was that workers were easily led. They were being duped by reformers to take part in strikes and demonstrations, when they should be at work providing for their families. A poster, headed 'EQUALITY!' printed in Knutsford at the time of Peterloo, read: 'Let every honest man, who has been misled by the itinerant orators and their vile publications, return to his duty and his home ...'

The working classes suffered greatly in the aftermath of the banking crisis during the winter of 1825. The failure of many country banks led to the widespread collapse of dozens of firms. One historian claimed the country's credit was only saved by the accidental discovery in the Bank of England of an unused box containing 700,000 pound notes, which had been put away and forgotten.

The cause of Catholic Emancipation was another political flashpoint. A strong undercurrent of anti-Irish and anti-Catholic feeling lurked in northwest England. The Irish rebellion (at a time when England was at war with France) was one reason; another was Irish immigration. There was an influx of workers desperate for employment and willing to undercut local wage rates.

George III's illness was exacerbated by anxiety over the cause of Catholic emancipation; he believed reform would conflict with his coronation oath. The King resolutely opposed Pitt on this issue and Pitt was forced to resign in 1801. But the issue continued to provoke debate. Distrust of Catholicism or 'Popery' was stoked up by the Anglican and Nonconformist churches. Anti-Catholic meetings were held in Cheshire, including one at Chester in April 1825. Two fine cheeses were presented to the Duke of York and the Bishop of Chester in June this year by some 'No Popery' Chester citizens to mark their approbation of these peers' opposition to Catholic reform. (The Duke of York's cheese weighed 132 lb.) In January 1829, another anti-Catholic meeting was chaired by Sir Harry Mainwaring in the George Inn at Knutsford.

Petitions from Cheshire against the reforms were presented to Parliament. John David Barry, the editor of the *Chester Courant*, was forced out of his job by the proprietor Mrs Monk in this year because of his liberal views on Emancipation.

The Duke of Wellington, well known for his opposition to reform in general, was deeply worried by the prospect of civil war. He pushed through the Catholic Emancipation Bill despite vitriolic opposition in Parliament, and George IV's qualms. One staunchly Protestant innkeeper in Knutsford was so incensed by the Bill's passage that he relegated the portrait of the Duke of Wellington, formerly hanging in pride of place as an inn-sign, to adorn a nearby pigsty. The head of Lord Eldon, one of the Bill's chief opponents, was given pride of place instead. The Catholic Emancipation Act finally received royal assent in April 1829.

Loyal Cheshire citizens took a keen interest in the Royal family. A full length portrait of George III, donated by Earl Grosvenor, hung in the Exchange at Chester, along with pictures of famous county men. The Prince of Wales was Earl of Chester, so his escapades in London and

Brighton were keenly followed in the newspapers. They provided much food for gossip in coffee-houses and inns.

During the autumn of 1806, the Prince of Wales stayed at Congleton. The Corporation and townsfolk presented him with a loyal address. The Prince's reply expressed his gratitude, and assured his subjects: 'the dearest wish of my heart, must and ever shall be, to promote the welfare and happiness of these kingdoms'.[7]

When George III celebrated his Jubilee in October 1809, everyone seized the opportunity to show their affection for their ailing monarch. An ox was roasted at Chester and there was a grand procession to the cathedral. At Macclesfield, church bells rang, flags flew, and a public dinner was held for over 1200 people. At Knutsford, according to custom, the streets were cleaned and decorated with beautiful patterns of coloured sand. The cavalry ('a fine troop') and infantry of the Knutsford Legion marched behind the Sunday school children to the church, where they listened to an 'excellent sermon' followed by 'God Save the King'. After the service, the Legion was reviewed by its commander, Lt. Col. Sir John Fleming Leicester. A feast at local inns was followed by a 'grand display of fireworks' and bonfire on the Heath. The evening was rounded off with: 'an elegant and well attended ball at the George Inn. A liberal subscription was made for the poorer inhabitants. To each man, woman and child, two pounds of prime beef were given, with a proportion of good ale.'[8]

Foreign noblemen and dignitaries visited the county. Prince William of Orange ('Slender Billy'), who had served with Wellington, came to Chester in August 1810. The Grand Duke Nicholas of Russia and General Kutusov explored the city during their northern tour of England in 1817. The Duke caused consternation at the Royal Hotel by asking for clean straw instead of the comfortable bed provided for him; he told the bemused manageress he was just an ordinary soldier, and preferred his usual billet. During his stay at Chester he visited the Shire Hall and Armoury, and enjoyed the obligatory walk around the medieval walls.

In November 1817 the death of Princess Charlotte, the Prince Regent's only child, caused huge national grief. The princess was greatly loved. Cheshire farmer James Higginson wrote sadly in his diary on 19 November: 'Princess Charlotte Interde at Winsor, a very Deplorable Day.' Many ordinary people dressed in deep mourning.

Princess Charlotte's husband, Prince Leopold of Saxe-Coburg, visited Earl Grosvenor at Eaton Hall in October 1819.

Princess Charlotte's death was followed by that of her grandmother Queen Charlotte twelve months later. The *Courant* reported her Majesty: '... expired with all the tranquillity of one who resigns herself to gentle slumber' (24 November 1818). The great bell of the cathedral and other church bells were tolled; many shops had half-day closing. The theatre, too, was closed.

Similar marks of respect were paid when George III died on 30 January 1820. The Cheshire papers announced the King's death with great sorrow. 'Farmer' George had occupied the throne for six decades. His popularity was undiminished, in spite of foreign policy mistakes, such as the loss of the American colonies. The *Chester Guardian* lamented the demise of such a 'respectable monarch,' and opined: '... the voice of posterity will unanimously pronounce George III to have been one of the most moral, honest, and upright of men'.[9]

The Prince Regent could mount the throne at last. But George IV faced a mountain to climb in terms of public relations. George III's well-known love of home and family life formed a stark contrast to his spendthrift son. The Prince had rebelled against an overly strict upbringing by leading a life of reckless boozing, gambling and womanising. Even though relations between father and son had been famously strained, the new King knew he had a tough act to follow. He said: 'I have the consolation of knowing that the severe calamity with which his Majesty has been afflicted for so many years, has never effaced from the minds of his subjects the impressions created by his many virtues ...' He promised his subjects: 'It will ever be my most anxious endeavour to promote their prosperity and happiness, and to maintain unimpaired the religion, laws and liberties of the kingdom.'[10]

The new monarch was held almost in contempt by his people. Nevertheless, Cheshire folk felt it their duty to mark his accession. There was much merriment at Malpas in February for the Proclamation of George IV. A procession of worthy citizens, accompanied by a band playing 'God Save the King', paraded through the town. The people cheered, helped by three hogsheads of beer to give a party atmosphere. The following month, the gentlemen of Northwich sent an address of condolence to the new King on his father's death, along with congratulations on his accession to the throne.

The coronation was postponed until 1821 because of the sensational trial of the new King's wife, Queen Caroline. This year witnessed the death of England's arch-enemy, Napoleon, on 5 May. As Bonaparte's star was finally extinguished, another was ascending. George IV was crowned King on 19 July 1821. The coronation at Westminster Abbey was one of unparalleled splendour. At Chester, the special occasion was marked with three triumphal arches erected at the ends of Bridge St, Northgate St and Eastgate St. A grand procession through the main streets, of the corporation and clergy, schoolchildren, clubs, the Royal Mail and other coaches, the military, and bands of music, gave the citizens a day to remember. Divine service was celebrated at the cathedral; the King and Constitution Club held a grand dinner at the Albion Hotel.

George IV embodied the contradictions of his time. A man of immense personal charm, he was capable of exhibiting a mean streak. As Regent and King, he set the tone for the spirit of the age, with all its sentiment, splendours and scandals.

It is time to begin our stage-coach journey through Regency Cheshire. Our travelling companions come from all levels of society: from elegant lords and ladies to pickpockets and murderers. We'll witness scenes of riots and reform; balls and bear-baiting; highwaymen and hangings – and hear the latest gossip along the way.

In this book I've followed the practice of previous authors, such as Venetia Murray[11] in using the term 'Regency' to cover the period from the year of the first Regency crisis in 1788 to the death of George IV in 1830. Like the Prince Regent, however, who let loose his stays when they felt too tight, I've expanded the timeline slightly where necessary in order to explain the historical background, explore future developments, or include tit-bits too juicy to ignore.

2

Changing Times

Although Cheshire was renowned for its rural landscape, industry had already made its mark. The cotton industry was a major employer and other manufactured goods included leather, ribbon, thread, gloves, buttons and shoes.

Water power was still used in corn mills like those on the Dee, and at some textile mills. But steam engines, those iron heralds of industrialism, were busily employed in salt-works and silk and cotton factories. George and Samuel Walker's corn mill at Chester was powered by a Boulton and Watt steam engine erected early in 1785. Samuel Oldknow was the first Cheshire cotton manufacturer to use a steam engine; it was installed in his Stockport mill early in 1791.

Chester's manufactories included a paper mill, rope-walks, tobacco and snuff factories; clay pipes were made in Love Lane. The city also had flourishing book and printing trades. But many of its manufacturing industries were disappearing fast. Traditional crafts such as clock-making and tanning had suffered. Glove-making had lost its former importance, and was hanging on by its fingernails. Most of the trade had moved to Worcester.

The few new industries which sprang up, such as cotton spinning, failed to gain a foothold. The Steam Mill in Boughton, built towards the end of the eighteenth century, was taken over by a corn miller in 1819. One probable reason why entrepreneurs didn't rush to establish new factories was Chester's lack of coalfields of its own. (There were some coal deposits on the county's eastern side, but salt was a far more important natural resource.)

The Chester and Nantwich Canal brought some heavy industry to the city. There were several iron foundries; one was near the House of Industry. Cole, Whittle & Co.'s foundry at Flookersbrook (1803) bucked the downwards economic trend and went on to become a success. One unusual addition to the Chester skyline was the 150ft high lead shot tower, built in 1801 when Walkers, Maltby & Co. established a lead-works by the Chester canal. The site also housed a large red and white lead factory and rolling mill, powered by steam.

Industry brought hazards as well as employment. Five men died in a very nasty industrial accident in Chester in June 1822. Mr Boult, a tobacco manufacturer in Cuppin St, was trialling a new high-pressure steam engine. The engine appeared to work well at first. But when the men attempted to run the engine again, the safety valve overloaded. A terrific explosion left the factory in ruins. The windows of nearby houses were broken, and the roof of a building fifty yards away was set on fire by smouldering lumps of fuel. Boult and four of his workmen were caught in the blast; all died from their injuries. Two of the men killed, Thomas and James Owen, were brothers.

Fire was an ever-present danger. There was a terrific blaze at the lead works in January 1821 and the Dee mills burnt down three times in succession. The coach manufactory on Foregate St belonging to Messrs Parry & Truss was razed to the ground down so often, the citizens must have set their watches by it.

The corporation maintained the city's fire engines, housed near the Exchange. The fire crews were organised in teams of six, each with a captain. A major fire in Bowers' oil warehouse in 1828 narrowly avoided burning down Northgate St and many properties nearby. The fire engines proved unreliable on this occasion; they almost ran out of water. Shopkeepers and local residents, young and old, fled for their lives. The blaze was finally extinguished, but the alarmed citizens demanded improvements to the fire-fighting facilities. The number of firemen was increased, and regular inspections of the fire engines ordered.

The long-established ship-building trade was another cause for pride: Chester-built vessels were reputed to be first class. Mulvey's shipyard built Mersey flats, and vessels of up to 500 tons: 'as complete and durable as those built in any other port of the kingdom; the materials are entirely of British oak'.[1] But Chester's port, like many of its industries, was fighting for its life. Until the end of the eighteenth century, Chester was 'superior' to Liverpool as a port, enjoying the lion's share of the Irish linen trade.[2] Large quantities of Irish linen were imported, as well as wood, hides, tallow, feathers, butter and other provisions. There was a small amount of foreign trade: mostly Portuguese wine, but also animal skins from Leghorn, fruit, oil and barilla (for soap-making) from Spain and Portugal, and timber and hemp from the Baltic. Vast quantities of cheese were sent to London, and groceries imported in return. Other exports included coal, lead, calamine, cast iron, and copper plates.

The prime cause of Chester's demise as a port was the navigation of the River Dee estuary, which had long been problematic. Constantly moving sands meant the channel shifted with wind and tide. Despite some attempts to improve navigation, including an artificial river channel from Chester to Flint in the 1730s, the city's commercial lifeline slowly stifled. Ships faced: 'difficulty and delay in navigating the river, which is nearly choked up with sand'. Another problem was 'the increasing commercial town of Liverpool, whose great consumption and intercourse offers a ready market to traders'.[3] Liverpool's transatlantic traffic, and better canal links, meant Chester's maritime trade sank without trace.

The city's role in the county was also changing. Chester lost its pre-eminence as the largest town early in the 1800s, even though its population was still growing. The population picture is a complex one. Towards the end of the eighteenth century, the town's population growth was slower than the national average. It seems people were moving away from Chester. Early in the nineteenth century, Chester's population only grew by approximately 1,000 people: from 15,100 in 1801 to 16,140 in 1811. However, there was a sudden sharp population increase over the following decade: by 1821 it was 19,940. This may have been because poor farm labourers came looking for work in the city. They had been hit by a double blow of land enclosures and high food prices during the Napoleonic wars. But their landlords (the farmers) were making a profit because of the same factors and they had more money to spend in Chester. Good times for the shops and associated industries in turn attracted more shopkeepers and traders, boosting the population. However, Chester's population growth slowed again after the early 1820s, perhaps because of the general trade depression.

As some of the county's old industries faded away, new industries took their place. The textile industries, which forced the pace of population change in Cheshire and neighbouring Lancashire, will be discussed in detail later. The success of cotton manufacture in Stockport meant it overtook Chester to become the largest town.

Stockport's spectacular growth was already apparent when John Byng visited in 1790: 'Astonishing is the increase of buildings about this town, and they go on most rapidly (Stockport contain'd, about ten years since, about 700 houses; now they exceed 2,000, which are insufficient to hold the inhabitants.)' The population figures leapfrogged from 14,830 (1801) to 17,545 (1811), reaching 21,726 ten years later. Cotton was the biggest employer and there was also fustian weaving, and a hat-making industry.

Macclesfield, too, was growing apace. The township's population doubled in the first two decades of the nineteenth century, from over 8,700 in 1801, to just under 17,750 in 1821. The town had a wide range of manufacturing industries and most of the population worked in the silk and cotton industries. Entrepreneur Charles Roe (1715–1781) and his partners built a foundry on Macclesfield common in the late 1760s for smelting and working copper. It was still going strong three decades later:

> On the said common there is also a large building, with an open counter-yard in the middle, of about 30 yards square, called the smelting-house, where they first melt down the copper ore, and make large quantities of shot or pellets; they also make large white bricks, of which they build their ovens, and deep large pots in the form of garden-pots, but much larger, to melt the copper ore in.[4]

Copper ore was washed and filtered in running water in the Calamine Houses, a large range of buildings one storey high. A windmill provided power for grinding the ore; the copper was made into sheeting, and used for ships and pan bottoms. Brass wire and nails were manufactured on the same site.

Col. John Byng (1743–1813), later the 5th Viscount Torrington, loved riding around Britain on horseback and he kept diaries of his travels. Byng greatly enjoyed his tour of 'Mr Roe's great copper works' in 1790. He saw the workers 'mixing, melting and flat'ning the copper' but commented it was 'a most unwholesome employ, for which the workmen, I think, are meanly pay'd, as the best earn but 14s per week.' However, by 1801 the works weren't earning their keep and they were wound down.

Brick-making was important locally and there were forty brick kilns on Macclesfield common. A colliery provided fuel for the town, kilns and copper works. Gritstone for slates, flagstones and gravestones came from a nearby quarry. The River Bollin powered a corn mill and some of the silk mills and a large brewery catered for thirsty workers.

Cotton manufacture transformed small villages into hives of industry. Dukinfield's population rocketed from 1,731 (1801) to over 5,000 (1821). It almost trebled in the following decade, reaching 14,600 in 1831. Stalybridge, a large village with a foot on each side of the Lancashire and Cheshire border, also became a booming cotton town. The same was true for the tiny village of Gee Cross, which grew into the town of Hyde: 'this village now resembles a small town, and the houses range along each side of the road for nearly a mile'.[5]

By way of contrast, the salt towns of Northwich and Nantwich were much slower growing; even by 1831, each town had only (very approximately) around 5,000 inhabitants. Northwich was also home to a ship-building industry. Pigot's *Directory* lists three ship-builders in the 1820s: two at Witton, and one based at Castle. Nantwich was no longer an important salt town, but many people were employed there making shoes and gloves.

In Knutsford, like Chester, not all attempts to introduce industry were successful. A manufacturer established a silk mill in 1770 in Silk Mill St, but it only survived a few years. Another silk mill, near the approach to Tatton Park, met a similar fate. A flax-spinning mill was more successful, but after a while flax was imported ready spun. (Spun flax was used to make linen thread.) The flax spinners then switched to cotton weaving when that industry became profitable. This, too, fizzled out, and by 1817 there was 'very little business done in the town either in the thread or cotton manufactures'.[6] Lack of access to the canal network is the likeliest reason Knutsford's industries didn't succeed in the long term.

As the county's population grew, its spiritual life faced new challenges. On paper, Chester seemed well supplied with churches. Cowdroy listed nine churches in the city (including the cathedral), six chapels for dissenters, a Quaker meeting house and a Roman Catholic church. He claimed: 'there can be little apprehension with regard to the spiritual welfare of the inhabitants.'

But the county as a whole was poorly served in the mid-eighteenth century, which seems surprising for a society for which religion was, in theory, a fundamental part of everyday life. Anglicanism was stuck in the doldrums. The diocese of Chester wasn't wealthy and few new Anglican churches were built. The population had long since outstripped the available facilities. Almost 90 per cent of Chester townsfolk didn't attend church at all in 1818.

The problem was worst in the fast-growing industrial towns. The only place of worship in Hyde was the old Presbyterian chapel at Gee Cross. Hyde had no Anglican church until the early 1830s so worshippers travelled to Stockport, Mottram or Denton. Wealthy industrialists helped erect new churches: cotton manufacturer Samuel Oldknow donated money and rebuilt Marple Chapel.

Church seats were available for less than 10 per cent of the population of the Stockport area. When Corry wrote his *History*, the town had ten places of worship, of which just two were Anglican churches. The newest church was St Mary's, built in the latest Gothic style in Runcorn stone on the site of the old parish church. This 'conspicuous and magnificent edifice' took four years to build; its first stone was laid by Wilbraham Egerton (of Tatton) on 5 July 1813. Later in the same decade, government funds were made available for new churches. The massive but beautiful, classically inspired church of St Thomas was built at Higher Hillgate during the 1820s.

By contrast, Methodism and the Evangelical movement were prospering. John Wesley (1703–91) frequently travelled through Cheshire as he journeyed to and from Ireland via the Parkgate packets. Wesley made several preaching tours and Chester had a number of Wesleyan chapels including one on John St (1811).

Methodism was especially popular in industrial areas. New chapels sprang up at places such as Congleton (1808), and Hyde, where cotton manufacturers, including the Ashtons and Howards, built a Wesleyan preaching house (1822). George Slater, who grew up in Gawsworth, wrote a memoir of his life which charted the progress of Methodism in the Macclesfield, Northwich and surrounding areas. His father (who attended the famous Camp Meeting at Mow Cop on 31 May 1807) lent the local Primitive Methodists a field for their prayer meetings. Slater senior later converted his old farmhouse into a meeting house.

The movement at Macclesfield was given impetus by a tailor, George Pearson (later a silk throwster), who converted to Methodism at the age of twenty-nine. After hearing Wesley preach, Pearson asked him to come to Waters Green. Wesley preached there and in Macclesfield, Congleton and Astbury in 1747 and the movement grew from strength to strength. Wesley's last visits to Chester, Macclesfield and Northwich were in 1790, the year before his death.

Methodism had a bumpy ride from Cheshire townsfolk during its infancy. At Northwich, preachers were often thrown in the canal near Witton. Preachers were pelted with mud and abused; they were even denounced as 'disorderly persons'.[7] Services were sometimes interrupted by angry mobs and stone-throwing, especially during the Napoleonic wars, when there were fears of Jacobins and Radicals hiding under every bed.

Preacher Jabez Bunting spent four years as a probationer on the Macclesfield preaching circuit. He wrote to a friend in 1800: 'I confess … I am much afraid of the Macclesfield pulpit and congregation, and I hardly know whether I dare make the attempt.'[8] Jabez overcame his initial nervousness and he married a Miss Maclaurie from the town. Mrs Bunting became 'the queen of Methodist Society'; she was a 'capital talker'.[9] Jabez Bunting and the Rev. Robert Newton opened the new Brunswick St Chapel in May 1824.

The Rev. Simpson (1745–99) was greatly inspired by Wesley and Methodism, although he remained within the Anglican Church. Corry attributed the vast improvement in the morals and manners of Macclesfield townsfolk to the preacher's influence. Simpson, a Yorkshireman, spread the good word to startling effect in St Michael's Church, Macclesfield. 'The zeal and sincerity of Mr Simpson, in the cause of evangelical truth, was offensive to many high-minded individuals in this town; they could not endure to be weekly reminded of their profligacy …'[10]

With great energy, but little tact, Simpson preached against 'whoremongers and adulterers' while a local baronet (Sir William Meredith of Henbury Hall), well-known for his gallantry towards the fair sex, was sitting right in front of him in the pews. This was considered extreme bad manners: how dare a mere curate find fault with the gentry's behaviour? The wealthier parishioners knew how to deal with the firebrand in their midst and they complained to the bishop of Chester that their curate was tainted with Methodism. Simpson was suspended from his post as second curate, and forced to preach wherever he could, in the open air or in people's houses.

Charles Roe was greatly taken with Simpson and even allowed him to preach in his dining room. However, Roe, a man of contradictory impulses, was very upset when his children followed more extreme forms of Methodism. He banished three of his sons from home, and only relented towards them on his deathbed. Despite the break-up of his family, Roe built Christ Church for Simpson to preach in, and 'as a durable memorial of his piety'.[11] Charles Roe still had an eye for a profit, though – the sale of graveyard plots and vaults within the new church brought him some extra income. Cooke's *Topographical and Statistical Description* gives us an impression of the church in about 1803:

> The new church, called Christchurch, was built in the year 1775, by the late Charles Roe, Esq., whose bust, finely executed in white and black marble, by Bacon, is placed above the altar, with an emblematic figure of Genius, weeping over him, with a cog-wheel in her hand; there is also an inscription to his memory. It is a very regular and elegant pile of building, 33 yards long, 22 wide, and ten and a half high, besides the tower and chancel; the tower is 42 yards high, six yards square within, and has ten bells. The church has a handsome organ, and a mahogany pulpit. In the church-yard which is open and spacious, over the family vault of Ro(w)e, is a handsome monument, in the form of a pyramid …

Manufacturing families like the Daintrys and Ryles of Macclesfield regularly attended Methodist services. John Ryle was the first Methodist to become mayor, and to be appointed as chief magistrate.

He helped fund the rebuilding of Sunderland St Chapel (the heart of Macclesfield Methodism) in 1798.

The Nonconformists of the Stockport area were also busy constructing new chapels, including Hanover Chapel (1821) and, four years later, the Wesleyan Chapel at Tiviot Dale. Other dominations were catered for, too. The Primitive Methodists had a small chapel (1825) in Steam Mill St in Chester. The Trinitarians founded a chapel on the site of the old Mechanics' Institute in Hyde (1814); the building was replaced by a new Congregational Chapel a few years later. The Unitarians, Quakers and Catholics each had a chapel at Stockport. Provision for Catholics was also on the increase, fuelled by growing numbers of Irish immigrants. The Roman Catholic Chapel on Queen St, Chester, built in 1799, had an increasing and 'respectable' congregation.[12]

The churches played a vital role in the provision of education for the poorer classes. The 'free' grammar schools founded in medieval times at places such as Chester and Macclesfield had only limited places for poor children; they were now almost exclusively for fee-paying pupils. The 'Free Grammar School' or King's School at Chester taught the classics and historian George Ormerod went to school there.

Macclesfield's 'free' grammar school on Back St dated back to the 1550s. The building was: 'elegant and spacious ... with a handsome dwelling-house for the headmaster, and has an open yard and an adjoining field for the boys to exercise in.'[13] The school had a good reputation. The headmaster, Dr David Davies, had a salary of £150 per annum as well as the house. But, as John Corry pointed out bitterly, the good intentions of the school's founder, Sir John Percyvale, were no longer in evidence: 'The very designation of *Free* Grammar School implies gratuitous instruction. This is not the case at Macclesfield.' The school took boarders as well as day pupils and wealthy local families sent their sons there. Charges were steep: a five guinea entrance fee, plus annual fees of thirty-five to forty guineas, depending on the age of the young gentlemen. Dancing, drawing and fencing classes were extra.

The free grammar school at Knutsford was in a state of crisis because of disputes over the curriculum. At the turn of the century the school's reputation was at rock bottom; the headmaster, Mr Lewis, was a jailbird, and his teenage son had to take over the school for a while. By Corry's time the Rev. Peter Vannett was in charge, and growing numbers of boys had enrolled. Forty boys were boarders and annual fees were 35 guineas. Only a few boys received free tuition.

Stockport's fifteenth-century free grammar school also took fee-paying pupils. By the 1790s it was falling into disrepair. The Goldsmiths' Company, who had endowed the school, built a new school on Greek St, run by Thomas Middleton. Although the school took boarders, boys from Stockport were admitted free.

At Northwich, the free grammar school at Witton founded by Sir John Deane in the sixteenth century was undergoing troubled times. Its income from endowments had fallen and it had great difficulty covering its outgoings. Quarrels between the headmaster and teachers meant that its English department, which was flourishing, in effect became a separate school for some time.

Congleton's long-established grammar school was only free for the sons of burgesses and of the town's freemen. The Corporation built a newer, more spacious building for the school in 1814 on land given by Sir Edward Antrobus. The school master had a minimum wage of £16 per annum as well as a house, garden and some land rent free.

There was no national system of education for poor children – their schooling was a matter of luck and location – but there were some free places at charity schools, like the ones at Dunham Massey and Nantwich.

The Blue Coat School in Chester (1700) was founded by Bishop Stratford. The main building was built in 1717. Twenty-five boys lived in the school and wore the blue coat uniform in Ormerod's time. Another sixty-five boys were 'day-scholars'; they wore green caps to distinguish them from the boarders. The blue coat boys were elected from the day scholars. Another charity, the Blue Girls' School at St Martin's-in-the-Fields, educated girls for a life in domestic service. They were taught washing, cleaning, plain cooking, sewing, spinning and knitting as well as the three 'R's. The girls' work was sold, and the proceeds used to buy them clothing.

Earl Grosvenor and his countess were patrons of a charity school (founded in 1811) by St John's churchyard. They sponsored places for 800 children: 400 boys at the Earl's expense, and 400 girls paid for by the countess. The children were kitted out with everything they needed: clothes, books and slates. On New Year's Day, the children feasted on roast beef and plum pudding, served by their teachers. Girls received a new dress each for regular attendance. The Earl gave book prizes for specially diligent or well-behaved children. In 1821, the boy who had arrived earliest for school each morning was awarded a copy of *The Great Importance of a Religious Life.*

Growing interest in educating infants led to some new Infant Schools paid for by public subscription, of which the Kaleyards establishment (1826) was the first in Chester. Mrs Swindells was the headmistress. The following year, the ladies of Chester held a bazaar in the Exchange and raised over £360 to help with funding. The school wasn't completely free: the children's parents paid a penny a week for each child towards the running costs.

Mrs Egerton of Tatton Hall at Knutsford sponsored a spinning school for orphans. The school-house, a neat mansion with a rustic thatched roof, was close by the large iron gates which guarded the entrance to Tatton Park. Eighty day scholars received free lessons in reading, writing and arithmetic; six orphan girls were fed, clothed and educated, and found places as servant girls once they were qualified.

If no charity school place was available, poor children went to their local dame school, assuming their parents could afford it. Adam Rushton, a farmer's lad who grew up to be a Methodist preacher, wrote his memoirs of his early life growing up in Higher Hurdsfield in the 1820s. While still very young, Adam went to the only day school in the district, run by 'Nanny' Clarke, an 'infirm old dame, with spectacles on nose'. Lessons were held in one room full of children: 'some at play, some in mischief, and some repeating lessons in the broadest and roughest dialect in Cheshire'. Discipline was imposed by means of Nanny's birch rod, which went 'swish, swish, all round the school'.

The churches supported an alternative to the dame schools, those 'modern seminaries of virtue', Sunday schools.[14] The main Sunday school movement really took off in the 1780s, pioneered by Robert Raikes (1736–1811) and others. But Cheshire had already shown the way. David Simpson set up one of the very earliest Sunday schools in 1778 for young silk and cotton workers in Macclesfield.[15] Simpson organized several classes at private houses on weekday evenings, where students learned to read and write; the more able students learned arithmetic. Students unable to attend in the week learned how to spell and read at Sunday classes.

At this time, education for the lower classes was still controversial. In the 1790s the splenetic John Byng, noting the growing number of Sunday schools in Cheshire, commented: 'I am point blank against these institutions; the poor shou'd not read, and of writing I never heard, for them, the use.'

Sunday schools were largely funded by two different societies and money was raised by public subscription. The British and Foreign School Society was the earlier of the two charities. Founded c.1808 by Joseph Lancaster, it was re-named the British Society in 1814. The National Society (1811) was founded by Andrew Bell. Lancaster and Bell both used variants of the monitorial system: a cut-price method of education. One teacher supervised and taught a lesson; the best pupils taught the same lesson to little groups of less able children, forming a kind of educational assembly-line. Economizing on teachers saved badly needed funds, which were used to buy equipment or build more schools.

In Chester, Sunday schools were encouraged by various denominations, such as the Wesleyan Sunday School in the Octagon Chapel on Foregate St. The Diocesan School on George St had over 200 pupils in Hemingway's day. A 'Sunday and Working School' for poor girls, founded by Dr Haygarth in 1787, was renamed the Consolidated Sunday School in 1816. Classes were held in a room in the Blue Coat School on Northgate St. Seventy girls learnt 'the rudiments of learning, and various branches of plain sewing'.[16]

Early attempts at educational provision for the masses were plagued by the contentious issue of religious control. Should schools be completely secular, or should religious bodies care for the minds of the rising generation? Macclesfield was turned into a battleground by various religious groups over the question of a new Sunday school. Following the success of David Simpson's initiatives, John Whittaker opened another Sunday school in Pickford St in 1796. The school soon outgrew its original premises, so Whittaker decided to build a brand new school in Roe Street. The storm broke when an appeal fund was launched. Whittaker and his friends wanted a non-denominational school, but the Anglicans kicked up a huge fuss. They were unhappy with the religious education the children received and they also alleged that children were missing out on church services while at Sunday school. After many heated debates in the local press, the Anglicans founded their own school in Duke St. This National School was a day school (the first in Macclesfield) as well as a Sunday school; it opened in 1813.

Meanwhile, Whittaker pressed on with his project. It was a great day in Macclesfield when the first stone of the Roe St Sunday School was laid on 21 April 1813. Workers in the town and its surroundings were given a day off. A procession lined up in front of the Macclesfield Arms and young scholars of the earlier Sunday schools thronged the streets. The parade included stonemasons and builders, the Masonic Lodges, and the Sunday School Committee. The school, an elegant new building with Tuscan columns, opened the following year. Over 2,450 children (girls and boys) attended between March 1814 and June 1815.

Adam Rushton learnt to read and write properly when he went to Sunday school. The children were also taught how to wash their hands and face. An old man kept the children's minds on their Bible studies by beating them with a staff. But Rushton loved his time there. He recalled the excitement of writing his first letters, and winning a prize: Thomas à Kempis's *Imitation of Christ*. Some children, who weren't keen on spending their Sundays in school, were discovered playing football in a nearby field. Their football was confiscated, and hung up in the schoolroom as a warning.

Congleton's Sunday school was first established in 1799, during the Rev. Brettell's ministry. After its inception, classes were held at Moody St, but later moved to Wagg St.

Some mill owners, such as the Ashtons at Hyde, had night schools for their child workers but, for many children, Sunday school was their only resource. Cotton manufacturer Henry Marsland began a Wesleyan Sunday school at Bullock Smithy. In Northwich, salt proprietor Thomas Marshall was vice-president of the new National School Committee. An 'excellent dinner' was held for fundraisers in 1818 to celebrate the opening of the school for the 'infant poor of the surrounding district'. Diners enjoyed 'every delicacy of the season, with an elegant dessert, supplied from the gardens of Winnington Hall, and choice wines'. The school had 180 boys and 127 girls on its books.[17]

In Stockport, Sunday schools were a runaway success, because the various denominations co-operated instead of bickering. By 1793 there were eight Sunday schools, including one at Chestergate and another at Hillgate. Just under 1,150 children were taught and the teachers were paid 1s 6d per day. The Hillgate school run by the Methodist Meeting House was extremely popular. By 1805, over 2,860 children attended lessons, and new premises were needed.

On 15 June 1805, the foundation stone was laid of the landmark Stockport Sunday School. The huge new building near Lower Hillgate was four storeys high; it taught up to 3,000 pupils free of charge. Another 2–3,000 children in Stockport were educated on Sundays at the three National Schools. Children learned the catechism and Anglican prayer book. Joseph Mayer, partner in a Stockport spinning mill, said his child factory workers learned reading, writing and arithmetic at the nearby Sunday school. By 1817 Corry could write triumphantly: 'about 7000 children are educated gratuitously by the active benevolence of the people of Stockport.'

The genteel classes were well catered for; those parents with sufficient funds sent their children to private schools (in addition to the 'free' grammar schools). Chester had over forty. A Mrs Courtney had a school in her house on Watergate St in the city in 1794, and Mrs Briscoe kept a ladies' boarding school in Queen St.

A grammar school which opened at Knutsford in April 1796 had a guinea entrance fee and yearly fees were eighteen guineas. Children over twelve years old received their 'board, lodging, instruction in the Greek and Latin languages, writing and arithmetic'.[18] The grammar school at Tarvin, run by a Mr G. Bagley in 1820, had very similar fees, but accepted young gentlemen under the age of ten; parents were charged £20 p.a. for their board.

There were only very limited opportunities for adults in the lower classes who wanted an education. Hemingway lamented Chester's lack of libraries accessible to the poorer classes; as a result: 'the extent of their reading is mostly confined to a newspaper.' Chester's General Public Library in Northgate St cost a guinea per annum to join. There was also a subscription library in the Exchange.

At Stockport, the first Mechanics' Institute, which opened in 1825, closed down less than two years later; its books were returned to their donors. This may have been because of the economic crash of 1826 as the Institute's members probably couldn't afford their subscriptions.

Macclesfield had had a subscription library since 1770 but again, it was too expensive for ordinary folk.

The middle and upper classes, of course, had far more opportunities to broaden their horizons, like the lectures on science given by the Philosophical Society (1815) in Chester. In November 1819, Mr Lester gave talks on optics in the Philosophical Lecture Room in Bollands Court and, the following spring, John Webster lectured on steam engines.

Touring exhibitions demonstrated nature's wonders. Mr Bird, a self-taught astronomer, visited Chester with his 'grand transparent Orrery, constructed by himself' in June 1818.[19] Visitors paid 2s 6d for lectures on astronomy in the 'Great Room' by the public library in Fletcher's Court.

As well as providing some education for the lower classes, the upper classes provided funds to feed and clothe the needy. Wealthy families such as the Grosvenors were expected to spend their money liberally and many such families took their social responsibilities extremely seriously. Money was donated to charitable subscriptions, or left as bequests.

At Chester, there were over thirty almshouses for the elderly in the 1790s. The most important foundation housed 'thirty decayed freemen' of the city. The men, who had to be over sixty years old to qualify for the charity, received an annual allowance of £4, and a new gown every third year. The men went in procession to church each Sunday.[20] Some funding for this charity came from the Owen Jones benefaction, founded in 1659. Jones, a wealthy butcher, donated the profits of an estate in Derbyshire for the use of poor members of Chester's craft guilds or 'companies' as they were known. The companies took turns to receive the money, beginning with the Tanners. The bequest only amounted to a few pounds at first, but the discovery in 1756 of a lead mine on the estate bumped up the annual profits to almost £400. This huge sum proved too tempting for sticky fingers, and was 'a *bone* of no small contention among the *rich* as well as *poor* freemen', as Cowdroy drily noted. There was a greedy scramble, like pigs round a trough, as each company's turn drew near. Some refused to allow any new members to join; others charged higher prices for new members. The money was shared out to rich as well as poor.

Other city charities were mismanaged, too, although this is too mild a term. Corruption was rife in the corporation during the eighteenth and early nineteenth century. Revenues intended for municipal charities were quietly siphoned into the corporation's coffers; less than half the charities' money was actually laid out on their behalf. The assembly's grasping grip on charity funds was finally ended by the Municipal Corporations Act of 1835.

Poor women were also cared for. Behind the Blue Coat School in Chester lay six almshouses for impoverished widows, run by a 'venerable matron'.[21] The Ladies' Benevolent Institution (1798) provided free medical care during childbirth for poor married women in their own homes. The women were given clean linen and sheets, soap, tea and sugar, and baby clothes if they lived in real poverty. Their babies were vaccinated against smallpox.

'Fallen women' who had 'deviated from the paths of virtue' and wished to be restored 'to a respectable station in society' could make a fresh start in Chester's Female Penitentiary, founded in 1827.[22] Patrons included Earl Grosvenor and the Bishop of Chester and £900 was raised by subscription to buy and fit out a building near Boughton. The inmates received food, lodging and religious instruction, and classes in useful skills such as reading, writing and needlework. The hope was that the 'penitents', after mending their ways, would find suitable work as domestic servants. But the institution was expensive to run, and wasn't an unqualified success. Either the path of virtue was too hard to rediscover once left, or the Penitentiary's regime was too strict. A large proportion of inmates left of their own accord, or were dismissed by the matron.

Macclesfield had three almshouses in Back St for women, founded in 1703. The houses were 'for the maintenance of three poor widows, who have their settlement in this town, with one penny a day for ever.'[23] There was a similar scheme at Weaverham; a bequest of £300 from Mrs Clowes of Liverpool was invested for six poor residents of Weaverham and their wives. If no suitable candidates were found, the vicar chose six deserving widows, or six old maids.

Long-established customs helped provide for the poor during the hard winter months. In Congleton, the tenant of the Corn Mill, in addition to paying rent, gave 30s, forty-eight loads of malt, and eighteen measures of barley flour to the poor at Christmas each year. The vicar and churchwardens of Weaverham gave Christmas cheer of bread and money to the poor.

The winter of 1819–20 was extremely harsh. At Chester, subscriptions were held for the relief of the 'necessitous poor'. Earl Grosvenor subscribed £100, and General Grosvenor and Lord Belgrave each gave £21. People were forced to pawn their furniture and even their bedding so they could buy food. To give an idea of the scale of the problem, about 4,900 people were relieved by the fund in just one week. Priority was given to those families subsisting on less than 5s per week. Potatoes, bread, bacon and coal were distributed to starving families.[24]

At other times when food was scarce, either because of poor harvests or trade difficulties, action was taken to feed the poor. This wasn't just from charitable motives. Urban populations in particular were increasingly less likely to bear their lot humbly, and much more likely to riot in the streets. Chester had a Corn Committee which bought large quantities of grain to make barley bread 'for every industrious inhabitant'.[25] Over 1,600 families were fed by this scheme. Plays like *Macbeth* were performed at the Theatre Royal for the benefit of the Barley Flour Fund.

Public health provision also depended on benevolent individuals. Chester Infirmary (1761) was founded by Dr Stratford. Pioneering doctor John Haygarth introduced separate fever wards for patients in 1783. The infirmary was attended by four physicians and four surgeons; over 450 in-patients and just under 900 out-patients were treated in 1816. But the four-storey building was poorly designed, badly ventilated and badly drained. Worse still, patients who were recovering were on the same wards as those newly admitted, with the obvious risk of fresh infection. At the end of the 1820s, £2000 was spent on rebuilding and upgrading the building. William Cole (the younger), the county architect, was commissioned to undertake the work; he also designed the new County Lunatic Asylum (1827–9) at Upton-by-Chester.

Stockport's new dispensary (1797) was built by public subscription for the town's poor and nine fever wards were added two years later. It evidently fulfilled a great need, because over 1100 patients were admitted during its first year.

For people too old and ill to work, or with no family to care for them, there was always the workhouse; Cheshire had around thirty such institutions in the 1770s. However, the vast majority of poor people received help under the 'outdoor' system; they were assisted from the rates while still living at home. The able-bodied poor were set to public works like road-building by the parish guardians to help reduce the poor rates. Waste land at Saltney was enclosed and farmed using pauper labour.

Although life in the workhouse was no bed of roses, the regime was in general kindlier during the eighteenth century than after the Poor Law reforms of the 1830s. Chester's House of Industry, built in 1757, was a large plain brick building between the Roodee and River Dee. This 'asylum for age and indigence' was home to the poor of several Chester parishes, but had fewer than 200 inmates in 1789.[26] Hemingway said the inmates were treated gently and humanely; their food was 'good and nutritious'.

Chester set an example in one burning question of the day: the use of little boys to sweep chimneys. The horrors these children suffered would make an angel weep. Their masters stuck pins into the boys to make them go up the narrow passageways and they even lit fires under them. Boys got stuck, were suffocated, or burned so badly that they died. The children rarely washed; they even slept on bags of soot. The soot caused a particularly nasty (and fatal) cancer of the scrotum. Boys as young as five were apprenticed to master chimney-sweeps. They were forced up chimneys which were still hot, and made to put out chimney fires. The problem was the design of the chimneys, especially in noble lords' great houses. The networks of flues were narrow and complex; some chimneys were only seven inches square. Many householders felt the best way to clean them was with tiny children (girls were used as well as boys, though this wasn't as common).

A bill to help the 'climbing boys' was passed as early as 1788; children weren't allowed to be apprenticed under the age of eight, had to be treated humanely, and should wash once a week. But the Act wasn't enforced, and was widely ignored. Some private individuals tried to help the boys and machines were invented to sweep chimneys clean. During 1817–19, several attempts were made to pass legislation banning the use of climbing boys.

In Cheshire, the Mayor of Chester, Henry Bowers, held a meeting at the Exchange in March 1818. A petition was raised to ask the House of Lords to pass the latest Act aimed at banning this 'cruel and unnatural practice'. Earl Grosvenor presented several petitions in March to help the children.[27] But the Lords temporized, claiming there wasn't enough evidence to support a ban. A report was commissioned, and the Bill abandoned.

Time after time, the House of Lords blocked each proposal to save the climbing boys. The problem was that in order to use machinery, the complicated chimneys of the rich would need some alterations, and this would hit them in the pocket. No matter what revolting tale of cruelty or harrowing evidence was put before them, the majority of their Lordships (in particular Lord Lauderdale) were inflexible, despite the efforts of more enlightened noblemen such as Earl Grosvenor to help the children. This social evil went unchecked for decades. The only way forward was at local level or via private charities. In April 1818, four master sweeps of the city of Chester were furnished with machines for sweeping chimneys.

Political questions were fought out in the pages of the local papers; they occupied many column inches. In Chester, the Tory *Courant* and Whig *Chronicle* were bitter rivals, engaged in a constant game of one-upmanship. The *Chronicle* editor was John Fletcher, who became Mayor of Chester. The *Courant* was a family business, run by Edmund Monk (and after his death, by his son John, followed by John's widow). There were many squibs in the *Chronicle* against the 'little noisy editor of the COURANT'.[28] Both papers rehashed court and social news from the London papers. Stories of animal sagacity were favourites, as well as scientific snippets and travellers' tales, such as the giant sea serpents reported in America. The Chester papers had a wide readership, spreading out across the county and into Lancashire, North Wales, Shropshire and Staffordshire.

Attempts to introduce a third newspaper were unsuccessful. The *Chester Herald*, founded in 1810 by Mr Cutter, lasted just three years. The *Chester Guardian*, founded in September 1817, had more success. The *Guardian* had several influential, wealthy backers 'who embraced nobility in their train' (this is Hemingway-speak for the Grosvenors). The paper espoused 'broad Whig' politics. Its editor, Mr Gorton, was given 'a salary which few provincial journals could bear', in Hemingway's opinion, despite Gorton's 'superior talent'.

Readers were treated to the usual round of journalistic ping-pong between rival Chester editors. The *Chronicle* accused the *Guardian* of being a Radical paper. The *Guardian* prematurely accused the *Chronicle* of being on its last legs in 1820. The editor pitied '... the sufferings of its last moments ... The dress in which it has for some time appeared before the public, has been barely decent.'[29] Unfortunately, despite the large sums lavished on it by its hopeful parents, the *Guardian* only survived for three more years; the market simply couldn't support a third paper.

The *Macclesfield Courier*'s first issue appeared on 2 February 1811. The money for its publication was advanced by two attorneys, a cotton spinning manufacturer and an ironmonger, so it had a Tory bias, as might be expected. However, despite its political leanings, even Corry (a confirmed Whig) admitted it was 'acceptable and amusing to the general reader'. After its publisher Jonathan Wilson's early death in 1821, the *Courier* had a succession of proprietors before merging in 1828 with the *Macclesfield Herald*, founded in 1825 by Joseph Swinnerton. The new venture went on to prosper.

In Stockport, the *Northern Express & Lancashire Daily Post* (formerly the *Manchester Express*) was printed at Hillgate House in 1821, but only had a very short lifespan. The first *Stockport Advertiser* appeared on 29 March 1822; it cost 4½d.

In those suspicious times, the laws against sedition meant Radicals had to be very careful about rushing into print to express their political views, or they could spend their days rotting in a prison cell. Men like Joseph Swann of Macclesfield were imprisoned for selling 'seditious' literature. Swann was sentenced to a total of four and a half years in Chester Castle in January 1820 after being found guilty of seditious libel, blasphemous libel, sedition and conspiracy. After being sentenced, Swann, who had already spent several months in prison awaiting trial, asked what had happened to his wife, who was 'taken up' at the same time he was arrested. But the court officials either couldn't or wouldn't tell him what had happened to her, and the poor man was left in suspense.[30]

Less dangerous and inflammatory works were available to readers and some of the great histories of Cheshire were written during our time period. George Ormerod (1785–1873) was a Manchester man. His monumental *History of the County Palatine and City of Chester*, in three volumes, was dedicated to the Prince Regent. It was first published in 1819.

The *Chronicle* editors wrote some landmark historical accounts. John Hickson Hanshall edited the *Chronicle* from c.1810 to 1824; his *History of the County Palatine of Chester* appeared in 1823. It was followed by Joseph Hemingway's *History of the City of Chester* (1831). Hemingway edited the *Courant* for several years after John Monk's death, before moving to the editorship of the *Chronicle* from 1824 onwards. He knew the city inside out.

John Corry's *A History of Macclesfield* was published in 1817; it was dedicated to Wilbraham Egerton. Corry also wrote histories of Stockport, Knutsford, Leek and Congleton.

Future novelist Elizabeth Cleghorn Stevenson (later Mrs Gaskell), born in 1810, was brought up in Cheshire. When she was just thirteen months old, she came to live in Knutsford with her Aunt Lumb. While a young lady, she spent many happy hours picnicking in the park of the Old Hall at Tabley.

Author Thomas de Quincey (1785–1859) paid a brief visit to Chester in 1802. He visited his mother, who lived at St John's Priory, after running away from school.

Some Cheshire gentlemen such as Thomas Legh of Lyme (1793–1857) were great travellers. Legh's *Narrative of a Journey in Egypt* was published in 1816. Another much-travelled Cheshire gentleman was Randle Wilbraham of Rode Hall (1773–1861) who was briefly engaged to Frances, Lady Shelley (1787–1873) before her marriage to John Shelley. Randle charmed her with fantastic tales of Jerusalem, Arabian deserts and Egyptian pyramids. Wilbraham almost died from fever while travelling in Persia.

Explorers like Sir John Thomas Stanley (1766–1850) of Alderley braved the icy northern wastes. His *Voyage to the Orknies* was published 1789. A Fellow of the Royal Society, he equipped a ship to make a scientific study of Iceland, and published two papers on the hot springs in Iceland in the *Transactions of the Royal Society of Edinburgh*. His nephew Arthur Penrhyn Stanley, born 1815, became Dean of Westminster and was a famous scholar and theologian.

One gentleman's story is a true 'ripping yarn'. Admiral Sir George Back (1796–1878) was born at Holly Vale near Stockport. He served at an early age as a midshipman on the ship *Arethusa*. During the Napoleonic wars, he was captured by the French and imprisoned at Verdun from 1809 to 1814. He sailed on an expedition to the Arctic with Sir John Franklin in 1818, went on another outing to the Polar Sea in 1819, and joined Franklin again in 1825. When supplies ran out in the bleak, icy wastes, he was reduced to eating old leather trousers and shoes. In 1833, Back mounted a search for Captain Ross's expedition, which had gone missing four years earlier. Back later published a book on his travels: *A Narrative of the Arctic Land Expedition* (1836).

When these gentlemen returned from faraway lands, they were doubtless astonished by the changes in the county which had taken place during their absence. Cheshire towns vied with each other to be 'dressed' in the latest style of elegance.

3

In the Latest Style

The late Georgian period marked a stylistic watershed in the appearance of Cheshire's buildings and inhabitants. Grecian and Gothic mansions and manors adorned the countryside. Spanking new public buildings swept away the mouldering relics of medievalism and brought space, light and elegance to town centres. Growing civic pride, and a determination not to be left behind by new fashions, led to 'makeovers' for places such as Macclesfield and Knutsford, as well as the main county town.

It would be difficult to top Cowdroy's enthusiastic 'puff' for Chester:

> There are few cities in Europe, or perhaps in the universe, which have a stronger claim to general attention, than Chester: the eye of the stranger will here find an ample field for admiration – the man of taste, who may honour it with a visit, will not depart ungratified – nor will the antiquarian search in vain for some rich and profitable treasures of investigation within its wall.

Chester was growing in importance as a tourist honeypot and the main Dee bridge was already struggling to cope with the increase in traffic. Welshman Thomas Pennant (1726–98) described Chester in the late 1770s: 'The approach to the city is over a very narrow and dangerous bridge, of seven irregular arches, till of late rendered more inconvenient by the antient gateways at each end, formerly necessary enough, to prevent the inroads of my countrymen, who often carried fire and sword to these suburbs ...'[1]

But instead of invading Welshmen, Chester's streets now welcomed raiding parties of shoppers. The famous Rows were objects of great curiosity to visitors, as had been the case for hundreds of years. Chester's inhabitants hadn't always prized them as they should. During the eighteenth century, the Rows were deemed dirty and unfashionable. They suffered a great deal of attrition, and even faced destruction. But now the Rows were once again recognized as an asset to the city's commerce; they were refurbished to maintain their character. Just as today, shoppers could: '... walk from end to end, secure from wet or heat, in galleries (or rows as they are called) purloined from the front of each house, open in front and balustraded ...'[2] A later visitor, Robert Southey, said the best shops were in the Rows.

Chester was the fashionable place to shop, with many high-class retailers such as gold and silver smiths, jewellers, clock-makers, wine and spirit dealers as well as clothes shops and ordinary grocers. Druggists and shoemakers, brewers and bakers, tailors and toy shops – the bewildering variety of goods available helped attract shoppers from a wide area. Home furnishings were available, too. George Haswell's paper-hanging warehouse in Newgate St, Chester, sold paper-hangings of 'the best fabric, choicest colours, and newest patterns'.[3]

Because shop development had progressed in a piecemeal fashion, old and new buildings were jumbled in a motley and 'grotesque' manner. For example, in Bridge St: 'Every gradation of architecture, from the rude clumsy wooden hut, to the open airy commodious hotel, is here displayed.'[4] The eastern side had a run of modern shops, mostly occupied by butchers. The western side of Bridge St was occupied by ironmongers, grocers, tobacconists and other retailers. Bridge St was also the coal market; long lines of dirty coal wagons caused traffic congestion, and were a dangerous nuisance to people and carriages. As time went on, shops such as baker's and butcher's premises, which sold day-to-day but less refined necessities, were gradually pushed away from the city centre.

Chester was the county's retail capital and it had the widest range and highest number of shops. But for everyday shopping, convenience was the biggest priority. Chester, Macclesfield and Stockport each had approximately fifty or more shops selling ordinary provisions in 1816. Although Macclesfield was smaller than Stockport, its shops offered a broader range of goods and more luxury items, perhaps because

Stockport shoppers took their custom to nearby Manchester. The working classes, especially in the industrial towns, formed a new, growing market; they wanted goods such as ready made or second hand clothes. Workers unable to make ends meet were regular customers at pawnbrokers, exchanging clothing or bedding for ready cash. They would redeem their articles on pay day, before beginning the same cycle the following week.

While retail businesses were flourishing, wholesalers had more mixed fortunes. The Irish linen trade was formerly a major player in Chester's business life. The Yacht Field near Watergate St had a roomy Linen Hall, built in 1778 for the sale of Irish linen at the summer and autumn fairs: 'It surrounds a large square area; on each side of which are piazzas, with numbers of shops well adapted for the purpose.'[5] The Hall contained 111 shops. But, after 1800, competition from Liverpool and a growing trend for English merchants to order directly from Irish manufacturers sounded the death knell for the linen trade. It was extinct by the 1830s.

Traders still came from all over Britain to the Chester fairs, but Hemingway, writing in 1830, lamented: 'the wholesale transactions … have been materially diminished'. The main fairs, which ran for fifteen days, began on 5 July and 10 October. Two weeks before trading began, a wooden glove was displayed on the outside of the Pentice building to mark the fair's opening. (After the Pentice's demolition in 1803, St Peter's Church was used.) The glove was taken down again when the fair closed. The first few days of the fair were once alive with activity as Cheshire and Welsh shopkeepers stocked up in order to supply their customers. Business was now mostly conducted during the fair's final week.

The trade decline was in spite of the construction of two new buildings, the Union Hall (1809) and Commercial Hall (1815), both near Foregate St, to accommodate Lancashire and Yorkshire merchants. The idea was to concentrate many different wares in a small area. Goods for sale included Lancashire cottons, hardware from Sheffield and Birmingham, Yorkshire woollens, Welsh flannels, Kent hops, as well as toys, trinkets and fancy goods. Hemingway attributed the drop in trade to retailers buying direct from factories, and 'the increased system of travellers traversing the country for orders'.

As Chester's population grew, new housing shot up inside and outside the medieval walls. Some well-to-do Cheshire families like the Mainwarings and Egertons still had houses in the city centre. But the centre became a less fashionable place to live. Ormerod mentions several 'large old mansions' in Abbey Square, Nicholas St and Stanley Place which in the previous century were town residences for the county families, but now housed less exalted residents. The richer classes decamped to grand new villas in the suburbs which catered for their desire for privacy and exclusivity. Poorer citizens didn't have this luxury: they were crammed into whatever accommodation they could find in the back streets. They lived in 'poverty, hunger and dirt', especially in the more industrial areas near the canal.[6]

Apart from the Rows, the remnants of medieval Chester were considered a mixed blessing to the city. The crumbling city gateways were demolished, but the walls were repaired and the walls walk took pride of place in tourist guidebooks. The expense of maintenance was met by 'murage' duties, a customs duty levied on all merchandise imported from overseas into the port of Chester.

By the 1820s, the circuit of the city walls was a 'delightful promenade, commanding views at once extensive and picturesque'.[7] The walls needed repairs in 1828 after a storm of terrible rain and hail undermined a section between Abbey St and the Phoenix Tower. A couple of years later, the walls and towers were smartened up still further. However, unlike the walls circuit, the ancient gaols were filthy and unhygienic. It took time, money and a wizard with stone to free the city from its medieval fetters.

Thomas Harrison (1744–1829) is the architect best known for changing the face of Chester during our time period. A Yorkshireman of humble origin, he studied in Italy during the early 1770s under the patronage of Sir Lawrence Dundas (of Aske Hall, Richmond), who was impressed by the young man's talent. Harrison's works brought a restrained classicism to the city, enough of it surviving so that we can picture Chester's rebirth in the 'true style of elegance'.

Harrison's first major project in Cheshire was the castle site. Chester Castle played several roles in county affairs. The civil and crown courts were held there, and an army garrison was housed inside. The county gaol housed debtors and felons, both those awaiting trial and those who had been convicted. The gaol was notoriously overcrowded. Thomas Pennant graphically described its horrors. In the daytime, guilty and innocent spent many hours together: '... in a little yard, surrounded on all sides by lofty buildings ... ever unvisited by the rays of the sun'. At night, three or four people were crammed together in tiny cells seven and a half feet by three and a half, ranged to one side of a 'subterraneous dungeon'. A tiny grate above each cell door provided the only 'ventilation' for these 'kennels'.[8] Prison reformer John Howard, who visited Chester in 1788, likened conditions in the cells to those in the Black Hole of Calcutta.

In the summer of 1784, the Cheshire Justices of the Peace at last decided to deal with the problem. (They were probably inspired by a typhus epidemic across the country the previous year which claimed some learned judges as victims.) The magistrates held a design competition for a new gaol within the castle. Thomas Harrison, now in his early forties, won the 50-guinea prize for his plans. Preliminary work began on site in 1788.

Harrison's new gaol was laid out in the shape of a half-octagon which fanned out from the Shire Hall. When the building was finally completed in 1801, conditions in the cells were far superior to those in Pennant's day. The gaoler's house looked out over an exercise yard and the cells, nine feet by seven feet, were built in two-storey blocks along the inside of the perimeter wall. During his north-west tour, Southey commented on how comfortably the gaoler at Chester was housed compared with his inmates:

> The new jail is considered as a perfect model of prison architecture, a branch of the art as much studied by the English of the present day, as ever cathedral building was by their pious ancestors. The main objects attended to are, that the prisoners be kept apart from each other, and that the cells should always be open to inspection, and well ventilated so as to prevent infectious disorders, which were commonly occurring in old prisons. The structure of this particular prison is singularly curious, the cells being so constructed that the jailor from his dwelling house can look into every one ... The apartment from whence we were shown the interior of the prison was well, and even elegantly furnished; there were geraniums flowering upon stands – a pianoforte, and music-books lying open – and when we looked from the window we saw criminals with irons upon their legs, in

> solitary dungeons: – one of them, who was intently reading some devotional book, was, we were told, certainly to be executed at the next assizes …

Although Harrison's design was very beautiful, it wasn't necessarily secure; five prisoners escaped in the spring of 1802, and another five absconded in November 1807.

Prince Pückler-Muskau visited the castle and gaol on New Year's Day, 1827. He wrote approvingly that the 'rogues and thieves' imprisoned there were well housed; the arrangements for them were 'most humane and perfect' with 'clean and airy' cells. Felons imprisoned for debt had a little garden in the courtyard for exercise; there were workrooms behind the cells, with a fire for comfort. The women's and men's cells were separate. While awaiting trial, prisoners wore grey uniforms; after their trial, they wore green and red. The prisoners' food varied with the severity of their crime. The humblest fare was usually bread, potatoes and salt, but on the day of the Prince's visit, the prisoners feasted on roast beef, plum pudding and ale to celebrate the New Year, by courtesy of the Mayor.

The crowning glory of the castle complex is Harrison's beautiful Propylaea Gateway, inspired by the Acropolis in Athens. The gateway, with its Doric porticos and elegant columns, is one of the high points of Greek Revival architecture in England. The first stone was laid in June 1811 by Lt. Col. Trafford of the Congleton local militia.

The old Shire Hall was also demolished. Harrison's new Shire Hall, with a grand façade of a Doric portico in fine ashlar stone, formed a harmonious whole with the prison buildings. Work continued on the castle site for the rest of the decade and a new armoury and barracks (the present day Regimental Museum) for the garrison was added.

Next on the city's architectural shopping list was the demolition of the last surviving medieval gate, the Northgate, which housed the city gaol. Like the old county gaol, it had a dire reputation. This mouldering pile had a dreadful dungeon thirty feet below street level. One famous prisoner was the martyr George Marsh, who was incarcerated here in the sixteenth century before facing an agonizing death at Boughton where he was burnt alive on 24 April 1555.

The poor wretches left to rot inside had only one means of ventilation: a system of pipes connected to the street, itself awash with muck and filth. Prisoners were kept in irons, chained to the floor and the felons' food allowance was a pennyworth of bread per day. Prisoners were allowed to beg for food during the daytime. John Howard said it was a disgrace that prisoners weren't fed properly in such an 'opulent city'.[9] Their spiritual needs were looked after by the chapel in the nearby Blue Coat School. When the Chester Canal (1779) separated the two buildings, prisoners couldn't go to chapel, so the 'Bridge of Sighs' was built over the canal in 1793 to solve the problem.

After much political bickering within the corporation over the choice of architect and cost of the work, the Northgate was replaced by Harrison with a 'light, elegant structure of white stone'.[10] A new city gaol and House of Correction, to Harrison's design, was built between 1806 and 1808, close to the medieval walls. Sadly, these buildings no longer survive.

Harrison was a very busy man in Chester in the early decades of the new century. The Exchange was refurbished, and the elegant Commercial News Room on Northgate St, built around the same time as the new Northgate, provided a quiet haven for gentlemen wishing to peruse the daily newspapers.

Cheshire churches were also given a touch of Harrison magic; the cathedral in particular was badly in need of restoration. It had been founded in 1541 on the site of the ancient abbey of St Werburgh but the chapter revenues weren't robust enough to maintain the building. The problem was the sandstone used for its construction. When Southey visited in the early 1800s, very little work had been done for over half a century: 'The cathedral is a mean edifice of soft, red, crumbly stone, apparently quarried on the spot; it would have been folly to have erected anything better with such wretched materials.'

When Hugh Cholmondeley became Dean of Chester in February 1806, he found the cathedral was indeed in a sorry state. Ormerod confirms: 'substantial parts were on the verge of decay, and many beautiful specimens of architecture, of a date as early as that of the original Norman foundation, were obscured by piles of rubbish.' The Bishop, George Law, appealed for funds to make good years of neglect and Harrison submitted plans for repairs, which were carried out in 1819.

Contemporaries like Batenham felt it was rather late in the day. He was sparing in his praise of the results:

> … some parts of the most distinguished and excellent parts were so completely ruined, that no art could repair or restore them … the repairs as they now stand were completed at the least possible expense, and which, although not happily harmonising with the exquisite skill of the earlier labours, are quite competent to the preservation of the remaining greatness of this stately national monument.[11]

Harrison also built a new Methodist church (1811) in Chester, and refurbished the exterior of St Peter's Church. Egerton Legh of West Hall, High Legh, commissioned Harrison to build a new chapel there to give thanks for the end of the war with Napoleon. Despite his wonderful public edifices, Harrison wasn't formally appointed as county surveyor until 1815; he was now seventy-one years old. Three years later, Harrison was asked to submit designs and estimates for a new bridge over the River Dee. The venerable medieval structure with seven arches, depicted in many old views of the city, desperately needed replacing. But it was many years before Harrison's ideas came to fruition.

Thomas Harrison's public works proved a stepping stone to success and his skills were greatly in demand for private homes. He built three houses in Chester, including his own. Dee Hills (1814) was constructed for attorney Robert Baxter and Watergate House (1820–1), an elegant mansion with fine views of the Roodee and Welsh hills, was built for the county's Clerk of the Peace, Henry Potts. A grateful corporation gave Harrison the land for his own new residence, St Martin's Lodge, completed around 1823; it overlooked his beautiful works at Chester Castle.

Away from the county town, Harrison gave Tabley House (near Knutsford) an up-to-date touch. The Leycesters of Tabley were a very ancient Cheshire family. John Leycester built the original family residence, the Old Hall, in the fourteenth century. The Hall had a very romantic situation on an island accessed by a stone bridge. Sir Peter Leycester (1613–78) was a celebrated historian and antiquary. The direct male line died out in 1742, but the fourth baronet, Sir Peter Byrne, took the name of Leicester. He felt the Old Hall was no longer convenient as a gentleman's residence. Sir Peter commissioned a new home, with tranquil views of the park and surrounding woodlands. Tabley House was built to John Carr's design in the 1760s. It was a real Palladian gem: 'a noble mansion ... on a magnificent style'. Tabley's stables were said to equal those of the Prince Regent: 'in convenience if not magnificence'.[12] Sir Peter's son, Sir John Fleming Leicester (1762–1827), became Baron de Tabley in 1826 and he played a very important role in county life. This notable patron of British art needed somewhere to display his wonderful picture collection. Harrison knocked three rooms into one to create a stunning new picture gallery, completed some time around 1810.

Cotton mill owner Peter Marsland asked Harrison to design his new home, Woodbank. Marsland's factory and Stockport home (a pretty mansion with gardens and greenhouses) were targeted by a Luddite mob in 1812. Marsland wanted to move his family to an out-of-town villa in more peaceful surroundings, overlooking the Pennines. Pevsner considered Woodbank to be Harrison's finest private house in the whole county.

Harrison's works were a wonderful legacy for future Cheshire generations. His obituary in the *Chester Chronicle* (3 April 1829) called him a 'highly distinguished artist' who 'in his professional character, had few equals'.

Cheshire was renowned for the large number of gentlemen's seats within its borders. Some ancient Cheshire families had died out, or were in decline, such as the Leghs of Adlington, who became extinct through the male line in 1781. Old blood was being replaced by new, however. As well as home-grown gentry, wealthy families from neighbouring counties had houses here.

Landowners and industrialists, anxious to be in the forefront of fashion, were caught up in the rage for improvement. As we have seen, successful manufacturers like Peter Marsland could afford to build elegant new houses. Lancashire mill owner William Turner bought the Shrigley estate from the Downes family in 1818 and built Shrigley Hall at Pott Shrigley in about 1825.

The Wyatt family of architects were in great demand with eminent Cheshire families for several decades. They used the classical style of architecture with great effect at places such as Tatton Park, Lyme Park and Rode Hall.

The Tatton estate near Knutsford belonged to the Egerton family for many generations. Samuel Egerton asked Samuel Wyatt (1737–1807) to enlarge the family home in the 1770s. The original plan was for a house with eleven bays. For some reason, the works didn't commence, but when William Egerton inherited the estate, the designs were revived. Building work began in 1789, and continued for many years. John Byng was unimpressed by the house: 'a patchwork thing, standing ill, with no plantation on the lawn'. He did enjoy his ride through Tatton Park, though: 'a grand domain of great verdure … with a noble lake'. The authors of *The Beauties of England and Wales* (1801), possibly with the need to please their noble subscribers, were more charitable in its assessment:

> The building is situated in the midst of a park, containing nearly 2500 acres of arable and pasture land. It stands on an elevated spot of ground, from the front of which a lawn gradually declines to the level of Tatton-mere, a fine piece of water … The designs for the house were given by Mr Wyatt, and are conceived in a style of elegant simplicity, but only part of the edifice is yet finished. The gardens are extensive; and the pinery is remarkably spacious, and well constructed.

After William Egerton died in 1806, his heir Wilbraham asked Wyatt's nephew Lewis to continue the works. Lewis Wyatt trimmed down the original design to a house with seven bays.

Lyme Park was home to the Legh family of Lyme. Thomas Peter Legh, MP for Newton and Colonel of the 3rd Lancashire Light Dragoons, became owner of Lyme in 1792. Thomas Peter only enjoyed the estates for five years. Before his death in 1797, he settled the estates on his natural sons Thomas and William. All Col. Legh's children were granted a special royal licence to bear the name and arms of Legh in 1806. Thomas Legh, later a famous Oriental traveller, was just four years old when he succeeded to the estates. His first wife Ellen Turner, while still a teenager, was the victim of a notorious Cheshire scandal, as we shall see later.

The Elizabethan mansion at Lyme Park, with its breathtaking setting and classically inspired façade designed by Giacomo Leoni in the 1720s, received mixed reviews from contemporaries. Byng complained the house was 'in the horrid taste and manner of Chatsworth, all windows ...' The grounds were in sad repair when he visited during the last decade of the eighteenth century, probably owing to the death of its owner Peter Legh (1706–87). The older trees in the park were dead or dying. Part of the grounds was a 'dreary swamp', and the rest overrun with rabbits. The sheep there looked half-starved.

The Beauties of England and Wales agreed that Lyme was badly situated, and was diplomatic about its architecture:

> The park is very extensive, but the situation ill-chosen, as the surrounding country is bleak, moorish, and unfruitful ... The plan of the building is quadrangular, but composed of very incongruous parts: the north and east angles are of the age of Elizabeth, or James the First; the south and west sides more modern, being erected from the designs of Leoni, in the regular Ionic order. Three sides of the inclosed (*sic*) court are surrounded with a piazza, which gives an air of grandeur to the whole edifice. The park is well stored with deer, and the venison is of a very superior flavour ...

Lyme was also famous for its ancient breed of wild cattle. Thomas Legh asked Lewis Wyatt to revamp and extend Lyme. A smart dining room was added, the drawing room updated, and the number of servants' bedrooms increased. The works were still ongoing when Ormerod wrote his *History*. Legh's collection of 'antique marbles and other curiosities' which he had acquired on his travels was on display.

Rode Hall, home of the Wilbraham family, was enlarged and extended by the third Randle Wilbraham (1773–1861). Randle, the second surviving son of Richard Wilbraham Bootle, inherited the hall in 1796. He began improvements three years later. Architect John Hope gave the building a smart stucco finish and a new entrance hall was constructed, ornamented with fashionable Tuscan columns. Lewis Wyatt added an elegant dining room some time during 1810. The grounds were re-landscaped and a lake gave a new serenity to the view.

Classical architecture was losing ground to the latest fashion craze: Gothic castles with medieval-style towers and battlements. The first Gothic mansion in Cheshire was probably Cholmondeley Castle. The old Cholmondeley Hall, which was on a very damp site, was taken down and the foundation stone of the new castle was laid in 1801. The main building was designed by its owner, George Cholmondeley, the fourth Earl (created Marquess of Cholmondeley in 1816). The castle was finished in 1804 and several towers were added by Sir Robert Smirke in the late 1820s.

Combermere Abbey (originally a Cistercian house) had been owned by the Cotton family since the Dissolution. Their home had a 'most romantic' situation, in a 'rich and well-wooded country'.[13] Sir Stapleton Cotton, flush with money after his sterling service in the Peninsular Wars, splashed out on a Gothic update of the abbey. Work must have finished by 1819, because Ormerod says the original walls were 'concealed by recent alterations in imitation of the pointed Gothic style'.

The most massive example of the fad for Gothic architecture lay just four miles from Chester. Eaton Hall was the family seat of the wealthy Grosvenor family. Sir Richard Grosvenor (1731–1802), the seventh baronet, became Earl Grosvenor in 1784. He laid out his money beautifying Chester, and paid for the new East Gate. The Grosvenors' spacious, handsome brick mansion at Eaton was built to William Samwell's design during the late seventeenth century. The gardens were laid out 'in the old formal style, with straight walks, and leaden statues. They are ... ornamented with several fine gates. The Park is well stocked with deer.'[14]

Sir Richard's son Robert (1767–1845) became the second Earl Grosvenor in 1802 when his father died. He wanted to 'keep up with the Joneses', and parade the family's vast wealth. He made sweeping changes to the old Hall. It was replaced by a Gothic leviathan lavishly embellished with pinnacles, buttresses and octagonal turrets. William Porden began creating the grand design in about 1803 and work continued for another decade. Freestone from the quarry at Manley was used for the rebuilding work. The building was further extended by Gummow in the 1820s.

Eaton Hall was on the tourist trail. Visitors were gushingly advised not to miss the 'magnificent mansion' adorned 'in the richest style'. According to the *Stranger's Companion*, the house was about 450 feet long, or almost 700 feet if the stables were included. Porden also gothicized the interior with a heavy hand. Paintings by artists such as Rubens and Benjamin West were on display; the library had a 'choice collection of books and manuscripts, many of them extremely rare and curious'. But the house wasn't pleasant to live in: its vast rooms were draughty and freezing cold. The new edifice wasn't to everyone's taste. Traveller Prince Pückler-Muskau came to see 'the wonders of Eaton Hall' on New Year's Day, 1827. He was scathing about the building: a 'chaos of modern gothic excrescences'. The Prince felt the interior furnishings were lacking in taste: 'All the magnificence lay in the gorgeous materials, and the profuse display of money.' A keen gardener and landscaper, the Prince gave the gardens short shrift: 'A number of "affreux" [hideous] little gothic temples deface the pleasure ground, which has, moreover, no fine trees ... the whole seems laid out in comparatively recent times.' The Gothic temple thus harshly stigmatized was specially designed by William Cole in 1822 to provide a focal point for a Roman altar. The altar was bought by Earl Grosvenor and displayed in the gardens at Eaton after it was unearthed in a field at Boughton in 1821.

Eaton Hall became a byword for magnificence. A Tarvin gentleman, Mr Dutton, wanted a handsome tombstone to honour his father's memory. The stonemason, Mr Reece, obliged with an edifice so ornate it overpowered the sensibilities of visitors to the churchyard. When Reece had finished his work, he sent Dutton a bill of similar epic proportions. Dutton refused to pay more than the £20 already agreed (a large sum of money then), and the dispute went to court. Learned counsel, with many witticisms on this 'grave subject', compared the tombstone to the Grosvenor residence: 'Gentlemen, if there is any objection to the architecture of Eaton Hall, it is because it is too flashy – so is the gorgeous tomb in question, heaped up with gingerbread work.' The case was settled in Dutton's favour.[15]

Beautiful Elizabethan houses such as Little Moreton Hall (residence of the Moreton family) still survived. But they weren't always treated with respect by their Georgian owners. A case in point was the sixteenth-century Bramhall Hall, home to the Davenports. John Byng was disgusted by its owner's lack of taste in giving the ancient black-and-white hall smart new sash windows. A servant maid told him that although his master, William Davenport, was a lover of antiquity, Mrs Martha Davenport had more modern tastes: all the rooms in use were furnished *à la mode*. It's perhaps just as well Byng didn't live to see the demolition of the house's Long Gallery during the 1820s.

A few days after his visit to Bramhall, Byng visited Dunham Massey, for many years home to the Booth family. The estates were inherited in 1736 by the Earls of Stamford, the Grey family. Byng had a taste for history and he hoped to find Dunham a venerable old mansion like Bramhall. He was astonished to discover Dunham was now a 'modern, red-brick, tasteless house, which I had not a wish to enter'. The Hall had been updated over half a century earlier by George Booth, the 2nd Earl of Warrington. Others were more complimentary; another writer called it 'one of the most beautiful residences in the county'.[16] The old and new parks had fine timber and herons nested in the mightiest and most venerable oaks. Byng was shocked to see trees in the new park being felled to make charcoal.

Another imposing Elizabethan mansion to undergo 'improvements' was Brereton Hall, home of the Breretons until the family died out in the 1720s. The estate was broken up and sold in 1817. After John Hyde of Howard bought the Hall in 1830, he removed the curving cupolas on the towers and replaced them with top-heavy battlements.

Despite these depredations, Elizabethan architecture enjoyed a revival around this time. The ubiquitous Lewis Wyatt built Eaton Hall in this style (at Eaton-by-Congleton) for the Antrobus family in 1829. Willington Hall was constructed in a similar fashion for Major Tomkinson during this year.

The spread of industry impacted on some estates. The old Cheshire family of the Dukinfields became extinct in 1758 with the death of Sir William Dukinfield-Daniel, third baronet and High Sheriff of Cheshire. After his death his wife Lady Penelope married John Astley (1720–87), the son of a Wem surgeon. Astley was a noted portrait painter. The estates became Astley's upon his marriage to Lady Penelope in 1775. He built Dukinfield Lodge on the banks of the Tame, facing the township of Ashton-under-Lyne. The spacious hall in the 'French Style' had a moat. The interior was adorned with many of Astley's own paintings. The house originally enjoyed a beautiful riverside view. Ormerod noticed that the factories and collieries of the increasingly industrial Ashton-under-Lyne 'have long since destroyed all appearances of picturesque beauty or of comfort'.

The Stanley family were very unlucky with their houses. The Stanleys' ancient residence, the Old Hall at Alderley, was greatly extended during the eighteenth century. The new addition burnt down in 1779. The family decamped to Park House, a farmhouse on the estate. A new house, Alderley Park, was built nearby in 1818 by Sir John Thomas Stanley (1766–1850). This house was demolished in the twentieth century after another fire.

What were living conditions like away from the great houses? Cheshire's inhabitants in the towns enjoyed some improvements to their quality of life as public utilities became a growing priority.

The eminent Chester doctor John Haygarth (1740–1827), who practised in Chester for over three decades, felt the city's climate was a healthy one. He estimated the city's mortality rate as 25 deaths per 1000 people in the 1770s, rather worse than for their Victorian descendants. (Sanitary reformer Edwin Chadwick gave the mortality rate for the whole county as 21 per 1000 in 1842.)

City sewerage was much the same as in medieval times. Although some houses had their own cesspits, the contents of chamber-pots, filth and rubbish from houses and shops were thrown in the rainwater gutters down the middle of the street. Walking was obviously extremely hazardous. The Chester Improvement Act of 1803 included provisions for new sewers and drains. Work began on the construction of rainwater culverts in Watergate St in 1807. Sewerage in other streets was improved over the next two decades.

Chester's water supply came from wells or cisterns and the River Dee. The pressure in the pipes supplied by the river was insufficient, however. Grumbles from the citizens led to the formation of a new Chester Waterworks Company in 1828. It installed new pumping machinery, powered by steam at Barrel Well Hill in Boughton.

Street lighting was by oil lamps, but the illumination they provided was poor. The Rows in particular were plagued by thieves, pickpockets and prostitutes. Gentlemen wanting to enjoy a quiet evening stroll along the Rows might find themselves shoved down the steps into the street and ladies who ventured abroad were even more vulnerable. By this time the Rows were cluttered up with many tiny shops and stalls. These were taken down by the authorities early in the nineteenth century to make the walkways lighter and more pleasant for shoppers.

The advent of coal gas lamps, installed by the Chester Gas Light Company (1817), helped to lessen the dangers of walking the city at night. However, it took over a decade before all the main streets were fully lit by gas. Towards the end of the Regency period, the Row tenants started a voluntary 'neighbourhood watch' scheme to make the walkways safer still. (The county didn't have a police force until much later in the century.)

Other Cheshire towns were smartening up with mixed success, because they were dependent on the goodwill of their ratepayers. Nevertheless, a new sense of civic pride was in evidence. Congleton Corporation demolished its old Town Hall in 1804, and spent £700 on a new 'Town Hall, Prison, and Collonade (*sic*).' A new workhouse, a 'neat and commodious edifice', was constructed seven years later.[17]

Knutsford's streets were clean underfoot thanks to the generosity of Lady Jane Stanley of Brook House. Lady Jane (1780–1803) paid for new pavements. This spinster, with very strict, high ideals, didn't approve of couples walking down the street with their arms linked. So she insisted the new thoroughfares should only be one flagstone wide: it was 'ladies first'. The *grande dame* perambulated the streets assisted by a gold-headed staff. She smartly tapped with her stick any non-locals ignorant of her rank who didn't give her precedence on the footpath. Lady Jane left money in her will to maintain the pavements.

One Cheshire village was so desperate for a change of image that it changed its name. Bullock Smithy lay on the turnpike road between Buxton and Manchester. This thriving village had a busy industrial community and a coaching inn. Unfortunately, its weavers and colliers enjoyed their time off with such enthusiasm that Bullock Smithy became a byword for riots and rowdiness. Its bad name began to cost the local businessmen money and they wanted it erased from the map. Accordingly, Bullock Smithy was given a makeover in 1795, and given a new name: the rural-sounding Hazel Grove. But it wasn't easy to change the name or its reputation for lawlessness: the village was still known as Bullock Smithy until it was officially re-christened in 1836.

Macclesfield re-paved some streets in the 1790s. The Corporation invested in a new Town Hall with Ionic columns designed by Francis Goodwin in 1823. However, fine feathers didn't necessarily make a fine 'bird' or modern town. Here, too, the streets were unsafe to walk at night. When the town suffered from a spate of robberies in 1812, the householders banded together and undertook night patrols for several months. Macclesfield Corporation passed an Act in 1814 appointing

Police Commissioners to improve the town's amenities. An ill-fated effort was made to provide gas lighting the following year. Five years later a new Gas Company was formed and the town centre was finally illuminated. A further Act in 1825 led to the main streets being paved and drained, and additional gas lighting installed. But the people of Macclesfield suffered from the same public health problems as other nineteenth-century towns. There was no decent sewerage. Privy middens were the norm for those families lucky enough to have their own privy – many had to use a public one. The streets were disappearing under excrement from humans as well as animals.

Unlike some towns like Frodsham, which were 'well supplied with many excellent springs of good water',[18] Macclesfield's burgeoning population suffered from inadequate supplies. Macclesfield had been in the uncommon situation of enjoying a piped water supply to some homes since the late seventeenth century. A programme to renew and extend the use of old lead piping began in the 1780s. But although cast iron pipes were now available, they were deemed too expensive, and alder wood was used instead. Unfortunately the alder pipes harboured all kinds of nasty diseases and from 1799 onwards they were gradually replaced by cast iron. However, many townspeople didn't have access to piped water. They filled buckets at public standpipes and wells, or dipped them in the River Bollin, before trudging home with their heavy load. Or they could buy water by the bucketful – Byng commented on the large number of water-sellers in the town.

The river and wells were also contaminated with sewage, because of the town's poor drainage. Macclesfield's worthies didn't feel public health issues were their responsibility. They were reluctant to raise the rates and nothing was done to remedy the situation. As a result, infant mortality was extremely high, with diseases like cholera and fever claiming victims of all classes. The workers huddled together in the town's industrial heartland were most vulnerable to illness.

In parallel with other towns, Stockport's improvements to local services were made at a snail's pace, impeded by ratepayers' reluctance to delve deeper into their pockets. Gas had been used to light the cotton mills for over a decade when the town's first private gasworks was established in 1820. Previously, the only lighting in the town centre was a few glimmering oil lamps, but by September 1825 there were four gas lamps in Underbank, and one in Bridge St.

As in Macclesfield, a few Stockport folk had piped water. The oldest part of town was supplied from open springs rising in Barn Fields. Water was collected into a reservoir behind St Peter's Church, and then piped into town. But elsewhere in Stockport people queued patiently at the public pumps in Chestergate or Spring Gardens, or bought water from water carriers. The population explosion meant the town's wells gradually became poisoned by raw sewage, with obvious consequences.

A local Police Act was passed in 1826 to enable streets to be lit, paved and cleaned. The Act also compelled the landlords of workers' cottages to supply water to their tenants. The town's factories were also thirsty for water. Henry Marsland bought up the water rights of the manorial corn mills in 1791. But growing water shortages led his son Peter Marsland to sink an artesian well in the yard of his Park Mills. The well was such a success, Marsland applied for an Act of Parliament for the right to supply the town and the Act was passed in May 1825. The new Stockport Waterworks began supplying fresh water two years later. The water was pumped into a reservoir at Woodbank and the supply was turned on for two hours each day. However, many workers remained the 'great unwashed' for decades yet: Stockport had no public baths until 1855.

Little interest was shown in improving working-class housing. Workers in places such as Watercoates (Macclesfield) and Heaton Norris (Stockport) were crowded together in damp, dark, dirty back-to-back houses and some lived in the dreadful cellar dwellings. Overcrowding was endemic. Undrained streets were swamped with rotting rubbish and ordure and open privies added to the general miasma.

Despite the risk of getting splashed by all the muck in the streets, Cheshire's inhabitants were keen to be dressed in the latest style. The local papers regularly featured the latest London fashions. The *Chester Courant* (4 January 1803) reported: 'The prevailing colours are Egyptian brown, green, crimson and amber. Caps or turbans are ... universally adopted; the latter ornamented with plumes of white or mixed feathers. In pelices [pelisses] silk has given way to kerseymeres. Straw hats are still worn lined with velvet.' The item about silk would have caused concern in the silk towns. The *Macclesfield Courier* (4 April 1829)

listed 'Female Fashions' for spring, culled from the modish *La Belle Assemblée* magazine. A 'poplin gown of apricot colour' was suggested for dinner dress.

Fashionable young ladies bought *Ackermann's Repository of Fine Arts*, especially recommended for the 'fair sex', from bookseller Mr Poole in Chester. This cheap, elegant magazine was 'the Mirror and Oracle of Fashion', crammed full of 'elegant Arts and Accomplishments'.[19] Another popular magazine was the *Lady's Monthly Museum* with its coloured fashion plates.

Milliners in Chester naturally looked to the capital for inspiration. F. Towsey, a hatter and hosier in Northgate St, sold 'Real London Hats'. However, some of the 'London' hats worn by Regency bucks or young ladies were probably made in Cheshire. Stockport hats were renowned for their quality and firms there supplied London merchants. There were forty-six hatters in the town in 1789. William Carrington had a works at Cale Green. George and Benjamin Lake had premises at Hope's Carr and Heaton Norris. Hats were still made by hand in workers' homes rather than in factories. Some of the finishing processes were done in the masters' warehouses, where materials and finished articles were stored. The masters 'put out' the work to the hatters, who had to return the goods by a given date. This day was treated as a holiday and the workers spent their wages at the Hatters' Arms or Jolly Hatters. The hatting trade was given a boost by the repeal of the hat tax in 1811, but, obviously, the industry was subject to the whims of fashion. Felt hats became increasingly unfashionable. Silk hats, made by firms such as Barlow and Shawcross at Reddish, and Christys on Canal Street, were more popular.

Beaver fur supplied by the Hudson's Bay Company was highly prized and became a top fashion accessory. In Chester, Shaw's 'Original London Hat Warehouse' offered 'an extensive and elegant selection of Ladies' Gentlemen's and Children's Beavers of the first quality'.[20] This was bad news for the unfortunate beavers, which were driven to the edge of extinction: over one million were killed for their fur in 1830.

Even ladies' maids hankered to be dressed in the latest modes but they preferred flimsy, stylish but impractical muslins to sturdy cotton gowns. This penchant for fashion dismayed their employers, who felt they were just aping their 'betters'.

Mill girls were well known for their love of finery: they spent a large portion of their wages on clothes. John Byng was bowled over by the young ladies of Stockport: 'Entering a town on a Sunday evening with all the damsels frisking around is very tremendous to a modest man … Nor did I ever see smarter lasses than I met in my stroll after tea; with their petticoats so short as to oblige them to turn out their toes and exert their best paces …'

As Jane Austen commented in *Northanger Abbey* (1818): 'Woman is fine for her own satisfaction alone.' The prime object of dressing modishly was to see and be seen. And Cheshire had no shortage of assembly rooms and genteel pleasure grounds in which to promenade in all one's finery.

4

High Life and Low

Regency Cheshire was no rural backwater; it enjoyed a busy social scene. Balls and assemblies had been held in the Exchange at Chester since the end of the seventeenth century. This large, handsome edifice (erected in 1689) had an elegantly fitted up Assembly Room, with an orchestra in the middle. Booth Mansion on Watergate St was another venue for assemblies during the 1740s. Later in the century, both Assembly Rooms had fallen out of favour with the gentry and they were abandoned to the less well-heeled classes. The Exchange now hosted 'winter assemblies for the trades-people' and it had a 'well-chosen subscription library'.[1] Tickets for the assemblies could be purchased at the White Lion Inn.

To accommodate the most modish gatherings, grand new Assembly Rooms were fitted out in the Talbot Inn, on the corner of Eastgate St and Newgate St. The inn was given a facelift in 1785 and re-opened as the Royal Hotel (now the Grosvenor Hotel). The Royal became the hub of a giddy round of fashionable entertainments. Ladies and gentlemen met in its coffee-room for a good gossip. Dancing assemblies were held fortnightly on Mondays from November to March in the 1790s; ladies on the subscription list paid 12s 6d for a ticket, plus 6d for tea. Card assemblies, which were held every Thursday, livened up the long winter evenings. The Royal was still going strong during the 1820s; it was commended for its 'excellent spacious assembly room … In this noble room large dining parties are frequently accommodated, and it is also often engaged for public concerts. A very superior subscription newsroom … forms part of this extensive establishment.'[2]

Knutsford, long considered a 'genteel place', was renowned for its elegant visitors during its annual races. Balls were held in an 'elegant assembly room' at the George and Dragon Inn, which also had a tea room.[3] A maidservant at the George assured one traveller that no tradesmen were admitted to the monthly assemblies there. Knutsford ladies went to the local parties and assemblies in sedan chairs, of which there were three at one time. The sedan chair originally donated by Lady Jane Stanley of Brook House was later used for May Day processions.

Congleton also had a beautiful Assembly Room, paid for by Sir Edmund Antrobus in 1823, it was built on to the Guildhall erected two decades earlier.

Newspaper advertisements give a good guide to the different kinds of entertainment on offer. Musical tastes were catered for; the *Chronicle* (9 January 1789) mentions eight subscription concerts to be held at the Royal Hotel Assembly Room. It cost a guinea for a gentleman's ticket; one for a lady cost 12s and 'strangers' were admitted at 3s 6d each. Doors opened at 6 p.m., and concerts started promptly at 7 p.m. The principal performers, from the Music Hall, Manchester, included Mr Haigh (first violin), Mr Hime (second violin) and Mrs Shipley (singer).

Spectacular music festivals were held at the cathedral to aid local charities and these events were very popular with the gentry. In the autumn of 1829, the festival was followed for the first time by a fancy dress ball at the Royal Hotel, which attracted an immense gathering.

As well as professional concerts, music enthusiasts enjoyed occasional concerts by an amateur choir, the Chester Choral Society, accompanied by an 'excellent organ'. The choir practised every week in the King's School at the cathedral.[4]

The top county families gave balls at home for their own social circle. Frances, Lady Shelley, said the Duke of Gloucester was a frequent guest at parties in the 'great Cheshire houses'. She attended a ball in 1805 at Vale Royal, the home of Thomas Cholmondeley. (Thomas was created Baron Delamere in July 1821. His wife Henrietta-Elizabeth became a great friend of Lady Elizabeth Belgrave, née Leveson-Gower.)

If, like Mr Darcy in Jane Austen's *Pride and Prejudice* (1813), you felt dancing was: 'a compliment which I never pay to any place, if I can avoid it,' you could watch a play instead. The Theatre Royal on

Northgate St, Chester, had a chequered history. Originally a chapel dedicated to St Nicholas, it was in turn a court-room, then a warehouse, before being converted into a playhouse. Each season began with a play 'by one of the first companies in the kingdom'.[5] *England Preserved*, 'a new tragedy never before acted here' opened in October 1795. The play was followed by a musical farce, *The Quaker*.[6] The theatre was smartened up in 1828 when it was leased by Mr Lewis. He increased the theatre's capacity by raising the ceiling and adding an extra tier of boxes; Hemingway proudly boasted the Royal was now 'one of the most elegant and commodious of any out of the metropolis'.

Famous actors and actresses from London trod the boards in the provinces. Master Betty, the 'Young Roscius', performed at Chester in November 1804. He received a mixed review from the *Chronicle* for his return visit eight years later. A packed theatre awaited his appearance with high expectations. 'Mr Betty made his entrée amidst thunders of applause, from an exceedingly numerous, and genteel audience. He is about five feet eight or nine inches high – extremely lusty ...' Although the first part of Betty's speech in his character of Achmet in *Barbarossa* was given in an 'affected, whining manner', he improved as the evening progressed; his performance became 'inimitably fine'.[7]

Actress Mrs Dorothy Jordan (mistress of the Duke of Clarence, the future William IV) appeared at the Theatre Royal in September 1789; she earned the princely sum of £130 for just four nights. She visited Chester again in December 1813. The immensely popular and successful tragedian Edmund Kean performed *Richard III* at the Royal in September 1815.

Audiences thrilled to shows such as the 'Grand Mechanical and Picturesque Theatre of Arts' in December 1819. A front seat in the pit cost 2s; the evening's fare began with 'A Voyage to the North Pole' and ended with 'A Tempest on the coast of Barbary'.[8]

Mr Handy's travelling circus must have been one of the liveliest and exciting shows ever to appear at Chester. For six nights only at the Theatre Royal, the audience thrilled to tightrope dancing, slack-rope vaulting, tumbling wire dancing, and the 'Original Child of Promise', who performed 'The World Upside Down' with candlesticks, chairs and 'Solomon's Ladder'. A Mr Robinson from the Royal Circus in London danced 'The Egg Hornpipe' over twelve eggs, while blindfold.

The evening concluded with 'The Ruins of Troy', performed by Mr Handy and 'ten capital performers'. As if these delights weren't enough, Mr Handy and his troop executed spectacular feats of horsemanship at the Circus in Crook's Lane every afternoon that week.[9]

The theatre in Macclesfield was very popular during the eighteenth century. But it was forced to close its doors after a charismatic local preacher, David Simpson, denounced theatrical performances as ungodly. However, the townsfolk must have missed the glamour and excitement of the stage, because when the Theatre Royal in Mill St opened in April 1811, it found a ready audience.

Regency gentlemen were sports mad. They pursued the pleasures of the 'fancy' – cock-fighting, boxing, the turf, the chase and so on – with great gusto. Horse-racing was hugely popular with the aristocracy and gentry and the Prince Regent himself bred horses. One of his successes was 'The Smoker', a famous Cheshire racehorse which belonged to Sir John Fleming Leicester. The race meeting in May at Chester Roodee was one of the highlights of the county's social year. The Roodee was a lush piece of pasture ground where cattle were allowed to graze in season. Races had been held there since about 1539, except for a hiatus during the Civil War and Interregnum. Around the time of the first Regency crisis, there was only one race run daily during race week: an endurance race, run in heats. Interest grew in short, fast races (as at modern circuits) with just one heat rather than several. By the time of George IV's coronation, sprint races had won out over the old-fashioned style of racing.

Chester races were held in high repute. Sports writer Charles James Apperley ('Nimrod') said the Roodee course was considered: 'far from being a good one, being on a dead flat, with rather a sharp turn near home, in consequence of which several accidents have occurred'. Nevertheless, the prizes at Chester were a huge draw; the course '... affords a good trial for young horses, and there is plenty of money to be run for by the old ones, who come out fresh and well'. The regular City Plate meeting (a race in heats) was won by Mr Ackers's 'Fair Forester' in 1803: the prize was a silver punch bowl worth 50 guineas. Five years later, the prize on offer had increased to an impressive 60-guinea silver cup.

New races were added to the Chester calendar during this period. The Earl of Chester Plate event began in 1802 and Charles Cholmondeley's horse 'Cheshire Cheese' won the 100-guinea prize for this race the following year. Two additional events, the Palatine Stakes and Dee Stakes, were founded in 1813.

Accommodation in the town, both inns and private rooms, filled up rapidly before race meetings and special balls, assemblies and plays were held during race week. Large numbers of less genteel folk also turned up in good time for the races: 'The usual attendants on this annual scene of gaiety, beggars, wooden-legged orators, flying-stationers, blind fiddlers, and raree-showmen, have already arrived ...'[10] Pickpockets were an unwelcome addition to the racing scene.

The first Earl Grosvenor (1731–1802) was a keen gambler and successful racehorse owner. Nimrod said Sir Richard was 'a great ornament to the English turf; he ran his horses honestly and truly'. The Earl spent a fortune building up and improving Eaton Stud; among his famous stud-horses were 'John Bull', 'Alexander' and 'Meteor'. He was said to have won over £200,000 during his career on the turf, but still hadn't covered his expenses when he died. The *Chronicle* reported his huge losses in just one year: 'Lord Grosvenor, on making up his racing accounts, finds himself, after all his success, no less than £200,000 minus for his amusements on the turf!'[11] Sir Richard's two best racers were 'Meteora' and 'Violante', said to be the best four-miler of her day. The Earl was a patron of the famous horse artist George Stubbs.

Earl Grosvenor's son Robert continued the tradition: his horses won prizes at Ascot and Doncaster as well as Chester. One of his jockeys, David Jones, was a witness in the famous trial of Dan Dawson, who was hanged in 1812 after being found guilty of poisoning racehorses. The second Earl Grosvenor donated race prizes and, along with other high-ranking gentlemen, was a patron of the Grandstand Committee. Subscribers bought £50 shares to raise funds for Chester's first permanent grandstand at the Roodee; a total of £2,500 was raised in 1817. The new stand was built to Thomas Harrison's design. The more genteel race-goers now had some protection from the weather, and the riff-raff were kept at a discreet distance. The Stand Cup race began the following year, with a very respectable 100-guinea prize. One fixture which became a firm favourite was a handicap race, the Tradesman's Cup (later the Chester Cup), first staged in 1824. This was another 100-

guinea race; it was won by Sir Thomas Stanley's horse 'Doge of Venice'. Stanley, of Hooton Hall, won many races at Chester with his specially trained horses.

The *Stranger's Companion* described the scene at the Roodee in the 1820s:

> The annual races … commence the first Monday in May, and continue five days, during which all is bustle and gaiety. The ground … is extremely well adapted for the diversion and convenience of the spectators: there is not perhaps in the kingdom a place so admirably calculated for giving accommodation and pleasure to everyone … The races are kept up with true sportsmanlike respectability … when the sport is once begun, nothing can equal the interesting effect which it gives. The people who have been casually spread over the ground, gather to the side under the wall, and range themselves one above another on the bank, and give an appearance very like an immense theatre, whilst the wall is surmounted by a large assemblage of fashion and beauty, collected from all parts of the city and neighbourhood.

One larger-than-life character often seen at Chester Races was 'Mad Jack' Mytton (1796–1834). The Squire of Halston Hall, in Shropshire, John Mytton was well known for his 'hunting, shooting, driving, racing, eccentric and extravagant exploits'. Heir to a fortune at an early age, Mytton had a 'lofty pride which disdained the littleness of prudence, and a sort of destroying spirit that appeared to run amuck at fortune'.[12] His usual diet was seven bottles of port wine every day.

Mytton went out hunting in all weathers in only the thinnest of clothing, with no underwear; he once followed some ducks across a frozen pond, stark naked. One evening, George Underhill, a horse-dealer, called at Halston after a visit to Chester fair. Mytton got Underhill really drunk, then tucked him up in bed with two bulldogs and his pet bear. This poor bear led a dog's life. Mytton once dressed up in hunting costume and rode the bear into his drawing room. The bear was put down after attacking a servant.

On another occasion, during Chester race week, Mytton and his friend Nimrod were enjoying supper one night in a hotel coffee-room (probably the Royal Hotel). 'A gentleman, who was a stranger to us all, was standing with his back to the fire, having drunk too much wine. "I'll stop him," said Mytton; and getting behind him unperceived, put a red-hot coal into his pocket.'

One Sunday evening immediately before race week, Mytton was caught gambling (which was illegal). He was playing at hazard (a game of chance, using dice) in a hired room, when the Mayor of Chester came in to stop the proceedings. Mytton coolly popped his winnings in his hat, put his hat on his head, and then walked calmly away, as if he was just a spectator.

Mytton blew half a million pounds (a fantastic sum then) in fifteen years; a large part of the money was spent maintaining his racing stable of fifteen to twenty horses and he had a number of successes at Chester. 'Anti-Radical', 'Habberley' and 'Euphrates' were just a few of his winning horses. 'Euphrates' won the King's Plate in 1823 and 1828. Another of Jack's horses, 'Halston', won the Tradesman's Cup the following year.

Unfortunately, Mytton's trainer and rider, William Dunn, was killed by a fall at the Roodee. Jack Mytton's successes there gradually declined, perhaps because he often raced his horses whether they were fully raceworthy or not. His horses also ran at Tarporley Hunt races, over a new course near Cotebrook in the Delamere Forest (where Mytton's stables were situated).

Mytton's daftest exploit ended tragically. He was afflicted by the hiccups while drunk. He attempted to frighten them away – by setting fire to his shirt with a lighted candle! Mytton was very badly burnt. He survived, but his faculties, already impaired by his heavy drinking, were badly affected. He died some time later in a debtor's prison.

At Knutsford, the annual races on the Heath had been running from as early as the 1670s; they brought wealth to the town as well as entertainment. The Knutsford Gold Cup was worth 100 sovereigns. The races were said to be 'remarkable for being honoured with a more brilliant assemblage of nobility and gentry than any other in the county; not excepting even Chester'.[13] However, John Byng peevishly declared the course was 'not large enough for a goose to run round'. When the course was extended in 1810, one horse bolted for the turn it was accustomed to run round and its jockey Thomas Day was killed.

Horse races were also held at Nantwich, Northwich and Sandbach and Farndon held flat races until 1803. The Tarporley Hunt races, founded circa 1776, were held at Crabtree Green until 1815, when Delamere Forest was enclosed. Races at Macclesfield were held in open fields by the London Road before a new course opened in 1828 at Town Field. Macclesfield's new annual race meeting was a three-day event in October, timed to coincide with the local Wakes; it was very popular.

Race days at Chester usually began with cockfighting or 'cocking' as it was known, to add to the fun. This revolting 'sport' took place at the cockpit on the outskirts of the city walls, near Souters Lane, but there were also cockpits in more central inns such as the Feathers. In rural districts, cockfights and badger-baiting took place in churchyards or inns. Cockfighting clung on at Hazel Grove right into the twentieth century. This was a gentlemen's entertainment; it cost five shillings per day to attend. Huge sums of money were involved: 'During the races at Chester, a MAIN of COCKS will be fought in the new cock-pit, St. John's-Lane, between Sir Peter Warburton, Bart., and Windsor Hanloke, Esq., for TEN GUINEAS the battle and TWO HUNDRED the Main.'[14]

The erection of a new building for 'cocking' at Chester in 1825 shows that even this late in the day, the sport was far from being in decline, despite being sniffed at by the tourist guidebooks as a cruel practice. The birds were prepared for battle by removing their combs, so their opponent couldn't grab hold of them. Their wing feathers were snipped and the tips sharpened and vicious spurs were attached to their feet. There was a really horrible version of the sport, 'cock-throwing', in which the feathered victim, fastened by its leg to a peg, was used as target practice, but thankfully this had virtually died out by the end of the eighteenth century.

The annual bull-bait at Chester was actually run under the auspices of the Corporation until Mayor William Cowper finally put a stop to its involvement in 1754. But the 'sport' was still going strong in 1789, near St Peter's Church: 'The Cross is famous for being the annual scene of exhibition of that *polite play* called a bull-bait; where four or five of these *horned heroes* are attended by several hundred lovers of that *rational amusement*.'[15] The bull was tied to a stake, then beaten with large wooden sticks and tormented by bulldogs. One year, when a poor, exhausted animal lay down after being wounded, these 'sportsmen' set fire to some straw underneath the bull to make it get up.

Although bull-baiting was forbidden in 1803 within Chester city limits, its adherents, nothing daunted, held bull-baits on the outskirts of the city boundary, at Boughton heath. The *Courant* gave a blood-curdling report (not fit to print) on the bull's sufferings at the Boughton bull-bait in August 1818: 'an exhibition as brutal as any we have heard of'.[16] There were also bull-baits at places such as Congleton, Middlewich, Nantwich and Hazel Grove. Bunbury had a 'bull-run' at its village fair, in which the unlucky beast was chased through the streets. Bull-baiting was still legal until 1835, when it was finally banned.

Bear-baiting had long been a favourite sport at Congleton. According to legend, the good townsfolk there sold the town Bible in 1621 in order to purchase a new bear when the old one died. Another slightly less scurrilous version of the story says the Corporation was saving up to buy a new Bible for the town chapel. After the town bear died, the Corporation decided this loss was the more urgent need, so they gave the money to the Bearward to buy a new bear instead. The story's commemorated in the old Cheshire rhyme:

Congleton rare, Congleton rare
Sold the Church Bible to buy a new Bear!

But by the turn of the nineteenth century, sports like bull-baiting and bear-baiting were beginning to be frowned upon. The authorities made strenuous efforts to ban them, not just because of the cruelty involved but also because of the public disorder which usually accompanied them. Stockport banned bear-baiting (and football) in 1826, but bear-baiting continued in the surrounding country districts, especially during Wakes week. George Slater remembered bear-baiting taking place at a pub in Gawsworth around this time.

Hunting, though more controversial nowadays, was a vital part of the social scene. The Cheshire Hunt was formed in the early 1760s by the Hon. John Smith-Barry of Marbury Hall. The hunt's first meet was always held at Sandiway Head; the kennels were nearby. One of Smith-Barry's hounds, Bluecap, was a legendary animal. His claim to fame was winning a 500-guinea race at Newmarket in September 1763; Bluecap covered the four mile course in eight minutes. When out with the rest of the pack, the high-speed hound was handicapped with a wooden weight round his neck so he didn't outstrip the other hounds and leave them far behind. Another story claims Bluecap ran from London to Sandiway Kennels – a distance of 180 miles – in just two days. A monument to Bluecap was, very aptly, erected on Speedwell Hill and the inn at Sandiway was named the Blue Cap in his honour.

Smith-Barry's nephew James took over the hunt in 1784, but was unpopular with his neighbours, so Sir Peter Warburton became the new Master of the Hunt in 1798. He shared the reins with other gentlemen including the Brookes and Mr Egerton. The Rev. George Heron took over in 1810, and although in theory he was Master until 1818, in practice Sir Harry Mainwaring of Over Peover was in charge from 1813 to 1837. The indefatigable Sir Harry hunted for four days a week over a vast area, despite being famously short-sighted (he had an eyeglass inside his whip handle). He kept kennels at Sandiway and Wrenbury as well as one near his estate.

January was a very busy month for the Cheshire hounds. The *Chester Chronicle* for 9 January 1829 detailed upcoming meetings at Wrenbury, Sandiway Head, Toft, Kinderton, Duddon Heath, Tarporley and Bartington Heath, all within a few days of each other.

Other notable Cheshire fox-hunters were the Tomkinsons, the Gleggs and Jack Ford. The Tomkinson brothers were commemorated in a hunting song by Rowland Egerton-Warburton as 'the Vicar, the Squire and the Major'. Henry Tomkinson was the vicar of Acton and rector of Davenham. The Rev. James was the aforementioned 'Squire' of Dorfold Hall. The 'Major' was William Tomkinson, the Peninsular War and Waterloo veteran; he built Willington Hall after purchasing the estate in 1828. Sir Thomas Stanley of Hooton also kept his own pack of hounds.

The Tarporley Hunt dates back to 1762. It was originally founded as a hare coursing club and the Tarporley foxes were safe until 1769. 'Many of the principal gentlemen of the county assemble at an annual hunt, the neighbouring heaths of Delamere Forest affording very favourable ground for the diversion'.[17] The Tarporley fox-hunters wore scarlet coats, green capes and green waistcoats and met at the Swan Inn.

Although fox-hunting was primarily a male sport, ladies like Lady Belgrave loved to follow the hunt along the roads, and sometimes even joined in the chase. The *Macclesfield Courier* (22 November 1828) described a hunt meeting at Duddon Heath. About 160 people, of whom seventy were clad in scarlet, attended the meet. Lord and Lady Belgrave, Lord Delamere and Sir William Watkins Wynn were present:

'The field had a very brilliant appearance.' After a chase of almost an hour, the fox saved himself by going to ground in the woods near Utkinton.

One famous meet was known as 'The Shavington Day'. This was a contest between rival packs from Cheshire, Shropshire and Staffordshire. Sir Harry Mainwaring's Cheshire hounds were hunted by Will Head. The packs met at Shavington Hall, near Crewe, in April 1829. Jack Mytton took part that day but he never hunted again after a bad tumble in which he was crushed by a horse. Unfortunately, Nimrod doesn't say which pack won the day.

The papers eagerly covered any sport. Prize-fighting was extremely popular. A 'Grand Fight at Chester' was held at the Navigation Cop between two tailors, Ben Piercy and Jack Pickering; a profession not normally noted for its belligerence.[18]

Less bloodthirsty sports were also much in vogue, such as the foot race held at the Roodee in 1828 between Edward Davies of Hope (near Flint) and Samuel Lewis of Cotebrook, near Tarporley. They ran the 160 yards for a prize of twenty sovereigns; Lewis won by several yards, much to the disappointment of the Welshman's supporters.

If visitors didn't have the time or means to visit the seaside to try the new fashion of sea bathing at places like Parkgate, they might try their hand at other water sports. Men enjoyed bathing or swimming in the Dee. Bathing was a dangerous pastime if you weren't a strong swimmer: a private of the 89th Regiment stationed in Chester drowned in 1818, after venturing out of his depth in the Dee near the Brewer's Hall. His companion survived after being rescued by some fishermen. Some men swam in the nude. 'We have received repeated complaints of the indecent conduct of persons bathing near the public walks, the banks of the Canals and the River Dee and Roodee Cop ... this is a very serious offence.'[19] This pastime earned one man two months in prison.

After the Peace of Paris was declared between France and the Allied Powers at the end of May 1814, a rowing regatta was held on the Dee the following month. The regatta drew thousands of spectators, so it was decided to hold one every year thereafter to coincide with the King's birthday. The regatta in June 1818 included a race for a silver cup (value £10), to be rowed for by four-man crews and an unusual event was a coracle rowing match. Church bells were rung at intervals throughout the day, and a good time was had by all. 'The river was completely covered with boats, some of which were manned by a few spirited town beaux, who in exhibiting their nautical skill made, we must say, a great *splash!*' Beer was on sale (sadly, some people over-indulged) and the 'beaux' smoked long pipes. Drinks and other goodies were available: '... cake, nuts, and oranges, ad infinitum, "imperial" pop, and barrelled cyder'. There was all the fun of the fair: 'round-abouts, and flying-coaches, all in motion, loaded by little children'. The Band of the Royal Cheshire Militia played some stirring marches and 'pugilistic exhibitions' provided more down-to-earth entertainment.[20]

A regatta at Lower Ferry in June 1824 provided a sad reminder of the perils of mixing alcohol and boating. Thirteen lives, including those of two young women, were lost when a boat full of partygoers tried to cross the Dee against a fierce tide. The vessel hit the chain cable of the sloop *Thetis*, and sank.

Chester also had some bowling greens, but this sport was more popular with the middle classes than the gentry. The walk round Chester city walls was a perennially favourite exercise. And of course there was no shortage of pleasant walks in Cheshire, such as Beacon Hill at Frodsham. There were also shooting 'butts' for archery at the bottom of the hill.

Visitors who flocked to Chester for the races might be lucky enough to witness another popular form of public entertainment: the hanging of condemned criminals. The inhabitants of the city were treated to more than their fair share of these disgraceful public spectacles because (for historical reasons) the city sheriffs had the responsibility for carrying out executions for the whole county, as well as the city.

Within living memory, the townspeople witnessed a Cheshire woman's horrific execution for 'petty treason': poisoning her husband. On 23 April 1763, Mary Heald was burnt at the stake. Mercifully, she was strangled by the executioner with a special chain before she was consumed by flames. Although this barbaric relic of medievalism appears to be an isolated case in the county, this particular form of execution wasn't abolished until as late as 1790.

Capital punishment wasn't reserved for major crimes such as murder: people were hanged for stealing goods worth just a few shillings. At the turn of the nineteenth century, there were still 160 capital crimes on the statute book. Even extreme youth was no mitigating circumstance, with children as young as six or seven being sentenced to death.

Public executions always drew huge crowds. On their last day on earth, condemned prisoners, weighted down with irons, were taken by the constable of the castle to the Gloverstone, just outside the castle. The prisoners were handed over to the city sheriffs, and paraded on a cart through the city to Gallows Hill at Boughton. After 1801, executions were switched to Northgate Gaol. The last execution at Boughton was a triple hanging; it was especially memorable, for all the wrong reasons.

In May 1801, convicted felons James Clare, Samuel Thompson and John Morgan were trundled through the streets in the usual manner. Clare, who'd vowed he wasn't 'born to be hanged', jumped from the cart. The crowd got out of his way, and he rolled down a gutter into the Dee. But Clare vanished beneath the waves, weighed down by the heavy irons on his legs. The drowned man was fished out onto the bank, then hanged anyway. In the meantime, his wretched companions on the execution cart were kept in suspense while the body was recovered. The dead and living convicts were strung up all together on Gallows Hill.

The new 'drop' or gallows at the Northgate was prone to malfunction. It prolonged the prisoners' suffering, so was nicknamed the 'drag'. This gallows was dismantled along with the old Northgate when the gaol was torn down. But there was no reprieve for those condemned to be 'launched into eternity', as it was euphemistically termed. Reluctant prisoners arriving at the beautiful portico of Harrison's new city gaol (1808) were greeted by a sinister vision: yet another brand new, up-to-date gallows. But the 'New Drop' wasn't much of an improvement, as we shall discover later. According to *Chester Chronicle* editor John Fletcher, thirty people were hanged at the New Drop between 1809 and 1822; they included William Tongue, executed in 1822 for raping a 9-year-old girl.

Executions were noisy, undignified spectacles. The execution of John Proudlove (highway robbery) and John Leir (burglary) in May 1829 was no exception. While the men were in their death throes (the unfortunate Leir took seven minutes to die), some 'ruffians' (probably pickpockets) 'were promoting a dog-fight immediately in front of the drop!'[21]

The new House of Correction adjoining Harrison's city gaol was for convicted petty criminals. Prisoners who had escaped being sentenced to transportation enjoyed a spell of hard labour instead. The chief House for the county was formerly at Middlewich, but there were also prisons at Stockport and Neston. Congleton's Town Hall contained 'a room for the confinement of debtors, and two arched dungeons for the temporary confinement of criminals, till they can be removed to the county gaol'.[22]

There were plenty of unwilling customers for the accommodation at Knutsford's new House of Correction. Following Thomas Harrison's lead, George Moneypenny's designs for the Sessions House and House of Correction were in Classical Revival style. The new buildings opened in October 1818. No doubt the criminals immured there were less than appreciative of the buildings' elegant lines.

The *Macclesfield Courier* (22 April 1826) reported that 192 people were committed to Knutsford for the sessions, with another thirteen people awaiting trial. The inmates included Mary Lomax, for stealing a blanket and linen sheet, and Thomas Brindley, for stealing three hens.

The youth of offenders was no excuse in the eyes of the law. In July 1828, two young lads, Samuel Jones (aged eleven) and Richard McDonald (twelve) were convicted of stealing linen at the midsummer Sessions. They were given six months in the Knutsford House of Correction – and the last week of each month was to be spent in solitary confinement.

Sixteen-year-old William Price, a 'notorious character', was sentenced to fourteen years' transportation for stealing six pounds of cheese and two caps. Price seemingly merited this draconian punishment because he had previous convictions for stealing a donkey, and for robbing a pedlar. His accomplices were treated more leniently: Thomas Jackson was sentenced to six months in prison, and 12-year-old Jonas Joinson sentenced to one week's imprisonment.[23]

The effect on offenders' families was devastating. The *Courant* (28 September 1819) gave a harrowing account of labourer Samuel Hooley's execution for burglary. Hooley (age sixteen in first reports, and nineteen in later issues) from Bowdon, was said to be 'young in years' but 'old in vice'. He had a last, traumatic meeting with his father:

'His grief was truly lamentable ... he could not even speak to his afflicted parent. The poor old man sat for nearly half an hour by his son, speechless; at last, after abruptly rising from his chair, with his face bedewed with tears, exclaimed in broken accents, "Farewell, my lad," and instantly hurried from the room.'

However, in practice, it seems the judges did sometimes make allowances for the age of offenders brought before them. James Smith, a 14-year-old found guilty of stealing a silver watch, was 'recommended to mercy' rather than facing execution.[24]

As well as fines or imprisonment, magistrates could impose alternative sentences on convicted felons or troublesome citizens. Older, medieval-style punishments were not yet a thing of the past. The stocks were still in use at many parishes. Two women were sentenced to sit in the stocks in the marketplace at Stockport in 1822. The stocks had been used within living memory when Heginbotham wrote his history much later in the century, although the pillory had long since fallen into disuse.

The iron brank or scold's bridle, that ghastly instrument of torture for silencing outspoken women, still survived in places such as Stockport, Macclesfield and Knutsford. Heginbotham says there were thirteen in the county. The brank in Stockport was hung on the toll-collector's door on market days as an awful warning to local women. The Stockport brank was notorious for being one of the most vicious in England. The metal 'gag' or plate which fastened down the woman's tongue was usually a flat metal bar. The Stockport gag had the added sinister refinement of sharp metal pins on the top and bottom; it must have caused agony to its helpless victims.

At Congleton, a husband could ask the town jailer to put the brank on his wife, then fasten the device to the fireplace. The poor woman was stuck there until marital harmony was deemed restored. The brank was still in use shockingly late during the supposed age of elegance. An Altrincham woman sentenced to the brank was carted round the streets in a wheelbarrow in 1820. In another case at Congleton four years later, Ann Rushton was 'branked' by the authorities for being rude to the churchwardens. These enlightened gentlemen paraded the lady through the streets, where she was insulted by the mob, before taking her back to the Town Hall to unfasten the brank and let her go.

'Scolds' also faced the ducking-stool, which plunged women into a stagnant pool; there was one at Macclesfield. Knutsford had not one but two ducking stools for 'brawling women' in the eighteenth century; no doubt they fell into disuse once Mrs Gaskell's 'Amazons' began their kindly reign. Some place names in the county still commemorate the 'cucking-stool'; one was used at Chester as a punishment for bad brewers. This was a kind of pillory, not a ducking-stool; the names became confused over the passage of time.

Petty offenders were publicly flogged at the town whipping post; the Stockport whip had nine lashes. John Hunter, a Manchester weaver, was convicted at Knutsford Sessions in July 1818 of picking the pocket of Joseph Mace of Heaton Norris. Sir John Thomas Stanley sentenced Hunter to be whipped once, and spend six months in prison. Hunter swore; he declared he would rather be hanged or transported than sent to prison. The 'depraved youth' then pulled off a shoe, which had an iron heel, and threw it at Sir John. He missed his aim, but soon regretted his impulsive action. Sir John consulted with his colleagues, then gave the 'hardened villain' a new sentence: two years in prison, and three floggings. Sir John ordered Hunter to be immediately whipped under the windows of the Sessions House, and later whipped again at Middlewich and Stockport.[25]

Whatever their station in life, high or low, the fates of the men, women and children who faced trial in the Cheshire courts were decided by the highest ranking members of society. Landowners and manufacturers served as magistrates, while workers who got into trouble might be tried by their landlord or employer. The usual suspects from the top county families crop up time and again on the grand juries at the assizes: Grosvenors, Cholmondeleys, Cottons, Wilbrahams, Davenports and Egertons.

Families like the Grosvenors wielded enormous power – and they were prepared to lavish vast sums to maintain the status quo.

5

A Vested Interest

For decades, Chester was the scene of violent political conflicts which brought the city into disrepute. A genteel visitor strolling round the city, guide book in hand, could see the physical scars left by the hotly contested elections of 1784 and 1812.

Our tourist would pause to admire the Exchange's exterior. The Exchange on Northgate St was used as a Town Hall and mayor's office, as well as for more frivolous occasions like assemblies. The quarter sessions and yearly elections for the mayor and other city officers were held here in a spacious room. The building was adorned with a cupola, and ornamented with plaques bearing carvings of the Royal arms and those of the Earl of Chester. The visitor's gaze would next be drawn to the fine, life-sized statue of Queen Anne. Unfortunately, Her Majesty had seen better days: the sculpture was badly damaged during election fever. Some ungallant rioters 'hostile to the corporation' had thrown stones and smashed Queen Anne's hand, globe and sceptre.[1]

Voter apathy was almost unheard of during the eighteenth and nineteenth centuries. Elections were literally fought over in the streets; blood was spilt and booze flowed in torrents. Polling days in Cheshire were no exception to the rule. Over £20,000 was spent on drinks by the Grosvenors in the contentious 1784 city election, to grease the wheels for their candidates Wilbraham Bootle and Thomas Grosvenor. This was double the amount spent by their Independent opponent, Mr Crewe. Unsurprisingly, the Grosvenors won the day.

The parliamentary system was ripe for reform. Only a very limited number of individuals were qualified to vote: the 'forty shilling freeholders', that is, those with property worth forty shillings or more. Bribery and corruption were fixed stars in the political firmament. Great lords spent fortunes wooing voters with cash, drinks and feasts. Gently born ladies had their own way of winning votes: Georgiana, Duchess of Devonshire (1757–1806), allegedly sold kisses for votes at the hustings.

Duels were fought over political questions. Even Prime Ministers felt compelled to defend their honour in person. William Pitt and George Tierney fought with pistols in May 1789 after a slanging match in the House of Commons. Both men deliberately missed (this was called 'deloping'). The Catholic Emancipation Bill sparked a duel between the Duke of Wellington and Sir Henry Hardinge (Earl of Winchilsea) in 1829. The Earl published a letter which accused the Duke of insidiously introducing Popery into every State department. Wellington demanded the letter be withdrawn; Winchilsea refused. Honour had to be satisfied, so the two peers met at Battersea fields on 21 March. 'After the necessary preliminaries had been settled, the parties took their ground. The Duke of Wellington fired first, but without effect. The Earl of Winchilsea then discharged his pistol in the air.'[2] The Earl gave Wellington a written apology. Although all ended well, public opinion was greatly shocked by this macho display.

Parliamentary seats were bought and sold like commodities (they were even advertised for sale in the newspapers). There was no secret ballot, so a would-be MP could check whether his money spent 'treating' the electors was well laid out. Another tactic was intimidation. Political candidates were usually landowners; tenants who didn't vote for their landlord could face higher rents or even eviction.

This was the age of 'rotten boroughs' like Old Sarum (Wiltshire), which sent two MPs to parliament, even though only a handful of people lived in this rural backwater. One of the greatest injustices was the lack of parliamentary representation in the growing industrial towns such as Manchester, Stockport and Macclesfield.

Cheshire had four parliamentary seats: two for the county as a whole, and two for the city of Chester. The Grosvenors of Eaton Hall kept a vice-like grip on politics at local and parliamentary level and they had a vested interest in keeping it that way. The fabulously wealthy Grosvenors, an ancient Cheshire family, acquired their riches through a prudent marriage in the seventeenth century. The third baronet, Sir Thomas Grosvenor (Mayor of Chester) married heiress Mary Davies; her marriage portion included the manor of Ebury in Middlesex. Their son Sir Richard developed part of this estate as Grosvenor Square (Mayfair) during the 1720s. This venture proved a wise and extremely lucrative investment. The Grosvenor success story reached even greater heights when George IV began to revamp Buckingham House in the 1820s. The new palace meant the portion of the Grosvenor estate which was still undeveloped had the potential to be a property goldmine. Lord Grosvenor moved swiftly; his new developments of Belgravia Square and Pimlico brought even more wealth to the family.

The family constantly added to their portfolio of investments, buying land, farms and property in several counties. They were major landlords in Chester. Commercial and domestic rents were kept low, but their tenants must have been uneasily aware that the situation could alter if they upset their landlords at election time.

If any proof were needed for the Grosvenors' political stranglehold on the county, their record of office speaks for itself. It was a family affair. Richard (the seventh baronet), who was created Earl Grosvenor and Viscount Belgrave in 1784, served as MP for Chester. His brother Thomas was MP for Chester for nearly forty years. After Thomas died, his sons (the Earl's nephews) Richard and General Thomas Grosvenor were both MPs; the general represented Chester for three decades.

The eighth baronet, Sir Robert (1767–1845), served as Mayor of Chester, and was an MP for the city from 1790 to 1802. Sir Robert was only twenty-three years old when he first entered Parliament. The ninth baronet, another Sir Richard (1795–1869), was also MP for the county from 1818 to 1830 (he was Viscount Belgrave at this time). To sum up, the Grosvenors held at least one but more typically *both* Chester city seats between 1780 and 1830.

The Grosvenor influence extended to corporation level, including the elections of the mayor and sheriffs. The assembly or corporation controlled the right to admit freemen to the city. Applicants obtained the freedom of the city upon payment of the appropriate fee. Political candidates would buy admission for their supporters so they had enough voters on their side. And the freemen had the right to elect the Chester city MPs. It was a beautifully balanced equation: control the assembly, and the city elections were a foregone conclusion.

The assembly almost invariably toed the Grosvenor line – it was a law unto itself. A major bone of contention was that the assembly was a 'closed shop' – it appointed its own mayor, aldermen and sheriffs. The aldermen 'took turns' to be mayor. Impartial observers couldn't fail to note that, for the best part of the eighteenth century, few faces unfriendly to the Grosvenors were elected to the corporation. Although many Chester citizens were happy to live under the umbrella of Grosvenor patronage, provided they spent their money freely (which they did), others felt fierce resentment. This was because the freemen of Chester believed they, not the assembly, had the right to elect council members.

The problem was the city's Great Charter (1506) of Henry VII, which set out the corporation's rights and privileges. This Charter, which gave the freemen a free vote to elect council officers, was confirmed by successive sovereigns, including Charles II in 1664. Unfortunately, after a legal dispute, in 1685 Charles II revoked the earlier charter, and created a new one. He put his own man, Sir Thomas Grosvenor, in charge of the assembly. King Charles also gave the corporation the right to select its own members; the freemen were no longer allowed a free vote to elect the city officers. The Grosvenor influence in the city became entrenched for centuries. The new charter caused much concern in Chester. During the eighteenth century, unrest grew in the city, stirred up by merchants and manufacturers who felt excluded from a share of the corporation pie of power and patronage. The corporation's high-handed attitude and dubious practices regarding city charities stirred up a hornet's nest of opposition.

Several court cases were brought to establish which charter was legal. The independent (i.e. anti-corporation) faction rejoiced in 1790 when the House of Lords decided that Henry VII's charter should stand. But this 'decisive victory' was met with lofty indifference by the corporation. They continued to self-appoint their own members, and took the case to court again, citing 'immemorial custom' to justify their actions.[3] The only real winners were the lawyers, of course. The independents simply didn't have deep enough pockets to match the seemingly endless financial resources of the corporation and its high-ranking friends. A noted opponent of the corporation, Ralph Eddowes, emigrated to America after losing £2,000 in these courtroom battles.

With the Grosvenors having such an all-encompassing reach, every little titbit of news concerning them made the papers. The citizens of Chester, so dependent on the Grosvenors' good offices, shared all their joys and sorrows with them. When the first Earl Grosvenor died on 5 August 1802, twenty-three carriages followed his funeral procession to Eccleston. The Earl was the oldest alderman of the corporation at the time of his death. The mayor and corporation occupied nine of the carriages and many of the earl's tenants followed on horseback.

There were huge celebrations at the birth of a son to Viscount Belgrave and his wife Lady Elizabeth in April 1823. An ox was roasted on the Roodee, and shared out with the populace, with twenty barrels of strong ale to wash it down. A grand dinner was held at the Royal Hotel, and a firework display at the Roodee the following evening. Sadly, baby Gilbert died a few months later. To the family's great joy a healthy son, Hugh Lupus, was born in 1825. The christening of the young heir (who grew up to become the 1st Duke of Westminster) was celebrated with a procession of six stage-coaches from Eccleston Church to Eaton Hall. The horses were gorgeously decorated, flags waved, the band played, and pistols were fired in the air. A ball for over 100 people was held in the Tenants' Hall, which was brilliantly illuminated and decked in flowers. The guests enjoyed sprightly country dances and modish waltzes as well as the slightly more formal quadrilles.

The county parliamentary seats were carved up between other eminent county families. Between 1785 and 1829 Sir Robert Salusbury Cotton, John Crewe of Crewe, Davies Davenport of Capesthorne, Thomas Cholmondeley of Vale Royal and the Egertons of Tatton shared the honours pretty equally. Cotton and Crewe were Whigs, Davenport an Independent and Cholmondeley and Egerton were Tories. The Grosvenor interest made itself felt in the matter of the county representation, too. The family supported the Tory Cholmondeley in 1796 to ensure he didn't make a grab for the Chester city seats.

The MPs for the city and county weren't hard-line party supporters. They kept an open mind on many issues, and weren't afraid to vote against their own party on matters of conscience. The Grosvenor family were keen supporters of the Tory William Pitt, but changed sides to the Whigs after his death in 1806. The second Earl was conspicuous by his absence when the arch-Tory Wellington visited the city and Combermere Abbey in October 1820. The Grosvenors' known independence of mind helped sweeten the pill of their all-pervading influence in Chester and reconciled many citizens to their reign.

However, the failure of the Independents to rein in the assembly and claw back their ancient rights, as they believed, left an undercurrent of anger which needed little encouragement to overflow into active hostility. The lower classes were keen to express their support for the rival factions. The Exchange was often the focus of 'disgraceful scenes' in which 'all the low ribaldry, coarse wit, and vulgarism' of the populace was vented on magistrates and other respectable citizens. The hustings for the city elections were erected between the pillars of the ancient building, where: 'many a broad and uncourteous joke has been played off, by our city wits of the lower grade, during those scenes of ardent conflict, when every tinker and cobler (*sic*) thinks himself of as high consequence and importance as any lord of the manor.'[4]

The tension between the Grosvenor/corporation faction and the Independents was fought out in the newspapers – and in open warfare on Chester streets. The Chester papers were, quite naturally, up to their necks in the turbulent waters of local politics. The long-established *Courant* was firmly Tory and pro-Grosvenor. When the *Chronicle* was first published in 1775, the new publication was given a frosty reception by Eaton Hall, no doubt worried it could prove a focus for opposition. The *Chronicle* certainly didn't mince its words about the Grosvenors and their puppets in the corporation. Its editor John Fletcher was imprisoned for six months after publishing some pithy but libellous comments on the council's tactics during the 1784 corporation elections, when the freemen were once more denied a free vote.

Things didn't always run smoothly for the Grosvenor interest. John Williamson, an Independent, was elected sheriff in 1804 after his opponent made himself unpopular in the city in the aftermath of a near-riot involving a press-gang. (The press-gangs, which kidnapped unwilling recruits for the navy, were hated by ordinary citizens.) But once Williamson was inside the charmed circle, he soon succumbed to its exclusivity, and lost his independent frame of mind.

But the worst was yet to come for the Grosvenors. The unthinkable happened in 1807 when an Independent candidate, John Egerton, was elected as MP for Chester. The Grosvenors' pocket borough was no longer sewn up. This was the political equivalent of an earthquake in the city. It was triggered by dissent between Grosvenor family members. The thorny issue of Catholic emancipation caused much heated debate throughout this period. Roman Catholics were forbidden to hold public office and they suffered many other injustices both here and in Ireland. The second Earl Grosvenor and his son Viscount Belgrave were firm supporters of emancipation. But many Cheshire folk were vehemently anti-Catholic. They felt the government's proposed new legislation had the potential to inflict lasting harm on King, church and country. (It must be remembered that as late as the 1850s, there was still a special service in the Book of Common Prayer giving thanks for deliverance from the Gunpowder Plot by extremist Catholics in 1605.)

The two members for the city for the five years prior to the 1807 election were Earl Grosvenor's nephews, General Thomas Grosvenor and Richard Earl Drax Grosvenor. But when the Earl discovered that Drax Grosvenor opposed Catholic emancipation, he was furious. He refused to let Drax Grosvenor stand as the Grosvenors' second candidate in the impending general election. Instead, the Earl sent an old friend, Colonel Thomas Hanmer, to canvass the city with General Grosvenor. The substitution was met with outrage by the corporation as well as the freemen. They didn't know Hanmer; he didn't live in Cheshire but, worst of all, Eaton Hall hadn't consulted them beforehand. As Hemingway commented: 'This procedure, to say the least of it, was not less uncourteous than impolitic; it was taken to be ... an insult to the freemen.' The corporation were also upset because many of them approved of Drax Grosvenor's anti-Catholic stance.

The few Independents in the corporation were quick to exploit this own goal by Eaton Hall. A deputation was despatched post-haste to Oulton Park, the ancient home of the Egertons. John Egerton, a popular figure with 'amiable and engaging manners,' was asked to stand in opposition to Hanmer.[5] He came from a good old Cheshire family with many links to the county town. When the assembly realized the tide of public opinion was firmly behind Egerton, it mustered its collective courage and backed him against Hanmer. The colonel was forced to withdraw and, on 6 May 1807, Egerton was duly elected as MP for the city. (General Grosvenor, of course, won the other seat.)

This momentous day was long remembered in the city. A song, 'The

Glorious Sixth of May', was written in its honour. But the Grosvenor interest wasn't so easily overturned. One of the assembly, William Seller, was next in line to be to be mayor and take his 'turn' according to the assembly's custom. However, he'd been a member of the deputation which had asked Egerton to stand. In the autumn after the election, Earl Grosvenor coolly announced his intention to act as mayor instead. He also informed the assembly that if Egerton were to be returned as MP for the city in the future, it should only be if backed by the house of Eaton as well as the assembly. This was a public slap in the face to Seller and the assembly and attitudes hardened still further.

Trouble flared again during the corporate elections of 1809. There were riots in the Exchange when the Independents in the assembly introduced their own candidates for mayor and sheriff; the Independents lost the vote.

One notable side-effect of the party rivalries was that the Chester newspapers switched sides. The Tory *Courant* lost its Grosvenor patronage after backing Egerton, probably because its owners approved of his stance against Catholic emancipation. (Although Egerton was an Independent in name, his politics were Tory.) The liberal *Chronicle*, too, changed tack: it took up the cudgels on behalf of the Whig Grosvenor interest. There was already no love lost between the rival publications. The changeover led to ever more vociferous and bombastic exchanges between its editors.

Party warfare now spilled over into every corner of the city, whatever the occasion. Even the assembly rooms, hotels and theatre weren't free from its malign influence. As hostilities intensified, the organizers of the winter assemblies at the Exchange fell out with the corporation. They decamped to the Independents' headquarters at the Royal Hotel, where they held a rival ball for the Egerton faction. The Independent faction didn't reign for long at the Royal, however. Earl Grosvenor bought the hotel in 1815 so he could use it as a family base for social occasions and at election time. Meetings were held there for the Whig Club founded five years later. The Independents were forced to switch their party headquarters to the Albion Hotel, which had an assembly room, in Lower Bridge St.

There were shocking scenes at the Theatre Royal after a Miss Holliwell arranged a musical concert. The Independent faction persuaded or paid the lady (who was in debt) to include the 'The

Glorious Sixth of May' as part of the performance, planned for 3 January 1810. This song, as 'every child in the city' well knew, was the Independents' battle-cry.[6] News of this intended insult soon reached the Grosvenor supporters. They bought tickets for the performance, determined to stop the odious melody being performed in public. As soon as the offending song was announced, a thunderous roar of shouts, boos and cat-calls erupted. The singer and musicians beat a hasty retreat.

An 1812 court case illustrates the liveliness of some of these political battles. The *Courant* explained the background to the proceedings, which 'excited much interest'. The question was once again 'whether the Grosvenor interest should be maintained against the franchises of Englishmen'.[7] The *Courant* editor surmised the case was a tit-for-tat prosecution after the citizens of Chester prosecuted some Grosvenor servants for 'committing several riots in support of his parliamentary interest'. The case followed an alleged riot in the Exchange Hall during the corporation elections in October 1810. The *Chronicle* (17 April 1812) also reported the court proceedings with great gusto. Labourers John Hassall, Joseph Cartwright and John Rogers were charged with riotous behaviour. The city's freemen had assembled in the Town Hall to elect a mayor and two sheriffs. But the lower orders wanted to have their say. The streets to the City Hall were blocked up with people: 'the greater part of whom were not freemen'.

Suddenly, uproar erupted in the Exchange as the labourers and their friends smashed tables and benches. A constable, Matthew Garner, tried to remonstrate with Rogers, who retorted: 'D-n you and the Corporation and all! I'm a man for you any day!' By this time a couple of hundred people had joined in the protests; dead cats and 'slough' (presumably muck) were hurled around. Witness William Woods testified that he had seen Cartwright dismantling a partition in the Hall by using a hammer to knock out the nails holding it together. Cartwright leapt up onto a table, shouting, 'Huzza, lads! No Yellow Bob! Turn him out!' The table was shoved against the seated Lord Grosvenor and General Grosvenor, who were forced to get up. (Yellow was the Grosvenor colour; the opposition colours were red and blue.)

The defendants were found not guilty by an 'upright and independent jury', the *Courant* triumphantly reported, because there was so much contradictory and conflicting evidence.

A Stockport man, Francis Philips of Bank Hall, was caught up in a major news story in May 1812. He was on the scene when Prime Minister Spencer Perceval was shot by a madman, John Bellingham, in the House of Commons. Philips helped to carry the dying man into an office. The Prince Regent asked Lord Liverpool to form a government. This administration went down in history as one of the most repressive on record.

As the general election of 1812 approached, there was never any doubt that General Grosvenor would win one seat for Eaton. The battle-lines were drawn over the second seat. Sir Richard Brooke was the Grosvenor candidate. Against the Grosvenors were Egerton and his running mate, Edward Venables Townshend. Of course, Egerton had declined to take up Earl Grosvenor's 'kind' offer to represent the house of Eaton.

No effort was spared by the Grosvenor and Egerton parties to wine and dine the people of Chester; it was 'open house' in all the city's inns and taverns. Egerton was said to have spent over £15,000; his opponents spent more than double this amount. The Grosvenors 'fought dirty' throughout this turbulent time. Some of the tenants on their estates who supported Egerton were evicted. Loyal tenants and workers swamped Chester in the run-up to polling day. Because the Grosvenors controlled the assembly, it was easy for them to create many more freemen to vote for them.

John Egerton fought the election on local issues; he played on the citizens' fears of Catholic emancipation. Egerton won by a narrow margin of twenty-seven votes.

'Teddy' Hall was an Egerton supporter and 'immoveable' foe of the Grosvenors. Edward was once a respectable citizen, but the excitement of the 1812 election proved too much for him. He was inebriated for weeks during and after the election. This colourful character became well known in Chester for his drunken antics. 'Teddy' taunted Sir Richard Brooke at the hustings. He dangled a 'dancing doll' from the end of a long pole while shouting: 'Egerton and no Grosvenor, Townshend and no Brooke; here's your Teddy!' The implication was that Brooke was a Grosvenor puppet. Edward was called Teddy ever afterward. The poor man never recovered from this binge and he spent the rest of his life walking the city streets.[8]

Hard on the heels of Egerton's election victory, the battle between the rival factions within the corporation led to scenes of high farce in the Chester streets in October 1812. The Independents, fed up with being sidelined within the corporation, put their heads together and assembled their own mayor, sheriffs and city officers. So on city election day, the citizens were treated to the novel spectacle of not one, but two corporations marching in pomp around the city. The ruling incumbents, resplendent in their robes of scarlet and ermine, had the advantage of possessing the historic city sword and mace and they were also firmly ensconced in the Exchange. The battle went to the courts and the lawyers had a field day once again. After a hugely expensive court battle, the Independents lost their case.

More bad news for the Independents lay in wait. Egerton's days as an MP for Chester were numbered. Sir John Grey Egerton (he had succeeded to the baronetcy after the Earl of Wilton's death) lost a great deal of popular support after voting for the suspension of the Habeus Corpus Act in 1817. This didn't go down well with the free-thinking citizens of Chester, who had petitioned against the Act's suspension.

News of the approaching dissolution of Parliament in 1818 immediately sent the Chester editors' blood pressure shooting sky-high. The leader writers sharpened their pen nibs and set to work. The candidates were General Grosvenor, now joined by Richard, Lord Belgrave to canvass for the house of Eaton, Sir John Grey Egerton, and lawyer John Williams, another Independent.

Sir John had the support of his election committee, who were rather like today's 'spin doctors'. In an advertisement in the *Courant*, they stoutly listed Sir John's qualifications: 'An independent, firm and conscientious discharge of his Public Duty, and a lively attention to the local interests of his Constituents.' They declared: '... the House of Eaton ought not to monopolise the Representation of the City of Chester ... the Liberties of the City should not be laid prostrate at the feet of one man.'

The *Courant*'s editor was Joseph Hemingway (John Monk had died in 1817 and his widow now owned the paper). Hemingway referred his readers to the elections of 1807 and 1812: '... we sanguinely concluded that he [Earl Grosvenor] would never again expose himself to the scorn, derision and indignation of the majority of the citizens of Chester'. The editor positively frothed at the mouth: 'The hydra-headed monster, Corruption, must be destroyed, and the flag of independence must again be hoisted.'[9]

John Hanshall, editor of the *Chronicle*, popped his head over the parapet and fired off a salvo. He challenged his rival editor to show that 'freedom in the election is incompatible with great wealth and rank in the candidate.'[10] Just a few years later, Hemingway would be writing from the other side of the political fence; he took over the editorship of the *Chronicle* in 1824.

The polls opened in Chester during the third week in June. The contestants were very close but Sir John took the lead in the polls for the first few days. The papers continued to take cheap shots at one another. The *Courant* (23 June 1818) claimed the *Chronicle* 'jumped the gun' by printing a letter of thanks to the voters from Lord Belgrave and General Grosvenor before the polls had closed. It also poked fun at the *Chronicle* for not printing the poll results. The *Chronicle* (26 June) in turn poured scorn at the other editor's 'lamentable imbecility'; the paper had gone to press before the results were known, so of course it couldn't publish the result.

As the close of the polls approached, the Independents' election committee discovered Egerton's support had sunk so low that he couldn't possibly win. So Egerton and Williams didn't appear at the hustings. When the results were announced the following week, Lord Belgrave and General Grosvenor were clear winners. They were triumphantly 'chaired' through the main streets, with a band of music in front of them, and their followers behind. The chairs, which dated from Queen Anne's reign, had 'the appearance of Indian palanquins'; they were decorated with ribbons, laurel and roses. Church bells rang, flags were hoisted on St John's church, and the fronts of houses were decorated with laurel and other evergreens. In the afternoon, the freemen who'd supported the Grosvenors enjoyed a dinner at their expense.[11]

Naturally, the *Courant* claimed Egerton's defeat was down to bribes from: '... a certain Noble Lord, whose money is reported to have freely circulated within the walls of our City'.[12] The *Chronicle* printed an indignant denial of the 'imputation of bribery'; General Grosvenor and Lord Belgrave had been 'wantonly traduced'.[13]

With feelings in Chester running at fever pitch, it's hardly surprising a report circulated that Sir John and Lord Belgrave actually fought a duel in late October. The cause of this 'Silly Duel'[14] was some verbal fisticuffs between the Grosvenor and Egerton factions at the mayoral election. When the two gentlemen met at dawn, Sir John's first shot wounded Belgrave in the pistol arm, but he wasn't badly hurt. Both Chester papers loyally dismissed the report as a hoax – an 'impudent falsehood' (*Chronicle*) and a 'wanton and unfounded statement' (*Courant*). Yet this supposedly imaginary duel is listed in J.P. Gilchrist's anti-duelling treatise of 1823, which lists all the principal duels fought since George III's accession.

Egerton petitioned parliament early the following year to have the election result set aside because of the chronic bribery and corruption of voters by the Grosvenors. The House of Commons upheld the election. This was a real blow to the Egerton family. The cost of the election contests was crippling them and they were forced to sell land and timber from their estates to meet their expenses.

Meanwhile, the Independents in the assembly made no headway against the Grosvenor faction, despite strenuous efforts. They tried to appoint their own candidate, William Seller, as mayor, but to no avail. The corporation election was again characterized by 'disgraceful and disorderly conduct'.[15] John Williamson, the former Independent who'd gone over to the enemy, was elected mayor instead.

The death of George III in 1820 meant Parliament was automatically dissolved and elections were held in March. There were the usual tussles, with fist-fights and drunken arguments in the street. The *Chester Guardian* commented drily: 'One peculiarity of Chester elections, is a total silence as to political general principles; this was the case yesterday, a fact which in the eyes of a stranger, gives an aspect to these contests very much resembling the quarrels of the servants in "Romeo and Juliet".'[16]

Mayhem broke out when General Grosvenor's coach hit a procession of Independent supporters on the Dee bridge; several people were knocked down and injured. The furious Independents believed it was a deliberate attack on them. The general and his friend Mr Long were dragged from the coach and they only escaped with difficulty from the mob. The traces of the general's horses were cut, and his carriage thrown off the bridge into the Dee, where it smashed to pieces. General Grosvenor's gold watch disappeared during the scuffle. The general and his companion sought refuge in the Bear and Billet inn until the streets were calmer. The general swore the collision was purely accidental: the post-boys were drunk, and unable to control the horses. Later that year, butcher Samuel Lloyd was acquitted of stealing the watch; he said he'd bought it for 5s from a 'sailor-looking man'.[17]

Lord Belgrave and General Grosvenor won the city seats again, no doubt thanks to the immense sums lavished on the usual treats for their voters. This contest was distinguished by the mystery of the missing mayor. When some young Egerton supporters tried to find John Williamson, so he could admit them as freemen, he was conspicuous by his absence. The mayor wasn't to be found either in the Exchange or his house. General Grosvenor won the election by a narrow margin. In July, the outraged Egerton faction petitioned against General Grosvenor's election. They were sure Egerton would have won if their supporters had been allowed to vote.

The election was once again allowed to stand, but the Independents won one victory, which must have tasted very sweet. John Williamson was tried and found guilty of corrupt practices (his disappearing act) in September 1821. He was given an impressive £1,000 fine, and imprisoned for six months. Williamson's conviction gave the Independent, William Seller, his chance to be mayor. The next year, he conducted an election of the city officers by the commonalty under the principles dear to every Independent's heart. A new corporation was voted in. But most unluckily, on the day the new assembly members were due to be sworn in, Seller, who had been in poor health for some time, was unable to attend at the Town Hall. The 'old guard' took advantage of his absence, and elected their officers 'as though nothing of the kind had taken place'.[18]

Battles continued to rage on the streets and in the courts over corporation elections until the end of the decade. Municipal reform had to wait until the mid-1830s, when the council voting system was overhauled by the Municipal Corporations Act.

The dissolution of parliament in 1826 meant Chester citizens must have held their breath. They faced yet another bitterly fought contest between the house of Eaton and the Independents. This time around, the violence between their supporters reached unprecedented heights.

Sir John Grey Egerton had died the previous year and his brother General C.B. Egerton and Edward Venables Townshend stood for the

The Temple in Eaton Hall gardens
(Engraving for *Ackermann's Repository of Arts*, October 1823)

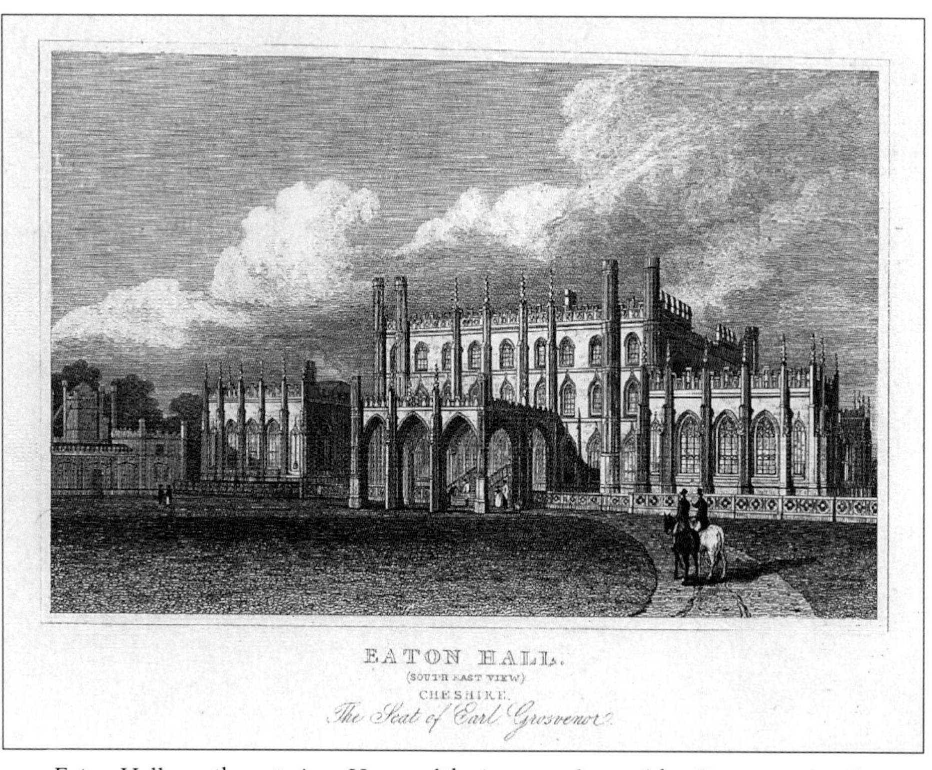

Eaton Hall, south-east view. Home of the immensely wealthy Grosvenor family
(Engraving by J.P. Neale, *c*.1818)

Ladies' fashions, evening wear, 1810
(French engraving by Camus, *c.*1830)

Men's fashions, winter wear. French modes were in vogue, even though England was at war with France (French engraving by Camus, *c.*1830)

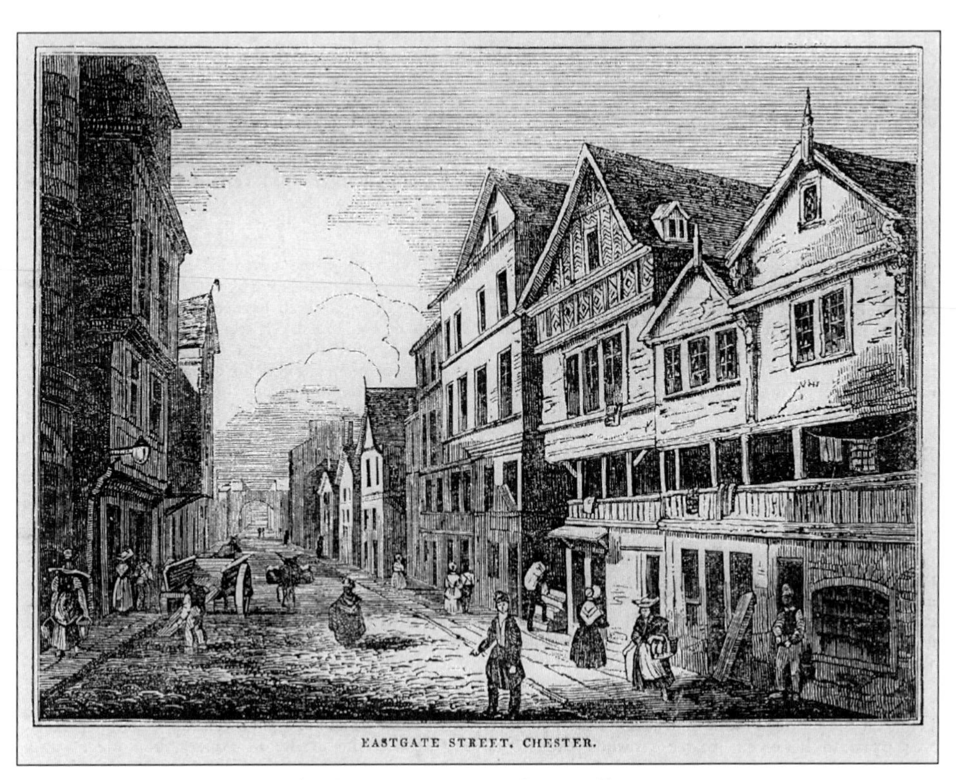

The Rows on Eastgate Street, Chester
(*Saturday Magazine*, 1836)

Harrison's Chester Castle works. The Propylea Gate is on the very far left. The county gaol, jury rooms and prothonotary's office are in the building on the left. The Shire Hall with its elegant Doric columns is to the right. The east wing (left) of the Hall was the military barracks; the west wing was the armoury
(*Stranger's Companion*)

Chester Grandstand (designed by Harrison) at the Roodee (*Stranger's Companion*)

28 THE STRANGER'S COMPANION

THE OLD BRIDGE GATE.

TAKEN DOWN IN 1781.

Old Bridge Gate, Chester (*Stranger's Companion*)

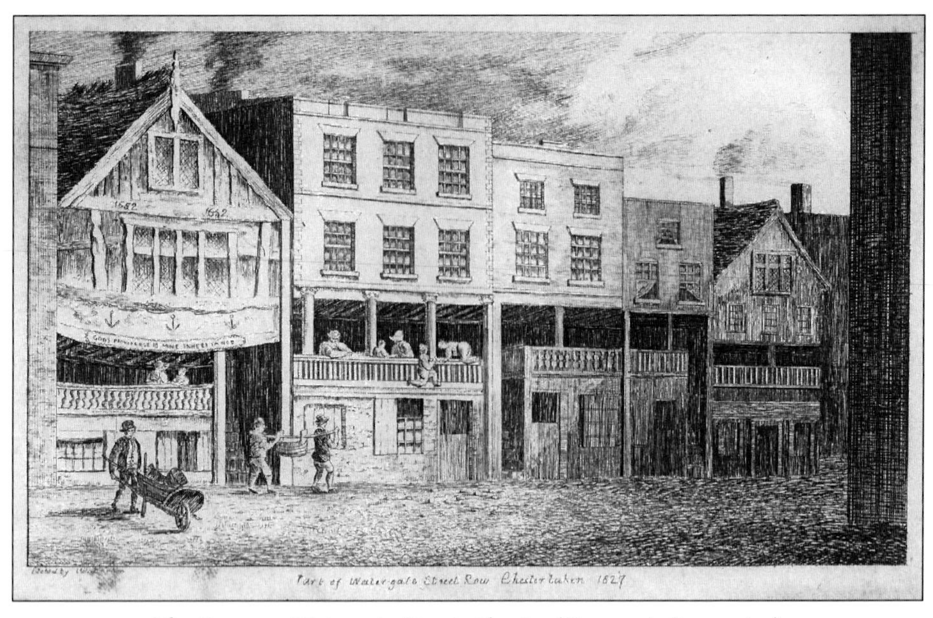

The Rows on Watergate Street, Chester (*Stranger's Companion*)

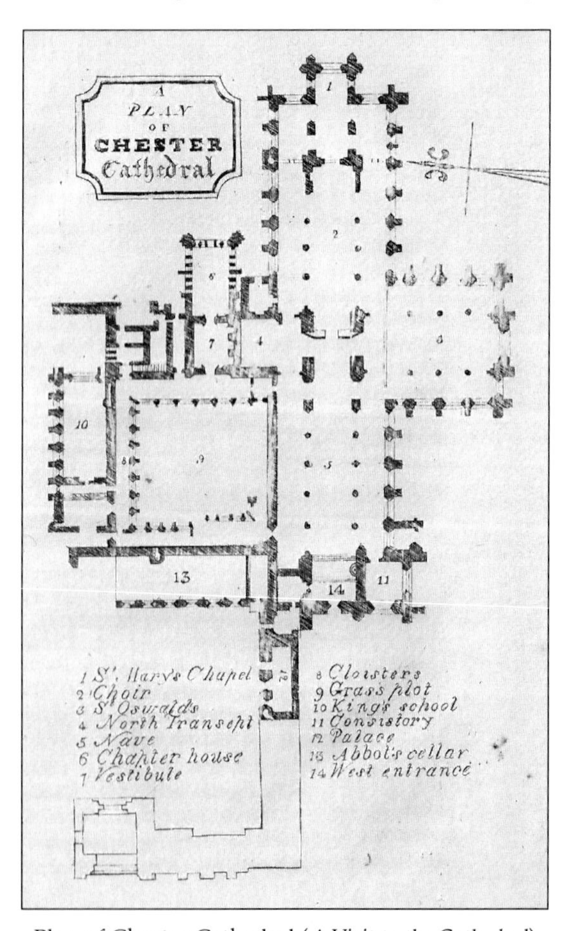

Plan of Chester Cathedral (*A Visit to the Cathedral*)

South East View of Chester Cathedral taken from the City Walls

South-east view of Chester Cathedral from the city walls
(Engraving by Batenham for *A Visit to the Cathedral Church of Chester*, c.1828)

South Entrance to the Cathedral

South Entrance to Chester Cathedral (*A Visit to the Cathedral*)

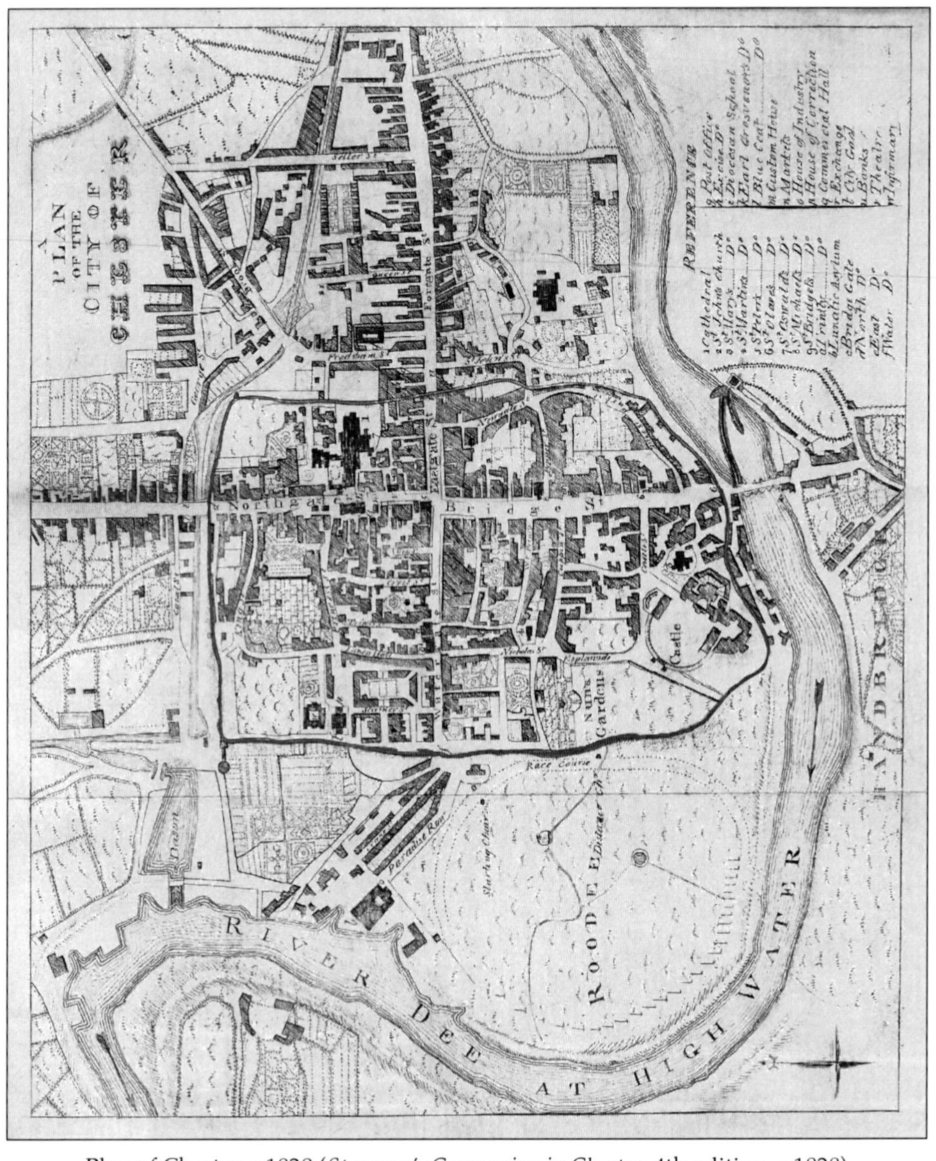

Plan of Chester, *c.*1828 (*Stranger's Companion in Chester*, 4th edition, *c.*1828)

Independents. General Grosvenor had withdrawn from the Chester representation and was standing for another Grosvenor 'pocket' seat in Hampshire. The Grosvenors were represented by Lord Belgrave and his brother, the Hon. Robert, who wasn't even in Chester. He was in Russia as part of the English diplomatic mission at the coronation of Emperor Nicholas.

As in previous elections, the Grosvenors spent freely – debtors languishing in prison had their debts paid so they could vote. Impoverished Egerton supporters were bribed by the Grosvenors' agents to leave town for a few days; even a pig was bought from a freeman for the princely sum of £22.

At first, it seemed as if the Independents wouldn't even bother to contest the seat and the election seemed decided before it had even begun. But their working-class supporters busied themselves on their behalf: a tinman, Mr Dutton, jumped on the table at the hustings and demanded the poll must be kept open.

For the first couple of days of polling, trouble between the rival factions was limited to a few minor scuffles when they encountered each other in the streets; no one was hurt. The Independents found they had much more support than they expected. Lord Belgrave had recently spoken in parliament in favour of repealing the Corn Laws and this was unpopular with his constituents, many of whom were farmers. (The Corn Laws protected Britain's farmers from foreign imports, and of course many Cheshire constituents were farmers. The laws forced up the price of corn, making bread dearer for workers.) So on the evening of Friday 9 June, General Egerton led the poll. His supporters, tradesmen and workers alike, linked arms and marched through the streets, waving banners inscribed 'Freedom of Election', 'No Bribery', and 'A Large Loaf'. The next day, the Grosvenor party entered the city through the Eastgate, followed by a long stream of carriages, with brightly coloured flags and banners flying. As they approached the Royal Hotel, the Independents arrived in the opposite direction, preceded by fife and drum, playing their favourite: 'The Glorious Sixth of May'. A battle royal commenced. The man leading the Grosvenor procession was knocked down and hurt; he was forced to seek refuge inside the Royal Hotel. Later that day, after leaving the hustings, Lord Belgrave was badly scratched by some ferocious women Independent supporters. (Women were involved in the party rivalries just as fiercely as men, even though they didn't have the vote.) Belgrave was said to be mortified because he'd been bottom of the poll for two days running.

Tempers flared afresh when General Grosvenor, arch-enemy of the Independents, arrived in Chester to cast his vote. He left his carriage outside Parry's, the brushmaker's shop, then walked into the hustings. There were some murmurs of resentment from the Independents, so when the general came away from the hustings, his friends crowded around him to protect him. Perversely, this really offended the Independents, who threw mud and dirt at the general's party. Shortly afterwards, paving stones were thrown at the Grosvenors, now making a stand at the south end of the Exchange. Even though the general's party was unarmed, it advanced towards its enemies. The mêlée now raged up and down the Chester streets, accompanied by a hail of stone-throwing. At length the Independents succeeded in clearing the streets of their rivals. Many people were badly wounded, including the town clerk, Mr Finchett-Maddock, who received a head injury. The battle left a 'scene of desolation' and the Exchange's windows were badly smashed.[19] That evening, the sheriffs posted up a notice that future disorder would be met by military force.

But the sheriffs' threat was ignored. By the evening of 21 June, the Grosvenors had gained ground, and led the polls. The Independents, facing the prospect of yet another defeat, were furious. As the hustings closed for the day, the sheriffs were met by a storm of rotten eggs, a dead rat, and other unsavoury missiles. The wooden timbers of the hustings were ripped up and used as weapons by the Independents.

Mayor John Fletcher read the Riot Act from the Exchange windows, but to no avail. Lord Belgrave only narrowly escaped from the rioters. The tumult continued until Fletcher called in a company of the 49th Regiment of Foot. The soldiers, with Fletcher and two aldermen leading the way, arrived at about six o'clock. The mayor read the Riot Act once more. This time order was restored. But the damage had been done. Many people, even women and children, had been wounded in the turmoil, and the windows of the Coach and Horse Inn demolished. The authorities decided enough was enough and the polling books were closed next morning. Lord Belgrave and Hon. Robert Grosvenor were elected as MPs.

The sheer cost of the elections was beginning to daunt even the house of Eaton. The perennial disorder cast a shadow on the reputation of Chester and the Grosvenors. Shocked by the sheer scale of the violence, Earl Grosvenor decided to bury the hatchet. In 1829, while no elections were under way and the city was quiet, the Grosvenors announced that in future, they would only field one candidate for the Chester city seats.

The death of George IV in 1830 meant another dissolution of parliament. When election time approached, Lord Belgrave withdrew from the city representation; only the Hon. Robert Grosvenor stood for the city. For the first time in years, the election went ahead smoothly. The Independents got their wish at last: their candidate Sir Philip de Malpas Grey-Egerton, nephew of Sir John, was elected. The election took place 'with great cordiality, and without the slightest appearance of opposition'.[20] However, this didn't mean the end of the Grosvenors' political ambitions. Lord Belgrave stood for one of the county seats instead, and was duly elected. (Wilbraham Egerton won the other county seat.) So the Grosvenors held one county and one city seat after the 1830 election.

While all-out war raged in Chester, elsewhere in the north west workers in the industrial towns with no parliamentary representation were busy agitating for reform. There were huge public meetings at Manchester and Stockport and the distress caused by the Napoleonic Wars led to a demonstration at Macclesfield. Over 2,500 people, including women and children, gathered at the Town Field on Thursday 2 January 1817. They drew up a petition to the Prince Regent detailing their discontent and expressing their disgust with the government. The petition is interesting, not just because it sheds light on how ordinary people viewed government, but because it gives a damning indictment of the political system: 'It is the opinion of this meeting, that the House of Commons does not fully and fairly represent the people of England ... if the Country was justly and fairly represented, it would be the means of alleviating our grievances and public distress.' And furthermore: '... a majority of those who call themselves Representatives of ten millions of persons, are returned by two thousand, six hundred and eleven individuals only'.

Another petition was drawn up by the Whigs in Macclesfield two weeks later. Its target was the House of Commons. The petition drew attention to the distress caused by the Corn Laws: 'the most pernicious Law ever made by a British House of Commons ... The want of Trade, and present high price of Bread, is most grievously felt by your petitioners.' The petition, which went on to beg parliament to give the people a just share of the representation, was signed by over 4,200 men and boys in Macclesfield and its neighbourhood: almost two-thirds of the male population.

Two years later, Lancashire and Cheshire workers paid a terrible price at Manchester during their quest for reform. As we shall discover, violence flared when the authorities, fearful of revolution, reacted by sending for military aid.

John Corry asked a pertinent question: '... what public body ever reformed itself?' Years of campaigning and much bloodshed was to pass before parliament bowed to overwhelming popular pressure and grasped the nettle of change. Cheshire folk had to wait for the Great Reform Act of 1832 before some of the political odds stacked against them were redressed in their favour.

6

School for Scandal

The Regency period was an age of scandal. High-profile affairs were viciously lampooned in satirical prints and no one's private life was safe – not even the Prince Regent. The polite world's sensational doings not only provided fodder for the gossip columns, but could also have long-lasting consequences, as a young officer from Cheshire discovered. A minor indiscretion by Colonel Stapleton Cotton greatly offended the young Prince of Wales and cost the young officer dearly.

The Prince didn't exactly set a good example to his loyal subjects. To begin with, he had an embarrassingly large number of wives. George III was determined his heir must marry well. But in 1785, the Prince secretly married Mrs Fitzherbert, a kind-hearted, motherly widow of good character. (The Prince had a penchant for more mature women.) The reason for all this secrecy? The lady was a devout Roman Catholic. The Act of Settlement forbade the heir to the throne from marrying a Roman Catholic. Another obstacle was the Royal Marriage Act. All the King's children under the age of twenty-five were required to gain the consent of their father and the Privy Council before marrying. If the marriage to Mrs Fitzherbert was legal, the Prince would have forfeited his crown. But the marriage was technically invalid because of the Royal Marriage Act. The Prince didn't care; he was madly in love. The secret ceremony was the only way Mrs Fitzherbert would consent to live in connubial bliss with him, even though they kept separate establishments.

His 'marriage' didn't stop the Prince enjoying a succession of mistresses, including the redoubtable Lady Jersey. The King, meanwhile, put pressure on his son to make a brilliant dynastic marriage and produce an heir. And he had plenty of leverage. The Prince was up to his ears in debt; among his many extravagances were the beautifying of Carlton House, and his first-class racing establishment. His father kept him on a very tight leash money-wise, but this hadn't stopped the Prince racking up debts of well over half a million pounds (an immense sum in those days). His creditors were baying for payment and even the money-lenders refused to lend him any more money.

The only way to persuade the King to increase the Prince's allowance and settle his debts was to get married. Most unfortunately for the Prince's future peace of mind, he didn't enquire minutely enough about the bride chosen for him: his first cousin, Princess Caroline of Brunswick (1768–1821). It's said that his mistress, Lady Jersey, influenced his choice, secure in the knowledge Princess Caroline would never supplant her in the Prince's affections. The King was very pleased with the match, but the Queen was dead against it: she had hoped the Prince would marry her niece.

Princess Caroline was a larger-than-life character: cheery, good-natured, highly talkative and confiding. But she was gauche, badly dressed, coarse, vulgar, loose-tongued and, fatally, seemingly unacquainted with the basics of personal hygiene. There couldn't have been a worse choice of bride for one of the most fastidious gentlemen of Europe. The moment he clapped eyes on his bride-to-be, the Prince demanded a glass of brandy. The Princess, for her part, far from home in a strange land, discovered her future husband was extremely fat, and that her newly appointed lady of the bedchamber was the Prince's mistress, Lady Jersey. But the people loved the Princess, and took her straight to their hearts.

It was a marriage made in hell. The ceremony on 8 April 1795 was a right royal farce. The Prince of Wales cried and had to be supported upright – he'd taken the precaution of downing several glasses of brandy beforehand. His bride claimed he spent his wedding night dead drunk in the fireplace. But somehow the ill-matched couple produced an heir to the throne; Princess Charlotte was born on 7 January 1796. His duty done, the Prince lost no time in separating from his wife. (It wasn't a formal separation as the King refused to allow it.) The separation went down very badly with the public, who expected the Royal family to live respectably. Nothing daunted, the Prince of hearts returned to the arms of his beloved Mrs Fitzherbert (he'd grown tired of Lady Jersey).

Now the Prince, like the proverbial elephant, never forgave or forgot anything he found unpleasant. Sir Stapleton Cotton of Combermere (1773–1865) was stationed at Brighton for two years with his regiment, the 16th Light Dragoons. In 1801, the young colonel married the beautiful Lady Anna Maria Clinton, daughter of the 3rd Duke of Newcastle. The newlyweds were frequent guests of the Prince of Wales at Brighton Pavilion.

Mrs Fitzherbert had a house on the Steyne. Although the Prince's affair (or first marriage, depending on your point of view) was much gossiped about, the Prince liked to keep his visits to her private. When the Prince hurt his leg, word spread that the injury occurred when he fell outside Mrs Fitzherbert's door, after paying her a night-time visit. Colonel Cotton heard the story. Believing it was true, he mentioned it in a letter to Lady Liverpool, who promptly retailed it to all the London gossips. The Prince somehow discovered who had spread the rumour and was very upset. The young colonel wasn't invited to the Pavilion again.

When Napoleon escaped from Elba in 1815, Cotton, now Lord Combermere, had been promoted. General Cotton had served ably as a cavalry commander in the Peninsular wars and he seemed the obvious choice to lead the cavalry against Europe's bogeyman. But the Prince Regent still harboured a grudge against Cotton. The command was given to Lord Uxbridge instead, despite an appeal by the Duke of Wellington. As Ormerod commented, 'A regent's foibles were barriers to justice stronger than all the power of a great public servant,' and so Lord Combermere missed out on a command at Waterloo. He was bitterly disappointed; right to the end of his life, he could never bear to hear Waterloo mentioned.

The Cheshire papers were happy to fill their pages with the latest titbits, like the very public scandal of the separation of the poet, Lord Byron, from his wife. In April 1816, Byron left England, never to return. Society cut him dead after dark rumours circulated about his emotional cruelty to his wife, and alleged incest with his half-sister Augusta Leigh.

Another juicy *cause célèbre* was the publication in 1825 of notorious courtesan Harriette Wilson's *Memoirs*. Saucy Harriette enjoyed amours with many Regency bucks like Lord Ponsonby and Beau Brummell. This resourceful 'lady' tried to blackmail her former lovers – if they didn't pay up, they were immortalized in print. The Duke of Wellington memorably told her to 'Publish and be damned!' Crowds mobbed her publisher John Stockdale's shop in London. The ensuing libel and damages cases kept the lawyers busy for many months.

Even Nelson, the nation's hero, wasn't free from the taint of scandal. His great love for Emma Hamilton was a major talking point. Cheshire-born Emma's story is an amazing one. Emily Lyon, a blacksmith's daughter, was born at Neston in April 1765. Her father died when she was still a baby, and she was brought up in Hawarden, Flintshire. Much of her early life is shrouded in mystery but at some point she changed her name to Emma Hart. There were few respectable paths to riches for an alluring, impoverished girl. Her striking good looks ensured her a career as a mistress. Charles Greville was one of her protectors. He introduced her to the painter Romney, for whom she sat as a model. Greville was the nephew and heir of Sir William Hamilton (1730–1803), ambassador to the court of Naples. When Greville was harassed by creditors, he gave Emma to Hamilton, knowing she would be well looked after. Emma, who loved Greville, was deeply unhappy at first. But this humbly born beauty staged a diplomatic coup – she persuaded the chivalrous, learned old gentleman to marry her. She became Lady Hamilton in September 1791 – but her murky past meant she could never be received at court.

Horatio Nelson (1758–1805) was married to the gently bred Frances (Fanny) Nisbet, who nursed him devotedly after he lost his arm in action off Tenerife. Nelson and Emma first met at Naples and their love blossomed after the battle of the Nile. They were besotted with each other. Sir William maintained a dignified front, as if nothing was happening. The unorthodox love triangle created a *frisson* in society. The brilliant naval commander's infatuation with Emma was also a source of wonder to his fellow officers. When Nelson returned to England with the Hamiltons in 1800, he received a hero's welcome from the public. But he was publicly snubbed by George III.

Nelson quickly made it obvious to Fanny that their marriage was over. Emma bore him a child, Horatia, in 1801. Despite high society's disapproval, Nelson adored Emma to the very end. At the battle of Trafalgar, with almost his last breath, he left Emma and his daughter to the care of the nation. Nelson's bequest fell on deaf ears, however. Emma soon ran out of money – economy had never been her strong point. Burdened with massive debts, she fled to Calais with her daughter Horatia. Emma Hamilton died in poverty in January 1815.

Meanwhile, the saga of the Prince's disastrous marriage was far from over. Princess Caroline had set up her own establishment at Blackheath. Her behaviour there with several gentlemen was so flirtatious and outrageous that she was accused of having had an illegitimate child. A 'Delicate Investigation' was ordered by the Prince in 1806. The commissioners found that the boy, whom the Princess had adopted, was the son of a docker. But the Princess was felt to be a poor role model for her daughter Princess Charlotte and the Prince used the Investigation as an excuse to curtail the meetings between Princess Caroline and her daughter. The Prince Regent probably believed he was protecting Princess Charlotte, but his decree endeared him even less to his subjects, who saw only that he was separating mother and daughter.

Princess Caroline, fed up with the Prince's restrictions on her life, left England to live on the continent in 1814, much to the Regent's relief. But although his hated wife was out of sight, stories of her indiscretion meant she was never out of mind. The Princess lost no time in enjoying life to the full, and thumbing her nose at her husband. Her relationship with her chamberlain Bartolomeo Pergami (or Bergami) was the talk of Europe. The Regent sent the 'Milan Commission' to Italy in 1818 to find out if the stories were true. But proving adultery, which was the best means of the Regent obtaining a divorce, wasn't easy, despite the wealth of gossip and circumstantial evidence.

The death of George III created what the *Chester Guardian* termed 'a curious and delicate emergency'. Would the Queen Consort, whom the new King detested, be crowned? George IV was determined he would never share the throne with her. The Queen's name was even omitted from prayers in the liturgy for the Royal Family. This measure greatly upset Earl Grosvenor, who was in any case no friend to the government. *The Times* (11 November 1820) reported that the Earl had declared that if he were Archbishop of Canterbury, and was asked to perform such an unjust act, he would have thrown the Prayer Book in

His Majesty's face. Not content with that, he said that if he had been one of the King's ministers, he would have trampled on the seals of office rather than remain in the administration.

The King gave the Milan Commission's evidence on the Queen's lifestyle, wrapped up in a green bag, to his ministers. He insisted they take action to rid him of his wife. A 'Bill of Pains and Penalties' was brought in. The case against the Queen would be heard in the House of Lords. If she was found 'guilty', the King would have grounds for divorce.

The court case was a public relations disaster. Caroline, in her role as wronged wife, had massive popular support. Cheshire was no exception. There was huge interest when the Queen returned to England, determined on taking her rightful place at the coronation. The *Chester Guardian* (8 June 1820) excitedly reported her arrival at Dover and her journey to Canterbury in an open carriage: 'All ranks vied in showing her the tenderness due to a persecuted woman, and the respect due to a Queen.' The editor was convinced she was innocent of any wrongdoing: '… this illustrious female has already been assailed by all that malice and perfidy could array against her, and she passed through the relentless ordeal, acquitted of the crime of which she was arraigned.' He declared the King's and his ministers' treatment of her was: 'anything but manly and generous'.

The Queen's trial was the scandal to beat all other scandals. Excitement was intense as the first day of the proceedings opened on 17 August 1820. What were the contents of the mysterious 'green bag'? For weeks and weeks, nothing else was talked about as each newspaper report brought fresh revelations about the Queen's goings-on. Hemingway says that in Chester, the proceedings against her 'nearly equally divided the citizens … many of the king's most loyal subjects were decidedly opposed to the measures of administration on this important question'.

In September, the trial was still the 'ruling topic of the day'.[1] Earl Grosvenor took part in the questioning of the witnesses in the House of Lords, but found it difficult to shake their testimony. One of the chief witnesses against the Queen was her servant Teodore Majocchi. He claimed the Princess had visited Pergami's bedroom; she had kissed him and Pergami even helped her with her bath. Fathers hid the newspapers so their young daughters wouldn't be corrupted by the 'vile catalogue of indecencies' printed each day as the Queen's dirty washing was laid bare for inspection.[2]

But nothing could dent the Queen's popularity. The strength of the people's support, and the House of Lords' lack of enthusiasm for the Bill, led Lord Liverpool to abandon it in November. The *Chester Guardian* was jubilant: 'We congratulate the country upon the signal triumph of justice, which has filled every honest and loyal bosom with joy.'[3]

There were huge celebrations across the country and Cheshire folk joined the merrymaking. In Stockport, a procession marched through the main streets to Great Underbank. A huge bonfire was lit at the White Lion Inn and an effigy of Majocchi was abused and burnt. Many houses in the town were illuminated to mark the occasion. At Tarporley, bells rang, the town was lit up and houses were decorated with laurel and white roses. Bread and ale were distributed to the poor and more effigies of the Italian witnesses against the Queen were paraded around and burnt in a bonfire at the bottom of Crane St. There were also bonfires at Nantwich and Parkgate. At Bunbury, a sheep was roasted and the Queen's health drunk with strong ale.

The Queen's triumph was short-lived. She was refused entry to George IV's coronation at Westminster Abbey and died shortly afterwards, as William Cobbett said, of a broken heart. She was mourned by the people, but her widower, the King, refused to order national mourning.

Cheshire had some home-grown scandals of its own. An earlier unsavoury tragedy was still remembered. In the late 1770s, Cheshire, so long famous for its cheese, acquired unwelcome notoriety for less wholesome fare – cannibalism. A 'most atrocious and perhaps unprecedented Murder' occurred at Congleton. Samuel Thorley, a butcher's assistant, murdered and dismembered a ballad-singer, Anne Smith. The unfortunate young woman's head and other body parts were thrown into a brook. Thorley reserved some of the fleshier parts, wrapping them up in his butcher's apron, and carried them to an old woman's house nearby. He told the old lady the meat was pork, and asked her to put it safe for him. Next day Thorley called again, and after asking permission to do some cooking, boiled up the 'pork' for his breakfast, and ate some.

In the meantime, Anne Smith's head, limbs and petticoat were discovered in the brook. Thorley coolly helped with the search for the rest of the body. A shrewd local man knew Thorley was a butcher and also knew that he liked to eat raw meat. The amateur detective soon 'put two and two' together, and guessed the murderer's guilty secret. The old woman was known to be a friend of Thorley's. Her house was searched and the other body parts were found there, and identified as human by a local surgeon. Thorley was arrested. He soon confessed to the 'savage act of diabolical cruelty', saying he'd been curious to see if human flesh tasted like young pig. He showed no remorse at his trial. After his execution on 10 April 1777, his body was hung in chains on a heath near Congleton.[4]

The whole range of human experience, from child abuse to bigamy, featured in Cheshire newspapers. The reports of the Chester Assizes and Knutsford Sessions catalogue many tales of misery and infamy. In 1823 John Kragon was executed for the rape of 8-year-old Jemma Ward, a worker at the Portwood factory. Kragon, who was identified by the little girl, insisted it was a case of mistaken identity: 'Oh! Am I to be hung! And to be hung for what! Oh! I've done nothing …'[5] He asserted his innocence to the last.

John Byng declared that 'country cities' enjoyed nothing but 'scandal' and 'abuse'. Cheshire had its fair share of adultery, because marriage was for life. Divorce was not only socially unacceptable, but also very expensive; only the upper classes could really afford it. One solution was bigamy. James Hampson (aged forty-four), a Stockport hatter, was transported 'for having married three wives, all living'.[6] Hampson obviously took to heart Dr Johnson's dictum that marriage was 'the triumph of hope over experience'. Hampson's fate didn't deter others, however. John Cotton, a Macclesfield weaver, was found guilty of bigamy and transported for seven years in April 1818.

Josiah Thornton of Brinnington became a bigamist at the surprisingly young age of eighteen. He got his girlfriend Ann Knowles pregnant but, because she was originally from Matlock, the parish overseers sent her back there so she wouldn't be a burden on the Cheshire poor rates. Meanwhile, the Matlock parish overseer heard that Thornton was planning to marry another young woman, Hannah

Pearson. The overseer arrested him, and Thornton was forcibly married to Ann Knowles on 11 July 1829. (Forced marriages were a consequence of legislation early in the eighteenth century to reduce the cost of illegitimate children to the parish rates; they were extremely common.) The young man was given some rum to fortify himself before the ceremony. But two days later, Thornton married Hannah at a church in Manchester. He was arrested, and later sentenced to two years' imprisonment and hard labour.

Among the lower classes, an unfounded belief persisted that it was legal to sell one's wife in the marketplace, provided she was sold for at least a shilling or more. These poor women were displayed for sale with a halter round their necks like cattle. One Twig at Macclesfield in 1799 was already married, but this didn't stop him buying not only one new wife, but two! It must have been a noisy household.

There were, of course, more permanent ways of disposing of an unwanted spouse. One of the most notorious cases was the sensational murder of farmer George Morrey (spelt Murray in early reports) by his wife and servant in April 1812. The *Chester Courant* reported the story in its usual measured tones: 'HORRID MURDER! IN CHESHIRE. On Sunday morning, the village of Hankelow, near Nantwich, was alarmed by a report, that George Murray, farmer in that village, having been found with his brains dashed out, and his throat cut from ear to ear!'

Shortly after midnight on 11 April, Morrey's servant girl Hannah Evans was woken by loud noises. She tried to escape from her bedroom window, but was stopped by Mrs Morrey, who came in carrying a lighted candle. Her mistress put out the candle, and grabbed Hannah's arm. Her mistress said there was murder in the house and if Hannah went outside she was sure to be murdered, too. When all seemed quiet, Hannah roused the Morreys' manservant, John Lomas and the two servants went to seek help from their neighbours.

But the murderers hadn't covered their tracks sufficiently. Suspicion fell on 20-year-old Lomas after a trail of blood was discovered from the dead man's bed to his own. A constable was sent for and the young man was arrested and taken to the nearest magistrate. Lomas declared: 'Well, I suppose I must be hanged.' He confessed the murder was planned by Morrey's wife Edith and himself. Lomas said: 'He had been urged to his horrid deed by his mistress, who wanted him to marry her.'[7]

When the constable heard this tale he went back to the farm to arrest Edith. The constable told her Lomas had confessed to the murder and implicated her and that she was under arrest. Mrs Morrey covered her face with her apron. Before the constable could stop her, she swiftly drew a razor from her breast, and cut her throat. But Edith didn't do a proper job – she survived. Mr Bellis, the doctor who had been called to view the dead man's body, stitched up her wound, and said it wasn't dangerous. When Edith was well enough to travel and face trial, the authorities' next problem was how to convey her to Chester Castle, where Lomas was awaiting trial. Popular feeling ran extremely high against her. So, fearing for her safety (an irony, considering she faced death by hanging), the authorities moved her 'with the utmost secrecy'.[8] A coach from Chester was sent to meet the carriage bringing her from Nantwich and it brought her to the castle. The *Courant* clearly entertained no doubts about her guilt. It primly highlighted the report that Mrs Morrey was dressed in full mourning, wearing widow's weeds.

Morrey and Lomas were tried on 21 August 1812 and nearly 4,000 people came to the trial. Both defendants were found guilty of murder, and condemned to death. Because Edith was pregnant, she was granted a stay of execution until her baby was born. (The child was probably fathered by Lomas.) Thirty-five-year-old Edith Morrey already had five surviving children; the eldest was fifteen years old.

John Lomas and Edith had a last, painful meeting the day before his execution. Their recriminations revealed the horrific details of George Morrey's final moments. Details of their conversation, in which they went over and over the events of that fatal night, were published, along with Lomas's confession. Lomas's 'Voluntary Confession' was taken down by Chester coroner Faithful Thomas. At midnight on that fatal evening, George Morrey and John Lomas each slept soundly in their beds. Edith woke John, and told him the time had come: he must kill his master. She had an axe all ready for the dreadful deed. At first John said no. He said they would be found out, and were 'sure to be hanged'. His mistress quickly reassured him; she said she would 'see him safe' and swear he was fast asleep. She'd send Hannah to wake him, so he had an 'alibi'. Lomas still demurred; he was afraid Morrey would wake up before he could reach the bed. Edith said she'd go in first, and signal when she thought George was soundly asleep.

At last, she gave the signal. The murderers advanced towards the sleeping farmer. While Edith held a candle, Lomas battered their victim three times with an axe. Suddenly, Lomas heard Hannah, the servant, get up. Edith quickly extinguished the candle, and Lomas ran to the door. Morrey cried out: 'Oh! Lord!' The injured man still lived.

Edith coaxed Lomas back into the room where he hit Morrey three or four times more with the axe. The guilty pair fled the room. But Morrey still wasn't dead – they could hear him groaning. Edith ordered Lomas to finish the job: 'John, he is alive; go and kill him.' Lomas, traumatised and exhausted, refused. The enterprising wife then found a sharp razor, and urged him once again to kill her husband. She put the razor in John's hand, gave him a push, and led the way. First, she checked on Hannah, who was sleeping soundly with the Morreys' children. Edith closed the door on them. Lomas returned to the Morreys' bedroom and found Morrey actually trying to get up off the bed. He seemed to recognise Lomas, and grabbed his shirt. (This awful moment especially haunted John afterwards.) Lomas pushed his master's hand away, and hacked at his throat: 'desperate cuts, and deep'. George fell to the floor and Lomas fled back to his own bed. He must have hoped it was all a dreadful dream.[9]

John Lomas's end was somewhat quicker than that of his victim. The *Courant* (25 June 1812) described the hanging: 'After the dropping of the floor, he struggled violently, but within a few minutes he was dead.' The following December, Edith gave birth to a little boy, Thomas. The baby was taken away from her to be brought up by Edith's parents, along with the Morreys' other children. On 23 April 1813, after the traditional hearty breakfast, Edith Morrey was hanged – exactly fifty years after Mary Heald was strangled and burnt for poisoning her husband.

Mere hanging wasn't enough punishment for condemned criminals; an even grislier fate awaited some. It was common practice for the bodies of hanged felons like Edith Morrey to be handed over to surgeons for dissection, as a means of teaching anatomy. Samuel Fallows, 'a good-looking young man', was found guilty of murder in April 1823; he had killed his pregnant sweetheart, Betty Shawcross, at Disley. The judge sentenced Fallows: 'to be hanged by the neck till you are dead, and after that your body will be given to the surgeons … to be dissected and anatomised'. In a final chilling indignity, after his execution, galvanic (electrical) experiments were carried out on Samuel's corpse before its dissection.[10]

Another sensational trial which created almost as much interest as the Morrey case was the 'wilful murder' of a handsome Northwich flatman, 21-year-old Richard Maddock. John Wakefield, a gentleman and salt proprietor at Winnington, was accused of fatally stabbing Maddock. Over 2,000 spectators packed into the court at Chester to see Wakefield's trial and more were crammed into the castle yard. Maddock's sweetheart, Elizabeth Woodward, a 'smart, good-looking girl', aged about twenty, was a key witness for the prosecution. She appeared in court dressed in a 'fashionable coloured gown, a straw hat with ribbons, and a drab woollen shawl thrown carelessly over her shoulders'.[11]

Elizabeth was a servant in Wakefield's home. He fell desperately in love with her. Wakefield offered to take Elizabeth to London, and 'keep me as a lady', she testified. She said Wakefield had threatened to shoot Maddock if he caught him on his premises. It was a classic 'love triangle'.

During Northwich Wakes, on the night of 8 September 1817, Wakefield (who kept a dagger by his bedside) discovered Maddock in the house with Elizabeth. There was a violent struggle and Wakefield forced Maddock outside. Later, another flatman found Maddock dying, about seventy yards from the house. A large number of workers gathered and they swore to have Wakefield's blood. By the time a constable arrived, an angry mob surrounded the salt proprietor's house. Wakefield was arrested but the murder weapon was never found.

Wakefield pleaded not guilty in court: he vehemently protested his innocence. Many eminent gentlemen queued up to give him glowing character references. Two of these witnesses, John Marshall of Green Bank and William Henry Worthington of Sandiway, were also on the Grand Jury at the trial! The jury, after due deliberation, found Wakefield guilty of manslaughter. The judge, commenting: 'You have hitherto supported a respectable situation in life,' gave him just six months in the 'common gaol'.

It is interesting to compare his trial with those of the poorer classes. Later that same year George Wood, a poor sailor from Cheadle, faced trial in Chester. Wood, who was starving, stole two pieces of muslin from Charles Sandford, a draper in Eastgate Row, Chester. He was in such a sorry state that he actually seemed pleased when arrested: 'Now

I shall have a bit of meat,' he said.[12] The judge, after listening to all the circumstances of the case, imprisoned Wood for six months – the same punishment handed down to the respectable John Wakefield for manslaughter in April.

The *Macclesfield Courier* (29 April 1826) reported a blackmail case. At that time homosexuality was described as a 'Detestable Offence'. Sodomy was a capital crime, for which four men had been executed at Lancaster in September 1806. One T. Wood, under pretence of using Mayor Thomas Brodrick's authority, tried to blackmail William Jackson. Jackson was charged with intent to commit an offence: 'not fit to be named amongst Christians'. He said Wood had used the mayor's name to extort money from him. Wood had produced a writ, saying the mayor would prosecute Jackson if he didn't give him £5. When Jackson refused, Wood said he would accept £2, and took Jackson's watch as security. Wood denied blackmail. He claimed he'd simply gone up to Jackson and said, 'I understood he had been with a soldier, and I then recommended him to clear the matter up.' Wood had also seen Jackson 'drinking with and treating the soldier'. The blackmailer could have been charged with obtaining property under false pretences, but the mayor clearly felt completely out of his depth in this case. He said, 'We shall dismiss the business [the case against Wood]. It is certainly a very extraordinary circumstance from beginning to end. One of you must tell great untruths – either you or Jackson.'

One mysterious murder was never solved, according to Knutsford historian Henry Green. The incident was said to have taken place early in the nineteenth century. The body of a well-dressed young lad, no more than fourteen years old, was discovered on the turnpike road between Knutsford and Ollerton. His throat had been cut. The gate-keeper of the Ollerton turnpike, when questioned, said a gig had travelled through in the middle of the night, carrying three people. Two of the travellers were propping up the other, as if he were ill. It must have been the already lifeless victim. Why was this child despatched so ruthlessly? Was he witness to a crime? Could he have been the heir to a fortune, perhaps the only obstacle between his murderer and a legacy? We shall never know.

A cheerier story is that of a respectable Cheshire farmer with a tender conscience. On a market day early in 1790, he called at the shop of Mr Poole, the Chester bookseller. The farmer put a shilling in

Poole's hand, saying 'he had owed it to him many years'. The surprised bookseller asked why. The farmer replied that 'When a boy, while buying a book-almanac in his shop, he had stolen another – the reflection of which had frequently given him much uneasiness.'[13]

The ball held after Chester Races seems an unlikely place for a scandal, but it made the national news in 1825. A Mr Rawlins and Mr Fitzgerald, both Irishmen, were thrown out of the ballroom by the gentlemen of Chester. They were said to have been behaving rudely and annoying the company. The aggrieved Irishmen didn't take their ejection lying down. Arguments and letters to the press over the night's events rumbled on for months afterwards. Rawlins instituted libel proceedings against the newspaper *The Age*, which claimed he had assaulted Lord Belgrave. Bow St warrants were issued for the arrest of Rawlins and Fitzgerald, and to ensure they kept the peace. But this storm in a teacup gradually blew over.

As Jane Austen's Henry Tilney (*Northanger Abbey*) declared: '… every man is surrounded by a neighbourhood of voluntary spies'. Everyone knew everyone else's business in the small, tightly knit town and village communities. It was vital to get on well with one's neighbours.

A scandal-monger in Huxley paid dearly for her gossiping. Sarah Fleet, a shoemaker's wife, was forced to apologize for 'divers scandalous words to the great injury and prejudice to the character of Mrs Mary Lewis', wife of a farmer at Aston. Whatever was said was obviously not only insulting but libellous. The aggrieved Mrs Lewis only promised to drop legal proceedings if Sarah paid all her expenses and apologized in print in the Chester papers.[14]

In the same issue of the *Chronicle*, there is a record of a very peculiar court case, in which a Poulton lady, Jane Johnson, was accused of witchcraft. Mrs Johnson and her husband John sued for damages after three Welshmen, Samuel and William Jones, and Thomas Speed, effectively kidnapped her. The defendants turned up at the Johnson house, claiming they had a warrant for Mrs Johnson, 'on account of her being a witch'. The men carried her off into Ruabon overnight, but she was released next day. It seems the lady's ordeal was caused by a dispute over rent and the Johnsons won their case for damages.

In the days when the merest whiff of scandal could mean a lady was completely ostracized by society, women had to be especially careful of their reputation. A gentleman's son wreaked havoc in the Astley family during the eighteenth century. George Hyde Clarke of Hyde Hall, near Dukinfield, eloped with pretty Sophia Astley. Her father, John Astley of Dukinfield Lodge, thought the world of her. But George's intentions weren't honourable and the young couple never married. They lived on Clarke's estates in Jamaica for many years and Sophia bore George two sons, Hyde and Robert. Sophia later married a Frenchman, M. Foncier. She lived at Wem, where she died in 1831. John Astley left his wayward daughter an annuity of £100, which would cease 'if she should at any time live or cohabit with that execrable villain George Hyde Clarke, Esq., of the Island of Jamaica'.[15] Her lover George later married an Irish lady. (Sophia's son Hyde Clarke served in the Royal Navy, where he had a distinguished career. Captain Hyde Clarke eventually settled at Hyde Hall and became a much loved leader of the local community.)

Ellen Turner's sensational story could have come straight from the pages of a Gothic novel. This young lady suffered what historian J.P. Earwaker described as: 'one of the most outrageous cases of abduction which has been chronicled'. Fifteen-year-old Ellen was the only child of William Turner and was one of the richest heiresses in England. Mr Turner, a retired Lancashire merchant, had recently purchased Shrigley Hall and was High Sheriff of Cheshire. The details of her abduction were widely published after the ensuing court case.

Edward Gibbon Wakefield (1796–1862) was the son of a writer, Edward Wakefield. A plausible adventurer and fortune-hunter, Edward Gibbon was a 'very elegant and personable young man, intelligent and well educated'.[16] Although Edward had never met Ellen, he had heard of her great expectations. His father was a widower living in Paris and the family were extremely hard up. The new lady in Wakefield senior's life was Frances Davies, the daughter of Dr Davies, a respectable Macclesfield clergyman. Miss Davies and Edward Wakefield got married, but for some reason Miss Davies continued to use her maiden name for the next few years. Frances Davies, her 'stepson' Edward Gibbon Wakefield, and his brother William, hatched a daring plot to kidnap Miss Turner.

The trio travelled to Macclesfield, where they wheedled their way into local society through Dr Davies's connections. Miss Turner was away from Pott Shrigley. She was at school in Liverpool, under the care of the Misses Daulby. Meanwhile, Frances ingratiated herself with Ellen's mother, who was in poor health. When the conspirators discovered Mr Turner would be away in London for several days, they sprang their trap.

First, they needed a getaway vehicle, so Miss Davies borrowed some money to buy a second-hand carriage. On 7 March 1826, Edward Gibbon Wakefield and a French servant, Thevenot, arrived at the school, bearing a forged letter from a 'doctor'. The letter said Ellen's mother was now dangerously ill, wanted to see her daughter, and that the doctor had sent his servant and carriage to convey her home straight away. The schoolmistresses knew about Mrs Turner's illness. They had no reason to suspect the letter was a hoax so they got their teenage charge ready for her journey home. Very soon the unsuspecting Miss Turner, filled with anxiety for her mother, sat in the coach, believing she was on her way home.

By some mishap the servant set off with Ellen but without Wakefield, but Edward and his brother met the coach at a Manchester inn. Edward introduced himself to Ellen for the first time and explained that her mother wasn't ill, but that the story was an idea of her father's, because he faced irretrievable ruin. This was the time of the great economic crash and many firms were going under, as Ellen knew. Wakefield told her that Daintry & Ryle's bank at Macclesfield had failed. Edward's tale about her father's money seemed plausible and she believed him.

By repeatedly telling Ellen her father was waiting for her, the Wakefield brothers got her first to Halifax, then Kendal. Along the way, Wakefield claimed he had a rich uncle, who had lent her father £60,000, but all had been lost. He said the bailiffs were after Mr Turner, and that he was now fleeing over the Scottish border. So on they went to Carlisle. Wakefield kept reiterating that if Ellen married him, his (fictitious) uncle would give them a handsome marriage settlement. Only then would her father be safe from being thrown out of the family home.

Young Ellen was now tired out. She had been travelling for hours and, terrified for her family's prospects, she finally agreed to Wakefield's proposal. She later told the court that his brother William had said: '… my father requested me, if I ever loved him, that I would not hesitate to accept Mr Wakefield as a husband … I was induced to consent by the fear that, if I did not, my papa would be ruined.'[17]

So far, Edward's plot was a success. Ellen and Edward travelled to Gretna Green, accompanied by William and the French servant. The 'happy couple' were married by the famous blacksmith David Laing. Wakefield now told Ellen her father, having heard about the marriage, had set off down south again. The poor girl (still worried sick about her father) was now dragged all the way from Gretna down to London.

In the meantime, news of Ellen's abduction had reached Shrigley. Her distraught parents were desperate to discover what had happened to her. When Ellen's abductor met a friend in London, he warned him the alarm had been raised. Wakefield, together with his new bride and William, sailed for France, where they would be safe from British justice. The Wakefields told Ellen her father had now sailed to Calais to escape his creditors.

The Turner family traced the kidnappers' footsteps to London, but her father, fearful for his daughter, became too ill to carry on. Ellen's uncle and the Turners' solicitor and family friend, Thomas Grimsditch, took ship for Calais. They were accompanied by a Bow St runner. The net was tightening on the newlyweds. The searchers caught up with the Wakefields in Calais. Edward, realizing the game was up, decided to brazen things out. He seems to have decided the best way of keeping Ellen (and her fortune) was to let her see her family, while insisting on his marriage's legality.

When Ellen's uncle explained her father's wealth was safe, she flung her arms around him in relief. Grimsditch and Ellen's uncle told Wakefield how poorly he had made his new in-laws. So Wakefield allowed Ellen to go home with them. He believed Ellen was his legal wife and that the Turners would have to drag him and their daughter through the courts to prove otherwise. He probably hoped they would give in gracefully rather than face the scandal.

Edward Gibbon Wakefield, William, and Frances Davies (now using her married name of Mrs Wakefield) were later arrested, and tried at

Lancaster. Ellen, a 'blooming, beautiful girl … gave her evidence with the most perfect clearness and precision'.[18]

The Wakefield brothers were found guilty of abduction and both were sentenced to three years in prison. William was sent to Newgate, and Edward to Lancaster Castle. Mrs Wakefield was found guilty. But the court, 'with unaccountable leniency', didn't punish her, perhaps because she wasn't present during the actual abduction.

The week-long marriage was deemed unconsummated. It was annulled by a special Act of Parliament the following May. But, strangely, Wakefield was far from being a social outcast after his release. He became an author and statesman, with a distinguished career in Canada and Australia. His obituary in the *Gentleman's Magazine* (1862) said Wakefield's crime 'made his fortune in every sense, and became the stepping stone to employment'.

Ellen Turner's story has a sad ending. Her family must have heaved a sigh of relief when in January 1828, she married the wealthy Thomas Legh of Lyme. The gossip at the time was that Thomas was on the point of paying his addresses to her when the abduction took place. Unfortunately, Ellen died in childbirth three years after her wedding; she was only nineteen years old. Her daughter Ellen Jane, born the previous year, eventually inherited the Shrigley estates, the prime cause of her mother's adventure.

Solicitor Thomas Grimsditch, who acted for the Turner family, and whose detective work helped to find Ellen, was conspicuous throughout the whole sorry affair for his coolness and tenacity. Grimsditch's sterling qualities had previously stood him in good stead as a member of the Cheshire Yeomanry. Many Cheshire gentlemen volunteered during the Napoleonic wars. But the foes they faced turned out to be much closer to home …

7

The King's Peace

The Revolutionary government of France declared war on Britain in February 1793 and fears of a French invasion of Britain surfaced early the following year. These fears were whipped to fever heat by an abortive attempt by the French to land at Cork in Ireland that December. More alarming still, 1,200 Frenchmen landed at Fishguard in Pembrokeshire in late February 1797. The landing party was quickly repelled by pitchfork-wielding Welshmen. Another French landing in 1798 in Ireland, where a rebellion had just been ruthlessly suppressed by the British, meant the Government had real cause for concern.

Anticipating an invasion, Prime Minister William Pitt (1759–1806) gave permission for counties to raise regiments in addition to the regular army, to defend King and country. Cheshire was to furnish 1,460 men for emergency supplementary militia as well as troops of cavalry, or yeomanry as they were known. The county also had a set quota for the ordinary militia, which was increased to 885 men in 1802. The militia and yeomanry were not usually expected to serve abroad; their role was to be trained and ready in case the threat of invasion became a reality. To fill the ranks of the militia, men aged between eighteen and forty-five were balloted; those selected had to serve for five years. If a balloted man had enough money and didn't want to enrol, he could pay someone to take his place. Unlike regular soldiers, militiamen's families could claim parish relief if they were in need.

Service in the militia wasn't popular, especially since the ballot was compulsory. Early in 1797, there was a riot at Carlisle on balloting day; a mob confiscated the ballot books and lists of eligible men and burnt them at the town cross. Back in Cheshire, several militiamen who had 'absented themselves' four years earlier from the Royal Regiment of Cheshire were offered a free pardon if they returned to their regiment.[1]

Volunteer regiments like the Chester Volunteers and Sale Volunteers were more popular. Volunteers and yeomanry who could prove they regularly attended drill practice were exempted from having to serve in the militia.

In Stockport, even old men turned out to defend their homes. The men, armed with pikes and dressed in long blue coats and cocked hats, were known locally as 'Pikemen' and 'Old Fogies'. Most of the Stockport Loyal Volunteers were infantrymen and there was also a cavalry troop and some riflemen, who dressed in green. Congleton Corporation voted the sum of twelve guineas in 1798 to help fund the Congleton Volunteer Association and a further eight guineas were added to the kitty in February 1800.

Some Cheshire citizens didn't take kindly to the Prime Minister turning Britain into an armed camp. A mercer at Macclesfield expressed his freedom of speech; he dubbed the volunteers: 'Billy Pitt's Dancing Dogs'. This was a great mistake, because many of them were his customers and they took great exception to his comments. And of course they were now armed! The hapless tradesman felt obliged to eat humble pie. He went to their parade ground and 'publickly asked pardon for his inconsiderate witticism'.[2]

Volunteers took their duties very seriously; they drilled and practised regularly. A member of the Stockport Volunteers (commanded by Major Holland Watson) was fatally injured while drilling on the exercise ground. Private Enoch Hill, aged thirty-six, in a 'singular calamity' was 'killed in the Ranks by the bursting of a Musket' on 21 February 1799. His troop erected a monument to the unlucky soldier, bearing the following commemorative verse:

> If crown'd with glory on the hostile plain,
> Sinks the brave Hero, for his country slain:
> On this plain grave let honouring tears be shed,
> For know its tenant for his country bled;
> Yet, nor in lands remote, nor with the foe
> Contending, felt he Death's resistless blow;

> But from the hope of Victory far apart,
> At home, a *shatter'd Musket* pierc'd his heart.

The story of the Cheshire Yeomanry begins during these troubled times. George Harry, 5th Earl of Stamford and Lord Lieutenant of the county, invited local gentry to a meeting at Northwich in November 1796. The 'numerous and respectable' gathering was held 'in order to receive Offers of Service from Gentlemen willing to accept Commissions in the Supplementary Militia, and in a Body of Cavalry to be raised' within the county.[3]

The meeting resolved to raise one infantry regiment of two battalions, and cavalry comprising six troops. The newly formed light cavalry corps was commanded by Colonel Sir John Fleming Leicester (later Lord de Tabley). Serving under the Colonel were a lieutenant colonel, a major, three captains, five lieutenants and six cornets. The Macclesfield Yeomanry Cavalry, captained by John Smith Daintry, was formed in June 1797 and the Nether-Knutsford Association appeared shortly afterwards. Elsewhere in the county, other corps were formed, independently of Sir John's troops.

Although they received a small amount of money for expenses from the government, gentlemen who volunteered paid for their own horse, uniform, pistol and sword. Each volunteer took the oath of allegiance. Many of the Yeomanry had farming commitments, so they had to fit in drill practice around their ordinary agricultural duties, such as bringing in the harvest.

Just like today's soldiers, the men were expected to keep their uniform spotless. They were fined 1s if they looked grubby and untidy when they turned up on parade. Officers and men were also fined if they missed roll call, or a drill, or were late, or drunk on parade (5s for troopers, 10s 6d for officers). So it would have been an expensive business if a soldier committed several offences at once.

At first it seemed the Yeomanry would only enjoy a mayfly existence, despite the growing threat of Napoleon Bonaparte, whose name was now on everyone's lips. After the Peace of Amiens, the Cheshire Yeomanry's strength was cut back although Knutsford and Macclesfield each retained one troop. Volunteers were disbanded and the Stockport Volunteers handed in their arms at the marketplace.

But in 1803 the fragile peace was shattered when Napoleon threatened Malta – France and England were at war again. Volunteer corps of cavalry and infantry were called for once more and they hastily re-formed. Men from all over Cheshire, from the largest towns to the tiniest villages, rushed to enrol. Crowds packed a public meeting at the Exchange in Chester in July that year and within weeks over 5,600 men had joined up. Subscriptions were held to help with the cost of uniforms and, on 1 September, the troops were inspected on the Roodee by Prince William of Gloucester.

By contrast, life in the militia was still unpopular. The *Courant* for 3 May 1803 carried a notice offering a total of 40 shillings' reward for the arrest of one Henry Harding, 'a butcher by trade', who had deserted from the Royal Cheshire Militia. Another militia man from Stockport, William Roylance, took drastic measures to get his discharge just three weeks after enlisting in a foot regiment. While 'in liquor', he asked an acquaintance, Robert Patterson, to pour vitriol (sulphuric acid) on his leg so he wouldn't be fit to serve.

The Yeomanry had many loyal men ready to enlist again. The indefatigable Sir John organized extra troops to join those at Knutsford and Macclesfield in June 1803. By the end of August, the Yeomanry had six troops once more: Northwich, Mere, Tabley, Knutsford, Macclesfield and Ashton Heyes (Ashton Hayes). More than 350 horses were needed for the cavalry; each troop contained forty-seven privates. The surgeon for the Yeomanry was Peter Holland. Holland (1766–1855) was doctor to the local gentry, and uncle to the novelist Mrs Gaskell.

Lord Grosvenor contributed £200 to the cost of another addition to the county's strength: the Western Cheshire Volunteer Cavalry, commanded by Thomas Crewe Dod, which had six troops. Stockport and Norton also provided one troop each of sixty men. If Bonaparte invaded, Cheshire now had a total of fifty-eight infantry companies (over 4,800 men), fourteen cavalry troops (over 730 men) plus artillery, ready and waiting.

The Chester volunteer infantry and artillery were inspected on the Roodee during the first week of December by Colonel Cuyler. They wore their new, 'uncommonly becoming' uniforms: 'red jacket with blue facings, white cloth waistcoat and small-clothes [knee-breeches], black gaiters' and a black cap with feather and ornamental 'military trophies'.[4]

The call to arms didn't go completely smoothly. There was uproar in Chester later that month when a naval press-gang seized Daniel

Jackson, one of the Royal Chester volunteers (who should have been exempt from navy service) and locked him up in the Northgate Gaol. His comrades in the volunteers, enraged by his seizure, broke into the prison and freed him.

In this year the Yeomanry acquired its distinctive badge of the Prince of Wales's triple feathers: a badge they wore with pride for centuries. The Prince gave permission for the regiment to be re-named the Earl of Chester's Regiment. Sir John provided a huge celebration for his troops in honour of this real feather in their caps. Their uniform comprised a dashing red and blue jacket, an undress jacket, blue pantaloons, and hessian boots, set off with cap and feather and white sword-belt. The commander for the district was Prince William Frederick, Duke of Gloucester. He reviewed the troops at Tabley in 1804 and presented the regimental standards.

Early in 1806, the Regiment was re-named the Earl of Chester's Legion after merging with the Knutsford Loyal Volunteer Infantry; Sir John Leicester was still in charge.

The threat from Bonaparte was no chimera; by the summer of 1806, up to 100,000 enemy troops were assembled at Boulogne. The doughty Cheshire men and their horses had to be ready for action. If the French invaded, warning beacons across the county would be fired. The Macclesfield, Tabley and Knutsford troops were to muster at Knutsford and the remaining troops were to meet at Northwich. Once all the men were assembled at the muster points, the officers would open sealed orders. Four days' rations were kept in readiness for action. A day's allowance for a man was a pound of meat, a pound of bread and four ounces of cheese; a horse's ration was twelve pounds of oats and ten pounds of hay. The men were to wear dress jacket and cap, with leather breeches. The men were also told to bring a greatcoat in case of bad weather, and to have ready other necessaries, including a flannel nightcap, a flannel waistcoat and one pair of flannel drawers.

While they waited for 'Boney' to attack, the Cheshire Yeomanry practised and drilled, at first at Seaforth near Liverpool, and later on the Roodee in Chester. Little did they realize they would soon find themselves facing their own countrymen rather than invading foreigners.

The cataclysm of the French Revolution had far-reaching effects in Britain as well as terrible consequences in France. At first, the more radical thinkers and young poets like Coleridge and Wordsworth welcomed the wind of change. But as the Reign of Terror reached its height, and the guillotine exacted a terrible toll, the ruling classes of Britain shivered in their shoes. Could it happen here? Would the working classes break their shackles and the streets run red with blood?

The authorities were terrified that the great mass of poor people was a slumbering monster which only needed a pin-prick to jerk it into angry life. Also, the authorities knew only too well how ill equipped they were to deal with widespread disorder if revolution reared its ugly head.

Government had several options to choose from to keep the King's peace. There was, of course, the regular army, then irregulars such as the militia and yeomanry, the night watch (as in Chester), and special constables or voluntary patrols. During the Luddite riots, the *Macclesfield Courier* (2 May 1812) reported that at Macclesfield and Stockport, a 'Nightly Patrole' composed of 'respectable inhabitants' was scouring the countryside to ensure there was no trouble.

There were no ordinary policemen as we know them today: the first professional police force wasn't formed until 1829, in London. Although a few Cheshire towns maintained their own police (Stockport had two constables), the county as a whole didn't have a regular force until 1857. Special constables, mostly respectable citizens, were enrolled by the magistrates for policing duties (usually unpaid), with powers of arrest to enforce order and disperse mobs if violence appeared imminent. But the special constables were hardly an effective fighting force in a real emergency, or when major civil unrest erupted.

During the aftermath of the French Revolution, the government flooded the English countryside with a vast army. New barracks were built, concentrated around the manufacturing districts. As a consequence, the regular army, backed up by militia or yeomanry, could now move swiftly into place when requested by local magistrates if there was a dire threat to civil order or private property.

The problem was that the property-owning classes, confronted by what they saw as alarming attacks on their authority, were only too quick to demand aid. The commanders of the regular army and the militia felt their men were dragged out of their warm beds by the magistrates far more often than was really necessary. The magistrates of this era appear to have been a particularly pusillanimous bunch, a trait which was to have tragic consequences at Peterloo. Magistrates 'cried wolf' so often, scenting rebellion where none existed and demanding military back-up over the most trivial of incidents, that some officers refused to turn out their men without a written warrant. Some senior officers also felt, especially when unemployment and hunger sparked conflict, that manufacturers should do more to help their workers in the first place instead of relying on the military to do their dirty work. In some instances, such as the Macclesfield spinners' strike of 1830, employers deliberately precipitated trouble by their intransigence. Sir Henry Bouverie, who commanded the army in the north at this time, was unhappy about the idea of using his troops to back up mill-owners who had created the conflict in the first place.

Because the cavalry were usually from the landed gentry, upper or moneyed middle classes (they had to have private means to afford a horse), their sympathies, rather naturally, lay with members of their own social stratum. The reverse was true for the militia men, who were drawn by ballot from the ranks of the common people. They were more likely to take the people's side if called in to quell strikes or food riots, especially if they were friends, family or neighbours.

In practice, this meant commanders weren't keen to use militia recruited locally as they might prove unreliable in an emergency. For example, in Cheshire in the spring of 1812, the Sheriff ignored a request from the Stockport magistrates to call out the militia, probably for this very reason. The Yeomanry cavalry, however, were deemed trustworthy; they could move swiftly and decisively on their mounts, and make short work of an angry mob. Over the next few years, the Yeomanry were in action so often their saddles must have been red-hot.

A combination of bad trading conditions, poor harvests (which meant high food prices), and war with America (which further exacerbated the trade depression) led to widespread distress in 1812 among ordinary people. The Yeomanry were sent for 'in aid of the civil power' to deal with riots in Macclesfield and Stockport, as we shall see presently.

After the Allies captured Paris in 1814, Napoleon abdicated and was exiled to Elba. Peace reigned again, the infantry regiment from

Knutsford was disbanded, and the Legion acquired yet another change of name: the Prince Regent's Regiment of Cheshire Yeomanry. The end of the war after Waterloo didn't mean the end of the Yeomanry, however. The peace brought a trade depression as the government cut back spending on food, clothes and arms for the troops. Widespread unemployment followed in its wake as soldiers and sailors returned home – 300,000 of them – and the manufacturing districts murmured with discontent again.

The increasingly paranoid and oppressive Lord Liverpool administration believed it faced a widespread underground movement plotting revolution. The government suspended the Habeus Corpus Act on 3 March 1817. People could now be imprisoned without trial. Civil liberties were under threat by the very government which claimed it was trying to protect its subjects.

But the common people had no vote, and hence no representation in Parliament. Their families were starving and they had to do something to highlight their distress. The workers attempted to publicize their unhappiness with their lot with a grand march on London. On 10 March 1817, approximately 30–40,000 people (accounts differ) gathered at St Peter's Field, Manchester. The majority of the crowd were starving cotton spinners. They naively believed that if they drew the Prince Regent's attention to their plight, he would personally intervene to sort out their woes. The original plan was for protestors to march all the way from Manchester to Carlton House in London, the Prince's residence, and present him with a petition. The men carried a few meagre provisions and rolled-up coats, rugs, and knapsacks containing blankets as they would have to sleep rough on the way. The workers were nicknamed the 'Blanketeers'.

The authorities swooped to nip the scheme in the bud. Cheshire Yeomanry troops from Knutsford, Tabley, Mere, Ashton Hayes and Northwich joined up with some units of dragoons and infantry at Sale Moor. They waited for orders, ready to pounce.

Shortly after the crowd had assembled, the Riot Act was read. The ringleaders of the march were swiftly arrested, and sent to cool their heels in the infamous New Bailey Prison at Salford. Some of the crowd, seeing the game was up, ran away through the narrow streets. Meanwhile, some marchers had already begun their long march to the capital, and were heading towards Stockport. More arrests were made along the route, and at Heaton Norris, but still the Blanketeers struggled on.

At Stockport bridge, they found troops from Stockport, a Macclesfield troop of Yeomanry, and the Life Guards waiting for them. To escape the soldiers, some Blanketeers jumped into the river, trying to ford it. The troops, seeing this, and realizing the streets of the town were now crammed tight, showed commendable restraint. They retreated from the bridge so that the people could cross the river safely. However, more Blanketeers were arrested in the town shortly afterwards and they were escorted to the New Bailey by the Stockport Troop.

The only fatality of the day was John James, a cabinet maker who lived in Old Rd, who wasn't even taking part in the march. He went out to see what was going on, and to secure his property. A soldier cut his head open with his sabre – James took two days to die. The jury at the later coroner's inquest returned a verdict of 'wilful murder', but the soldier involved was never identified and charged.

A few hundred Blanketeers continued on to Macclesfield. Here they found the second troop of Macclesfield cavalry awaiting their arrival. More arrests were made. Many of the tired, dispirited workers (some already faint from hunger and weariness) gave up and went home. Approximately 500 marchers made it as far as Ashbourne in Derbyshire before being turned back by Yeomanry. Just one man, Abel Couldwell from Stalybridge, found his way to the capital eight days later and handed in his petition.

A writer for the *Chester Chronicle* witnessed the arrival in the city of twenty-one Blanketeers arrested at Heaton Norris.[5] Their coach was escorted by the Earl of Chester's Cavalry. The prisoners were charged with committing 'seditious and treasonable practices'. Despite the general alarm caused by the disturbances, the reporter obviously felt sorry for the Blanketeers: 'We never recollect seeing a more wretched looking set of beings; some of them are mere boys.' The high hopes of the Blanketeers were dashed for ever. But the sad story of their ill-fated march set an important precedent: the authorities had shown it was possible for cavalry and militia to disperse a vast crowd with minimum casualties.

The Cheshire Yeomanry's role in the infamous 'massacre' of 'Peterloo' (the name was an ironic reference to Waterloo) is rather more controversial, and difficult to untangle. In July and early August 1819, the authorities in Manchester were alarmed to hear that large numbers of men had been seen drilling military-style on the moors and along the roads. The real reason for this sinister development was that the people were just practising marching. A huge mass meeting of parliamentary reformers was planned, and the Radicals wanted to present an image of a united, respectable appearance to the world, rather than be painted by the press as a disorderly mob. The meeting was planned for 16 August. The star speaker invited was Henry 'Orator' Hunt, dubbed a 'designing Villain' by the *Chester Chronicle*. The gentlemen of the press were invited, and thousands of people were expected: one of the biggest public meetings ever gathered together at that date. Shortly before the assembly, Hunt tried to surrender to the authorities, but they refused to arrest him. So there was no genuine pretext for stopping the event.

The authorities mustered their forces. During the first week in August, the Cheshire Yeomanry and other regiments were put on full alert. But on 7 August, Sir John Fleming Leicester wrote to the Home Secretary, Lord Sidmouth, asking to be excused from going to Manchester because of a 'grievous calamity'.

The previous night, Tabley House had been set on fire: '... tho' whether accidentally or Maliciously is I believe at present uncertain; and the whole spacious offices of every description burnt to the ground – the House only being saved by the most hazardous exertions of my Neighbouring Tenantry'. The fire was a terrific shock to Lady Leicester, who was already in poor health. It was fortunate the Leicesters' children were staying away at the time, because their rooms were 'levelled to the ground'. A letter from fellow officer Captain Daintry to Sir John on 22 August shows the colonel's suspicions had hardened: 'I am surprised to hear you say you have reason to believe that your house was set on fire by some of these deluded reforming scoundrels.'[6] Whatever the cause, the fire's impact and Sir John's subsequent illness meant he was unable to lead his regiment at the Manchester meeting.

The Manchester magistrates had no shortage of military strength, both regular and irregular regiments, ready to back them up. The officer in charge of the area, Lt. Col. L'Estrange, had at his disposal various troops of the 15th Hussars (cavalry), the 88th and 31st Foot (infantry), the Royal Horse Artillery, the Manchester and Salford Yeomanry, and the Cheshire Yeomanry, who at this time comprised eight troops (about 600 men). The men were expecting trouble. Tradition has it that some of the Yeomanry made their wills before leaving for Manchester. Sir John Fleming Leicester, still severely ill in the aftermath of the Tabley House fire, was unable to attend; his men were led by Lt. Col. Townshend.

On the morning of 16 August, the Cheshire Yeomanry mustered at Sale Moor (on the county border) before riding into the city and taking up their allotted position in St John St, a couple of blocks away from the Radical meeting in St Peter's Field. Everything seemed in order and troops surrounded the Field. In addition, several hundred special constables were stationed in several locations. Some men were posted on the Field itself, around some makeshift hustings for the speakers, and also on the roads into the city.

By great good fortune (although doubtless he didn't think so as events unfolded) John Tyas, a reporter for *The Times* who'd been sent to cover the meeting, got a ring-side seat of the meeting's early stages. Tyas and other reporters, including John Saxton from the *Manchester Observer*, were on the hustings together with other Radical notables; one was Stockport reformer James Moorhouse, a coach proprietor.

'Orator' Hunt, wearing his trademark white hat, got ready to begin his speech. An estimated 60–80,000 people – men, women and children, even babes in arms – were now jam-packed together on St Peter's Field. There was a large contingent from Stockport (mostly weavers), including a women's group. The sun shone and the crowd was in holiday mood, waiting peaceably for the 'great man' to speak.

The eyewitness accounts of what happened next at Peterloo are extremely confused and contradictory, to say the least. It seems the Manchester magistrates were completely unnerved, not only by the immense size of the crowd, but also by the almost military-style discipline with which they arrived in the town. Convinced a major insurrection was planned, they panicked, and requested the military to assist their deputy chief constable, Joseph Nadin, with the arrest of Hunt.

The Manchester and Salford Yeomanry Cavalry, who had been refreshing themselves in nearby hostelries while they awaited orders, were sent in first, under the command of Hugh Hornley Birley. 'Orator' Hunt had barely begun his speech when the cavalry hove into view. They were trotting rapidly, and brandishing their sabres. Understandably, the crowd became nervous. Hunt calmed them down, and asked them to give three cheers for the soldiers. Nadin, accompanied by special constables and cavalry, began to force a way towards the hustings to arrest Hunt. The crowd tried to make way for them but the people were so tightly packed together that it was impossible for many of them to move. The cavalrymen's horses grew frightened; the Yeomanry began to hack their way through the gathering. Even women and children weren't safe. Screams pierced the air as sabres sliced into flesh and many in the panic-stricken crowd were trampled underfoot. Hunt and others on the hustings were arrested and escorted off the field.

John Tyas only mentions the Manchester and Salford Yeomanry Cavalry taking part in this stage of the massacre. After Hunt was safely in custody, the cavalry, full of glee, shouted: 'Have at their flags!' They struck out wildly at the flag-bearers in the crowd.

Tyas said the Manchester Yeomanry now completely lost their temper and lashed out in all directions. John Saxton, the Radical newspaper editor, narrowly escaped being run through. Tyas, witnessing carnage all around him, not unnaturally began to fear for his own safety. He and his companions asked a constable to protect them. They were promptly arrested and taken to a nearby house, which at the very least preserved them from injury and may have saved their lives. Unfortunately, it meant Tyas didn't witness the rest of the dispersal.

During these chaotic few minutes, L'Estrange and the 15th Hussars, and the Cheshire Yeomanry, who were stationed further away and hence had further to travel than the Manchester and Salford Yeomanry, arrived on the scene. Utter confusion and disorder reigned. The petrified Manchester magistrates, seeing the Manchester Yeomanry were now hopelessly entangled with the crowd, told L'Estrange the people were attacking the Yeomanry. They ordered him to disperse the meeting.

Another eyewitness account gives a version of the early stages of the meeting which differs from that of Tyas. (It was written by an anonymous gentleman who was at the meeting with a Yeomanry officer, who sent it to Sir John Fleming Leicester.) The witness said that while the Manchester and Salford Yeomanry and constables were engaged in a 'general battle' in front of the hustings, two troops of the Cheshire Yeomanry and some of the 15th Hussars rode onto the field, but from a different direction to that of the Manchester Yeomanry. They advanced towards the crowd and special constables all mixed up together by the hustings. They: 'charged this crowd (constables as well as others indiscriminately) and many of the constables were ridden over and much hurt, and one of them was killed'. (This was one of the special constables from Manchester, Thomas Ashworth.) 'While all this was going on',

Hunt, Johnson, and some women were seized and taken away. 'The rest of the Cheshire Yeomanry', who had been stationed elsewhere, and the remaining regular soldiers and their artillery, 'then came up.' There was still a large crowd remaining on the field (either because they wouldn't or couldn't get away). The newly arrived troops drove them 'entirely off the field', except for those already killed or wounded.

Another version of that fateful day was written by Samuel Bamford, a Radical weaver from Middleton, who was in the thick of the action. His memoirs, *Passages in the Life of a Radical*, were written up years after the event. Although he was no friend to authority at the time of the reform meeting, Bamford clearly states that it was the Manchester and Salford Yeomanry who charged the crowd and were responsible for the carnage in the early stages of the 'massacre'. The 15th Hussars and Cheshire Yeomanry appeared on the scene 'soon after the attack'. He commented, however, that: 'the latter, as if emulous of the Manchester corps, intercepted the flying masses, and inflicted some severe sabre wounds'. Bamford said the Hussars tried to use the flat of their sabres rather than the sharp edge. Major Dyneley of the Royal Artillery, who arrived late on the scene accompanied by his six-pounder guns, confirmed that the Stockport Troop of the Cheshire Yeomanry used their sabres.

Henry Lomax, landlord of the White Lion at Stockport and a member of the Yeomanry, gave evidence the following March at Henry Hunt's trial for attending an unlawful meeting. He testified that he saw:

> People in confusion at St Peter's Field ... He was there an hour, or an hour and a quarter, but observed nothing particular, except the people running away. Some were down, and could not run, but it was not the Cheshire cavalry that did it ... The people had nearly all gone when the Cheshire Yeomanry got on the ground. Their swords were drawn, before they entered the field, by order of the commander, but not because they saw anything. They did not interfere with the remaining few.[7]

Some witnesses claimed stones and brickbats were thrown at the cavalry; the forces of order certainly didn't escape unscathed. Three of the Cheshire Yeomanry, including Mr Broadbent, were injured, and one of their horses was killed.

Without the assistance of a time machine, it is probable that no one will ever know for certain precisely what happened on that fateful day. A consensus has never been reached, either by contemporaries or historians, on the fatalities and casualty figures for Peterloo. The authorities gave a figure of five or six deaths at the most. Other historians estimate the number of deaths as between eleven (including three women) and fifteen people. At least 400 people, about a quarter of whom were women, were injured in the dispersal. There were over a hundred wounds from sabre cuts and this fact tells its own tale. Other injuries occurred as people were crushed and trampled, either by the cavalry horses or the rest of the crowd in the mad panic as they fled. It's said that many of the wounded were too terrified to seek medical help in case they were arrested for being at the meeting. Meanwhile, Hunt, who had received a slight sword cut, was sent to the New Bailey prison with John Tyas and some other prisoners. Tyas was set free the following day. He found the city quiet, but a report of a riot at Oldham sent the Cheshire Yeomanry scurrying away to that district. On the same day, there was working-class unrest in Macclesfield when a couple of thousand men ran amok in the town. The Riot Act was read by the Mayor; a mob attacked the printing shop of the Macclesfield Courier. Thomas Grimsditch, the Yeomanry officer we met previously, had all his front windows broken. One of those arrested during these riots was a Waterloo veteran, Ralph Wright, who was later given six months in prison.

Peterloo was a propaganda coup for the Radicals. But the authorities refused to allow an enquiry into the actions of magistrates and military. In Manchester, 'a numerous and highly respectable meeting' of the more die-hard loyal citizens was held three days after Peterloo at the Star Inn. They drew up a letter of thanks to the Manchester magistrates, borough-reeves and special constables, and 'several military bodies' for 'securing the public safety … and suppressing the disorderly and tumultuous assembly on Monday last'.[8] It seems only fair to reiterate that the assembly was perfectly orderly and quiet until the magistrates sent in the Manchester and Salford Yeomanry.

The magistrates, glowing in the consciousness of a job well done, as they thought, publicly thanked the Cheshire Yeomanry on behalf of the inhabitants of the city, and praised the conduct of the Manchester and Salford Yeomanry. Members of the government maintained a united front, no matter what their private feelings as to the prudence of the Manchester magistrates. The Lord Chancellor, Lord Eldon, commented that 'the magistrates must be supported; but they are very generally blamed here'. Home Secretary Lord Sidmouth wrote to the Lord Lieutenants of Lancashire and Cheshire to express the Prince Regent's 'great satisfaction' with their 'prompt, decisive, and efficient measures for the preservation of the public tranquillity'. The Prince Regent was also pleased with the 'conduct of the magistrates and civil authorities of Manchester, as well as the officers and troops, both regular and yeomanry cavalry'.[9]

A special vote of thanks to the Yeomanry from the Grand Jury of the County Palatine was published in the Cheshire newspapers. While there was outrage in Manchester, the publicly expressed opinions in Cheshire were that the Yeomanry had done their duty well; any blame should be laid fairly and squarely on the shoulders of the Manchester and Salford Yeomanry. The *Chronicle* (20 August) declared: 'The Cheshire Yeomanry distinguished themselves throughout these dreadful proceedings with great forbearance ...' The *Courant* (31 August) printed many testimonials to the 'zeal and alacrity' of the yeomanry 'during the late rebellious Meeting at Manchester'. The Northwich Troop was met with a round of applause on their return.

The day after Peterloo, Stockport officer Captain Newton wrote to Sir John Leicester, who wasn't present. He reported that: 'The crowd were yesterday dispersed in a very effectual manner.' The Stockport Troop had captured two of the Reformers' flags, which were later burnt in the town marketplace. Yeomanry officer Captain John Hollins also wrote to say his men 'conducted themselves in general in a very praiseworthy manner'.[10] But some Yeomanry members were intimidated and threatened in the backlash against the 'massacre'. (Joan Leach quotes Sir John Leicester as saying Peterloo made the Yeomanry 'obnoxious to their neighbours'.)

The Whig Earl Grosvenor (on the opposite political fence to the government) obviously felt sorry for the Peterloo victims. He contributed £50 to the relief fund for the sufferers. He commented in a letter that he was a 'friend to the principles of universal justice and humanity, which involves the great maxim of equal law to the rich and poor, to the magistrate who executes, and people who obey it'.[11]

One inference which may be drawn from Peterloo is that of the

Englishman's basic instinct for peace and lack of real revolutionary ardour. As Samuel Bamford pointed out the day after the massacre: 'If the people were ever to rise and smite their enemies, was not that the time?' Yet there was no general uprising in protest at the authorities' actions. Nevertheless, 'Peterloo' was a rallying cry for Radicals and Whigs for many years to come. And it was never forgotten by the Lancashire and Cheshire families mourning their loved ones.

The month after Peterloo, the Loyal Knutsford Volunteer Infantry re-formed and rejoined the Yeomanry. Sir John Leicester was still in overall charge of the regiment, now the Prince Regent's Cheshire Volunteer Legion. The Prince Regent knew Sir John well: he was godfather to his first son, George, who became captain of the Tabley Troop in 1827.

As this eventful year closed, the Legion was stronger than ever. It now included troops from Dunham Massey and Altrincham and had a total of eight cavalry troops and four infantry companies.

Clothing and equipping the Yeomanry and their horses cost a great deal of money. When the government refused to provide any more funding for some additional troops raised at Stockport and Macclesfield in response to the 1812 rioting, Sir John very generously agreed to find the money himself. A bill dated May 1812 for ammunition for Macclesfield Troop lists flints, powder, 'bulletts', cartridge paper, labour for making cartridges, and other sundry items, which amounted to £7 7s 6d.

Another pay-list gives wages for Captain Newton's Troop when the men 'were assembled on duty at Stockport from 15th February to 16th February 1819 in aid of the civil powers'. Officer Lt. H.E. Howard received £1 4s 2d for the two days' duty. Trumpeter William Orme and 'private men' like John Dodge and John Hunt each earned 10s, that is, 5s per day. (For comparison, a handloom weaver in 1819 earned approximately 9s 6d for a full week's work.)

The extent of Sir John's generosity in equipping the men becomes clear from another document from his personal papers, which itemizes the cost of equipping: 'a private of HRH the Prince Regent's Regiment of the Cheshire Volunteer Legion'.

In November 1819, the horse's saddle alone cost £2 14s 9d; the whole of its equipment, including breastplate, bit and bridle, came to £7 0s 11d. The yeoman's drill jacket cost £2 1s 6d and he also needed a dress jacket, boots, spurs, sash, gloves, cloak, hat, wellington boots at a guinea a pair, etc.: £11 13s 8½d in total. So it cost a grand total of £18 14s 7½d to kit out just one man and his horse.

At this time the yeomanry wore smart grey pantaloons, a blue jacket with scarlet collar and cuffs, gorgeously decorated with silver braid and regimental buttons, and a black 'shako'. (A shako is a plumed, cylinder-shaped peaked military cap.) The trumpeters wore bearskin caps. The fashion of the day meant pantaloons were cut to an extremely tight fit (leaving little to the imagination), so yeomanry also carried a 'sabretache'. a bag fastened to their sabre belt to act as a pocket for personal possessions. The overall effect was extremely dashing; it was a truism that men in uniform caused many a female heart to flutter.

In 1820 the Prince Regent became King at last and the Legion asked if its name could follow suit. He graciously acceded to their request and it was re-named the King's Cheshire Volunteer Legion in March.

The deaths at Peterloo didn't put a stop to civil unrest. As we shall see, the Yeomanry were called out again to riots in Macclesfield in April 1824 and Captain Daintry and his men were hurt by flying missiles. A member of Northwich Troop, Mr Arrowsmith, was injured during disturbances at Ancoats in Manchester in the spring of 1826. Many yeomanry units were disbanded across the country in December 1827, but the Cheshire troops' role was still considered essential. Two years later, further riots by striking silk weavers in Macclesfield were quelled by Manchester and Stockport cavalry. The rise of Chartism meant that the Cheshire Yeomanry's policing duties were still necessary during the reign of William IV, and continued into Victorian times.

While the yeomanry and militia were in demand for the thankless task of policing the county, soldiers in the regular army served bravely on distant foreign shores. The 22nd (Cheshire) Regiment, first raised at Chester in 1689, had a long and distinguished service record. Among many other battle honours, men from the regiment were at Dettingen (1743) and fought under General Wolfe in the famous attack on the Heights of Abraham at Quebec (1759). They also served in the

American War of Independence (1775) and saw action at Bunkers Hill. The 22nd Regiment was renamed the 'Cheshire' by George III in 1782. After a tour of duty in Ireland in 1790, the Regiment was sent all over the world. It served in the West Indies, South Africa, India and Mauritius in 1810, when the island was captured from the French.

One member of the Cheshire Regiment who performed feats of awe-inspiring bravery was Sgt. John Shipp (c.1784–1834). A motherless boy from Suffolk, he enlisted in the army at about the age of thirteen (his birth date is uncertain) under new 'experimental' rules. Certain regiments were allowed to boost their numbers up to 1000 rank and file each with pauper boys aged ten to sixteen. Boys were offered a guinea and a half if they enlisted. Parishes were only too pleased to relieve themselves of the burden of unwanted boys on the poor rates; all they had to do was pay the children's travelling expenses to the appropriate recruiting depot.

Shipp joined the 22nd when it was temporarily stationed in Colchester after its stint in the West Indies. The Regiment needed to increase its strength, as it suffered heavy losses because of the unhealthy climate in the West Indies – hundreds of men had died from 'yellow jack' fever. A keen, likely looking lad like Shipp, who'd always wanted to be a soldier, was quickly snapped up.

In 1805, the British were embroiled in a war with the Mahrattas to defend British interests in India against Revolutionary France. The 22nd Regiment and others were under the command of Lord Lake at the Siege of Bhurtpore. Although he was already wounded, John Shipp volunteered to lead three 'Forlorn Hopes'. (The 'Forlorn Hope' was the initial storming party in a siege; few were expected to survive, but those who did usually received a promotion for their gallantry.) Shipp was slightly wounded leading the first storming party. As the second Forlorn Hope fought its way through, he received a serious head wound which nearly blinded him. The doctors refused to let him fight for a while, which meant he had to sit and watch his comrades' 'desperate hard struggle' in the next suicidal attempt on the fort's defences. Despite his injuries, Shipp insisted on leading the final Forlorn Hope:

> I had not been on the breach more than five minutes, when I was struck with a large shot on my back, thrown down the bastion, which made me lose my footing, and I was rolling down sideways,

> when I was brought up by a bayonet of one of our grenadiers passing through the shoe, into the fleshy part of the foot ...

A soldier who helped Shipp onto his feet was shot and killed. Shipp regained the top of the bastion, but an explosion blew him off into the ditch, where he lay unconscious for some time. Although John Shipp lived to tell the tale, the twelve men he led all died. His Regiment's sacrifices were in vain. The siege was unsuccessful; hundreds of men were killed, and thousands wounded.

During the course of his career, John Shipp was twice commissioned from the ranks (a unique achievement in those days of patronage). He later served in the Night Watch at Liverpool, and became master of Liverpool Workhouse. He died in 1834.

The Cheshire Regiment suffered more losses at Jamaica in 1827, when it lost many men to the infamous 'black vomit'.

Closer to home, Cheshire men like Captain Barra, commander of the Stockport Troop of Yeomanry, saw action in the Peninsular wars. He served with the 16th Lancers in Spain and Portugal. Captain Barra and other members of the Yeomanry were Waterloo veterans.

William Tomkinson (1790–1872) of Dorfold Hall was a lieutenant colonel in the 16th Light Dragoons. Tomkinson was badly injured in 1809 during Wellington's crossing of the Douro and he received medals for his conduct at Waterloo. His troop leader Major Clement Swetenham (1787–1852) of Somerford Booths (near Congleton) also saw plenty of action in the Peninsular wars and Waterloo. Richard Egerton (youngest brother of Sir John Grey Egerton of Oulton) was a major, and later a lieutenant general; he served as aide-de-camp to Lord Rowland Hill.

Sir Stapleton Cotton served under Sir Arthur Wellesley (later the 1st Duke of Wellington) at the battle of Talavera (1809). He led a cavalry charge by the 14th Light Dragoons. Cotton's cavalry brigades played key roles at the battles of Fuentes de Onoro (1811) and Salamanca (1812). Sir Stapleton was wounded in the arm in a 'friendly fire' incident at Salamanca, when he was fired at by a Portuguese sentry. Luckily, his arm was saved.

When Commander-in-Chief in India, Cotton (now Lord Combermere) succeeded at Bhurtpore where Lord Lake had failed two decades earlier. Combermere began a bombardment of the seemingly impregnable fort on 23 November 1825. He was equipped with vastly more men and better artillery than Lake and, in January the following year, a mine destroyed a key part of the fort's defences. Troops poured into the breach and the fort surrendered shortly afterwards. Wellington himself said Combermere achieved 'a military feat which had never been surpassed by any army on any occasion'.[12]

Lord Combermere's equestrian statue still guards the entrance to Chester Castle and the monument lists his military achievements. The county's soldiers who died during these stirring times should never be forgotten; men like Lt. Col. Edward Currie of Chester, a Peninsular veteran who fell at Waterloo. There must be many others whose names were never recorded. The pity is that Waterloo wasn't the last time Britain's soldiers made the ultimate sacrifice on a foreign field while defending these shores.

8

The Golden Age of Coaching

The great coaching days seem full of glamour and excitement: the toot of the guard's horn; smartly turned out carriages; hustle and bustle while the horses were changed at roadside inns. What was it really like travelling in those times?

Travel was notoriously slow and treacherous right up to the mid-eighteenth century. In theory, there were two systems of road maintenance. Since Tudor times, local parishes were responsible for keeping roads repaired. Each parishioner was expected to contribute to road maintenance with the sweat of his brow, labouring on the road; wealthier parishioners paid cash instead. The General Highway Act of 1773 reinforced local obligations and ten surveyors (unpaid and not necessarily qualified) were appointed to look after every parish's roads. But since most roads were used by through travellers, road maintenance was unpopular with parish ratepayers. Poorer parishioners dragooned into road-mending were unskilled, and begrudged time spent away from their usual work. As a result, roads were badly neglected in many areas. Commerce was literally at a standstill if roads became impassable during the winter.

The turnpike system came into use after 1663 to help relieve the burden on parishes and the two systems ran side by side. Private trusts borrowed capital so they could adopt and repair roads (or more rarely, make new ones). Tolls from travellers helped pay off the trust's debt and went towards the road's upkeep. Trustees often included the local gentry (whose power and influence was essential to the turnpike's success), businessmen and well-heeled farmers.

Those locals with disposable income could 'subscribe' to, or more precisely invest in, the trust's mortgage bonds and receive interest on their investment.

Journeys became punctuated by the innovations of signposts, toll-gates and milestones. But a turnpike road wasn't necessarily a good road; many trusts were badly run, and never recouped their initial investment. Some major routes were encumbered by such large volumes of traffic that the trustees were unable to cope. Travellers' coaches overturned in vast ruts or got bogged down deep in mud. Arthur Young (1741–1820), who travelled widely in Britain and on the Continent, frequently lamented the horrors of the roads and the very real risk of injury.

Thomas Pennant, looking back to his youth, said that in 1739 the Chester stage to London (pulled by six horses) took a whole day just to travel the first twenty miles from Chester to Whitchurch. Sometimes eight horses were needed to pull the stagecoach through the bog and mire and the stagecoach finally reached London a bone-shaking six days later. In the 1750s, the so-called 'Flying Coach' from Stockport to London took four and a half days to complete the distance.

After the middle of the eighteenth century, huge strides were made and the turnpike system was extended and upgraded. John Metcalf (1717–1810), also known as 'Blind Jack of Knaresborough', was responsible for several new Cheshire roads. His works included the link from Whaley to Buxton in Derbyshire, and the route from Macclesfield to Sheffield via Chapel-en-le-Frith (1779).

A free-for-all followed the General Turnpike Act (passed in 1773, the same year as the Highway Act) which expedited the setting up of turnpike trusts. Hundreds of trusts were set up along all the major routes and by 1823 nearly 25,000 miles (over 20 per cent) of British roads were turnpiked. But there was no centralized control of the turnpike trusts, so the resultant road system varied hugely in quality.

By 1790, Chester had new turnpike roads to the most important neighbouring towns: Whitchurch, Northwich, Warrington and Birkenhead. However, many of the roads on the Wirral peninsula weren't upgraded until the mid-1820s.

Thomas Wedge, writing in 1794, commented that the 'great public roads' in Cheshire 'in general, are not very good; being most commonly rough pavement, called causeways, or deep sand. Within the last twenty years improvements have been made, and greater attention has been paid than formerly was to the private roads.' He described the roads looked after by the parishes as 'generally bad for carriages,' especially in clayey areas. A small pavement at the side of the roads for horsemen meant they were able to trot along easily, unlike the coaches.

The most important coaching inns in Chester were the White Lion, the Yacht and the Pied Bull. Passengers on the nightly Royal Mail coach to London began their journey at the White Lion: a twenty-eight hour journey in 1789. They paid three guineas to sit inside, or £1 11s 6d to sit on the outside of the coach exposed to all weathers. Travelling 'outside' was perilous but much cheaper. The *Royal Chester* took thirty-six hours to reach London via Nantwich, Lichfield and Northampton; the fare was two guineas inside.

Goods were sent long distances by the ponderously slow 'fly waggons', such as the one which left for London from the Wool-Hall Warehouse on Northgate St bright and early at four o'clock every Wednesday and Friday morning in the 1790s. The Wednesday waggon went by Stafford. On Fridays it travelled via Stone and Lichfield; the six-day journey terminated at the Castle and Falcon, Aldergate St.

Coach travel continued to improve as the turnpike roads were upgraded, thanks to the efforts of Thomas Telford and John Loudon Macadam (the 'Colossus of Roads'). In 1803, the *Royal Chester* post-coach to London left the White Lion at six o'clock in the morning on Sunday, Wednesday and Friday, arriving in London at eight o'clock the following evening. It now cost £2 12s 6d to sit in comparative comfort inside, and £1 12s 6d 'outside'. The *Telegraph* (a famous post-coach) from Chester to London, Bath and Bristol via Birmingham departed from the White Lion on Tuesday, Thursday and Saturday mornings at four o'clock, reaching its destination at six o'clock the following evening.

The chief inn at Macclesfield was the Macclesfield Arms. The town was on the busy London to Manchester route and was a regular stop for the *Defiance* and *Telegraph* coaches as well as the mails. Local businessmen enjoyed 'convenient accommodation' on the *True Briton*, which left the Bull's Head at six o'clock on Tuesday, Thursday and Saturday mornings for the Manchester market. Bulkier goods went by local carriers or for longer distances by 'Pickford's Fly-Waggon, which carries bales and parcels of goods to and from London, and the intermediate towns'. (The Pickford family firm was based at Poynton.) There was also a daily 'Express Coach' to Birmingham.[1]

Stockport was fortunate to be on one of the first turnpikes in the county, the Manchester to Buxton road (1725). Trans-Pennine routes and links to the south soon followed. Towards the end of the eighteenth century, local cotton manufacturers felt more up-to-date links were needed to serve their businesses. The Marple turnpike was completed in 1801 and, the following year, an extension from Marple Bridge to Glossop was approved by Parliament. The important thoroughfare to Liverpool via Northwich and Warrington was turnpiked in 1821, and other local routes were upgraded.

By this time Stockport's narrow, steep streets were becoming so choked with coach traffic that drastic action was needed. Wellington Road was 'the greatest improvement ever made' in the town.[2] The new turnpike, constructed by the Manchester & Buxton Turnpike Trust, bypassed the traffic bottlenecks and encouraged fresh industrial development. Wellington Road ran from Heaton Chapel in Heaton Norris to Rowcroft Smithy at the south end of Stockport. The Wellington Bridge across the Mersey, with its eleven arches, was a vital link in the chain; the road and viaduct cost £36,000 to construct. The bridge opened on 3 July 1826: a public holiday was declared, and 800 Sunday school students feasted on wine and buns.

The fastest way to travel was on the mails. The first Royal Mail coaches appeared in 1784. They usually carried four passengers inside and two outside.

> Every coach has its guard, armed with a blunderbuss, who has charge of the mails; he has a seat affixed behind the coach, from whence he overlooks it, and gives notice with a horn to clear the road when anything is in the way, to bring out the horses when he approaches the end of a stage, and to be ready with the letter-bags when he enters a post-town. Guards and coachmen all wear the royal livery, and the royal arms are upon the coaches.[3]

Letters were the 'Internet' of the day and news of loved ones, births and deaths, fortune or failure, all came by the mail-coaches. Thomas de Quincey (1785–1859) wrote: 'The mail-coach it was that distributed over the face of the land ... the heart-shaking news of Trafalgar, of Salamanca, of Vittoria, of Waterloo' (*English Mail-Coach,* 1863).

Author William Hazlitt (1778–1830) loved to see the mail-coaches begin their journey: 'The horses paw the ground and are impatient to be gone ... Even the outside passengers have an erect and supercilious air, as if proof against the accidents of the journey; in fact, it seems indifferent if they are to encounter the summer's heat or the winter's cold, since they are borne through the air on a winged chariot' ('The Letter-Bell', *The Mirror,* 1831).

If you wanted to know the latest news, such as a royal wedding, the mail-coach guards were sure to know. Lady Jane Stanley at Knutsford loved to keep abreast of the times, and discover the freshest gossip before anyone else in town. She paid the guard of the mail-coach which regularly passed by Brook House a 5s reward to fire off a pistol whenever there was any hot news as the coach galloped past her home. A manservant was then hurriedly despatched to the inn where the mail-coach changed horses; the guard was paid, and the servant rushed back to Lady Jane with the latest tit-bit, or a newspaper hot off the presses.

Coaches and coachmen were household names. Mail-coach drivers were regarded as heroes by all classes of society. Young 'whips' of the gentry even dressed like them; they considered it an honour to sit and chat with the coachman on the box-seat. It was an even bigger honour to be allowed to drive the coach; the young gentlemen even raised their hat to the passengers, and accepted tips from them. Some very eminent gentlemen, including peers of the realm, loved driving the public stagecoaches. One notable whip had his teeth filed to leave a large gap so he could spit like a regular coachman.

One evening early in the nineteenth century, Robert Southey travelled from Birmingham to Manchester by mail-coach. He left us a vivid portrait of his journey through Cheshire:

> We saw this quiet pastoral country to the best advantage; the sun was setting, and the long twilight of an English summer evening gives to the English landscape a charm wholly its own. As soon as it grew dark the coach-lamps were lighted ... We meant when evening closed to have forsaken the roof and taken our seats withinside; but the places were filled by chance passengers picked up on the way, and no choice was left us. Star light and a

> mild summer air made the situation not unpleasant, if we had not been weary and disposed to sleep; this propensity it was not safe to indulge; and the two hours after night set in till we reached Manchester, were the most wearying of the whole day.

The years 1815 to 1840 are often called the 'Golden Age' of coaching. Journey times shrank and coaches were better designed and more comfortable to ride in. Speed was king.

The bulk of Chester's coaching trade had switched to the Feathers Hotel, 'an inn of very superior character' in Bridge St, by the 1820s.[5] The new *Wonder* coach left the Feathers every evening at seven o'clock in 1828. It stopped at Birmingham at 4.30 the following morning so the passengers could have some refreshments and it reached the Bull and Mouth in London three and a half hours later.

The London to Holyhead mail traffic, which came through Chester, was important for the city's prosperity. From Chester, the mail went along the Holyhead turnpike via Mold, Hawarden and Holywell. Even though it travelled by night, and stopped en route, the Holyhead mail reached an average speed of nine and a half miles per hour. Old John Scott was one of the drivers along this route. When he had a particularly 'sticky' or unwilling team of horses the only way he could coax them up Penmaenmawr hill (thirty-six miles from Holyhead) was to hit the horses with the whip so slyly that they couldn't hear the crack of the whip coming.

Yet the Holyhead road was in a bad way; seven different turnpike trusts were in charge of it, and as a result, its surface was in poor condition. The North Wales roads in general were 'rough, narrow, steep, unprotected, mostly unfenced, and in winter almost impassable'.[6]

In 1808, the Post Office proposed to send the London to Holyhead mails along a shorter route, via Shrewsbury instead of Chester. But because the Welsh roads were so atrocious, vast sums were needed to upgrade the route and the plans were put aside for a few years. Work finally began in 1815, and continued for fifteen years. Thomas Telford's new road went from Shrewsbury to Holyhead via Llangollen, Betws-y-Coed and Bangor. The Holyhead mails now reached an average speed of ten and a half miles per hour, allowing for stops along the way. Telford also improved the coast road from Chester to Bangor, which formed part of the mail route from Dublin to Liverpool.

The loss of the Holyhead mails was a major blow to Chester. However, despite losing out to Shrewsbury for long-distance traffic, Chester was still a busy coaching town for local traffic; it served the whole of the north-west region. The number of coaches leaving grew from seven per day in 1801 to twenty-six per day in 1831. At the latter date, four coaches left the Feathers Hotel for London every day. Local passengers enjoyed a choice of three daily coaches to Manchester, and five to Liverpool.

By the 1830s, the *Telegraph* travelled from London to Manchester in just eighteen and a quarter hours. But if journeys were shorter and the ride more comfortable, travelling wasn't necessarily more pleasant. Very little time was allowed for meals. Mail-coaches were timed to the minute, and the passengers were too. Breakfast had to be gobbled up in ten minutes, and dinner in just twenty. If service was slow, the poor passengers were whisked back into the coach before they had finished their boiled beef and potatoes.

Away from the main roads, life proceeded at a slower pace, especially if the driver was keen to oblige his customers. Nimrod tells the story of the *Shrewsbury and Chester Highflyer*, which often took twelve hours to travel the forty miles between the two towns. After leaving Shrewsbury promptly at eight o'clock in the morning, the coach might pause at Ellesmere so a 'commercial gentleman' could transact his business. Or if a 'real gentleman' wanted to pay a morning visit to his friends, there was all the time in the world. The coachman, Billy Williams, was a 'wonderful favourite with the farmers' wives and daughters along the road' and he was offered many a pork pie to break his journey. The coach stopped for two hours for dinner at Wrexham, whose inn was 'famous for ale', but Billy was willing to stretch a point if asked. 'The coach is ready, gentlemen,' he'd say, 'but don't let me disturb you, if you wish for another bottle.'[7] No wonder the coach didn't reach Chester till eight o'clock that evening. Later in the century, coaches covered the same distance in less than four hours.

The quality of inn food was rather hit-and-miss and travellers naturally remembered which hostelries fed them well and visited them again. The Unicorn Inn (later the Hogshead) at Altrincham put on a real spread for John Byng in a clean, white-washed room. He tucked into roast beef and potatoes, cold pigeon pie, and cheesecakes, and ordered a gooseberry pie to round off his meal. Byng's favourite

Cheshire inn was the snug and comfortable Ram's Head at Disley: 'a neater and more cheerfully situated inn I never saw … The stables are excellent; the brown bread and cheese so good, the water so cold, the decanters so clean and the bedrooms so nice that I wish'd to make a return …' Byng had less elegant fare when he stopped for dinner at the Old Angel Inn in Macclesfield in June 1790. His 'pot-luck' turned out to be boiled bull's buttock, but luckily he was extremely hungry and made short work of it. That afternoon, Byng went on to an 'excellent' inn at Knutsford, the George and Dragon, where he enjoyed a much more refined repast: 'spatchcocked eel, cold fowl, cold lamb, tarts and custards'. Next day, however, he grumbled at the poor quality of the cheese, which he claimed was a common occurrence in Cheshire: 'as if all the good cheese were sent to London …'

The most luxurious way of travelling long distances was by post-chaise, but the charges were dear. The 'post-boys' (mostly men) who rode the horses wore beaver hats and yellow or blue jackets. Posting-houses, where horses were exchanged for fresh ones, didn't usually cater for ordinary coach passengers. Depending on the route, fees ranged from 12d to 18d per mile for a pair of horses, but could reach as much as 2s 6d per mile.

Inn-keepers hired out the 'Yellow Bounders', as they were known, to genteel folk who wished to travel privately. In Jane Austen's *Sense and Sensibility* (1811), ambitious social climber Lucy Steele is anxious to impress Mrs Jennings: 'Not in the stage, I assure you,' replied Miss Steele, with quick exultation; 'we came post all the way …'

Most people travelled by stage or mail-coach; the bill of fare was less expensive. The first stagecoaches appeared shortly after the mails were introduced and the guards were clad in scarlet, as on the mails.

A 'hack' post-chaise was rather like a taxi: both horse and vehicle were hired. Hemingway says 'several one-horse chaises' had recently set up business in Chester in 1830. Travelling by 'hack' was rather looked down on, since anyone with even the slightest pretensions to gentility owned their own horse and carriage.

A huge variety of vehicles, some more fashionable than others, whizzed down the high roads: phaetons, curricles, cabriolets, whiskeys, gigs ... the list seems endless. The Prince of Wales was a keen handler of 'the ribbons', and set the fashion. His favourite carriage was a high, single-bodied phaeton called a 'highflyer'. Prinney and other young bucks loved to race their highly sprung carriages down the public roads, with bets, of course, laid on the outcome. These vehicles were very dangerous to drive, but the Prince and his chums enjoyed testing their skill. They often drove 'four-in-hand', that is, with four horses pulling the carriage.

Private coaches were a visible display of wealthy families' income; they were beautifully turned out and sumptuously upholstered. Families such as the Grosvenors and Cholmondeleys had their coach doors embellished with the family crest or monogram. Horses were carefully matched for appearance as well as speed. Coachmen and grooms wore family livery and were immaculately dressed and their highly polished coat buttons sported the family crest, too. Coats were carefully tailored to fit over waistcoats with vertical stripes. White leather breeches were worn over spotlessly clean top-boots and the ensemble was completed by a black hat. Coachmen still wore tricorne hats, even though they were now considered old-fashioned. A 'box' coat with several capes protected the coachman from the vagaries of the weather.

Coachmen prided themselves on their turnout. At Overleigh in January 1792, Mrs Cowper's coachman took the carriage and horses down to the River Dee at the toll-house near the bridge to wash them. But he took them beyond their depth and the tide swept the footman and horses away to their deaths. The coachman survived by clinging on to the carriage for dear life.

Commercial coach-horses were worked till they dropped and those working the busiest routes only lasted a few years. There's a good story about the Liverpool Mail, said to have occurred in 1807, which demonstrates the amazing stamina of these horses:

> As the Liverpool Mail Coach was changing horses, at the Inn at Monk's Heath, between Congleton in Cheshire and Newcastle-under-Line (sic), the horses, which had performed the stage from Congleton, having just been taken off, and separated, hearing Sir Peter Warburton's fox-hounds in full Cry, immediately started after them, with their Harness still on, and followed the chase to

> the last. One of them, a blood mare, kept the track with the Whipper-In, and gallantly followed him for about two hours, over every Leap he took, until Reynard ran to Earth, in Mr Hibbert's plantation. These spirited horses were led back to the Inn at Monk's Heath, and performed their Stage back to Congleton, the same evening.[8]

The authorities' morbid fears of insurrection indirectly caused a nasty accident at Macclesfield. In January 1820, after a report that Radicals were going to attack the mails, the postmaster asked for a military escort of Lancers for the mail travelling from Macclesfield to Stockport. As the coach was going down Beach Lane, which was very wet, the coach horses took fright at the Lancers' flags. The coach was upset in the middle of the bridge and passengers, coach and soldiers plummeted over twenty feet into the Bollin. Luckily, the passengers escaped unhurt, but soldier Thomas Davies was badly injured and mail guard James Davis broke his leg.

Highwaymen were more likely to attack the mails than Radical sympathizers. The 'gentlemen of the road' had long been the bane of the county. During the eighteenth century, one silk manufacturer gave protection money to the highwaymen infesting the London road. Because silk goods were so valuable, they were usually accompanied by the manufacturer on their fourteen-hour journey to London. Willoby (*sic*) Ashbrook, silk throwster and Mayor of Stockport in 1779, paid the highwaymen so he could travel unmolested; he was given a secret password to use if stopped.

Legend has it the infamous Dick Turpin himself made an appearance in the Bowdon area and he robbed a lawyer on the Altrincham to Chester road. After relieving the lawyer of his valuables, Dick galloped at top speed on his trusty steed Black Bess to the Kilton Inn at Hoo Green (near Mere, Knutsford). He began playing bowls with some gentlemen on the Green, commenting loudly on the time of day, to give himself an alibi. When the crime was later investigated, the magistrates compared the time of the alleged robbery with the time of the bowling match. They refused to believe that any horse could cover the distance within the time needed to establish Turpin's alibi and they dismissed the charges.

Highwayman Edward Higgins's exploits were kept alive in folk memory for many years. He lived in Knutsford in a house opposite the Heath. He kept his own horses, and gave every appearance of being a well-to-do gentleman who enjoyed the social round but he indulged in a spot of housebreaking as well as highway robbery. When the police came to arrest Higgins in Knutsford, he escaped so swiftly and completely, a story circulated that he must have had an escape tunnel from the house. Higgins met an ignominious end when he was found guilty of housebreaking in Wales: he was executed in 1767. Mrs Gaskell's story *The Squire's Tale*, which appeared in *Household Tales*, was inspired by his exploits. Higgins's skeleton is said to have been preserved and displayed in a museum in Manchester. Highwayman Higgins's home can still be seen in Knutsford and another local celebrity once lived in the same house – 'Mad' Jack Mytton, the sportsman who frequented Chester Races.

The mail-coaches were very tempting targets. Highwaymen who got caught were executed and their bodies were hung in chains on the gibbet as an awful warning. The rotting remains of malefactors were all too common sights on journeys; in 1792, Byng saw the body of a weaver hung in chains near Stockport. The weaver, John Dean, had murdered his wife, who was seven months pregnant.

One frosty winter's night in January 1796, post-boy John Stanton, a teenage lad, was carrying the Warrington mail when he was stopped at Dunham on the Hill by two men on horseback. The men made him dismount, rifled through the bags, and tied him to a tree. They told him some men were watching him and would cut his arm off if he tried to escape. Stanton eventually freed himself, and ran back to Chester. The perpetrators, Thomas Brown (aged twenty-six) and James Price (nineteen), were 'launched into eternity in the presence of an immense multitude' in April 1796.[9] Their bones whistled in the wind on Trafford Green for over twenty years afterwards. It was probably their remains which revolted Southey as he came into Chester by coach.

The gibbet was taken down in April 1818. The *Chronicle* reported the event in forensic detail: '... a considerable portion of the muscular parts adhered to the thigh of Brown. Nearly the whole of their bones remained, and in the skull of Price, a Wren had built its nest.'[10] Interestingly, when Hemingway wrote his *History of Chester* over a decade later, the wren had changed into a robin; perhaps the historian felt Robin Redbreast added a splash of colour to a grisly story.

As the nineteenth century wore on, highwaymen were no longer the menace they had once been, but thieves still took fearful risks for gold. The General Post Office offered a £50 reward after mailbags were stolen from the Chester mail while changing horses at the Eagles Inn at Wrexham in April 1819; letters were opened and banknotes taken. Ordinary travellers were robbed, too. Mr Collins, a carter, had his pocket book stolen at Bowdon while travelling on the road between Manchester and Northwich. Joseph Walker, aged twenty, was executed in May 1819 for this theft. He maintained his innocence to the last: 'I die as innocent of the crime as the babe in its mother's arms.'[11] Three years later, highway robber George Groom was executed after a brutal assault on an old man.

Despite the newspaper stories, however, it seems Cheshire folk felt confident enough to go out and about. Byng was surprised to see young women riding alone around Knutsford: 'Why, within fifty miles of the devilish metropolis, they would all have been robb'd and r(aped).'

The weather was a less glamorous but much more likely threat than highwaymen. Coach drivers, guards and outside passengers were exposed to everything the British climate could throw at them. Snow was one of the biggest perils. Whatever the weather, the mails had to get through. *The Times* reported the mail-guards declared 'they never experienced so severe a night' as that of Friday 8 February 1799.[12] The Coventry, Chester, Shrewsbury and Worcester coaches were stuck fast in the snow; the guards abandoned their coaches and continued on horseback. A snow storm in November 1807 accompanied by high winds left drifts so deep the Chester mail, after leaving St Asaph, needed six horses to climb Rhuallt hill. After three hours' heroic struggle the coach was only halfway up the hill, so it was decided to abandon the attempt. The Macclesfield to Ashbourne road was under almost three feet of snow. The wind was so fierce that the Manchester mail needed six horses all the way and it was almost overturned several times. A rider carrying mail from Buxton to Macclesfield had to ride through snow up to his horse's stomach.

The devastating floods of July 1828 created havoc with coaching services as well as causing loss of life and dreadful damage to crops. The horses of the Chester coach to Manchester were belly-deep in floodwater along a mile of the turnpike road. The Birmingham mail and *Eclipse* coaches travelling to Manchester were re-routed through

Stockport because the water was five feet deep on their usual route. Northwich was particularly badly affected by the floods. The River Weaver burst its banks, inundating shops in the lower part of town and destroying salt merchant R.P. Hadfield's warehouse. A house in Witton St fell down and many inhabitants who took refuge in the upper storeys of their homes were rescued by ladder from boats. No coach services could pass through the town.

In September the following year, two passengers were killed in a flood at Smallwood, near Lawton Gate, after nearly twenty-four hours of heavy rain. When the *Rocket* mail-coach arrived at the bridge, in the early hours of the morning, the stream it crossed was so swollen that the bridge was barely visible. Nevertheless, the coachman cracked his whip, and urged his horses forward. Just as the coach was crossing the bridge (which had recently been repaired), it gave way. Coachman, coach and passengers were hurled into the dark, turbulent depths of the river. The coachman, Mr Ball, was badly kicked by the terrified horses, but managed to scramble his way to the river bank. One of the horses was drowned. The guard, T. Moreton, was carried away downstream. He saved himself by grabbing a tree-branch, and clinging to it until he was eventually rescued. Meanwhile, three passengers were trapped underwater inside the coach. One slim young man wriggled his way through the coach window, and escaped. The other unfortunate men were too stout to climb out, and perished. In spite of the mail-guard's terrible ordeal, the mail still had to be delivered. The letters were recovered from the vehicle, and the guard took them to Liverpool, arriving on the afternoon of the same day the accident happened. 'True grit' indeed.

The roads were dangerous for pedestrians, too. In April 1826 a 2-year-old boy, the son of Charles Hopwood of Stockport, was run over and killed by the Macclesfield *True Briton* coach. The child was playing in the road near his home on Lancashire Hill and the coach driver was unable to pull up in time.

As if the weather, highwaymen and ordinary accidents weren't enough to contend with, passengers were put at risk by the competitive spirit between the drivers. The Chester coach to Shrewsbury was upset in April 1812 and almost all the passengers were 'severely hurt'.[13]

The drivers of the Holyhead mail and the Chester mail, Thomas Perdy and George Butler, were charged with murder after a fatal accident in August 1819. The two mail-coaches happened to pass along the road. As soon as the drivers caught sight of each other, they whipped their horses into a gallop. As they went downhill near St Alban's, Butler, driver of the Chester mail, turned his leading horses in front of the Holyhead coach, even though there was plenty of room to pass. The Holyhead mail crashed; passenger William Hart was killed, and the others injured. The two drivers had plenty of time to cool down and kick their heels in prison before coming to trial the following spring. They were found guilty of manslaughter and sentenced to a year in jail. Three years later, another mail-coach driver was charged with manslaughter after the Chester mail overturned on its way to Holyhead, as a result of driving too fast through Halkyn. One of the outside passengers died 'in great agony'.[14]

Politician Thomas Creevey (1768–1838) had heard such poor reports about the Chester mail that he went out of his way to avoid it on a visit to Croxteth. Writing in 1828, he told a friend:

> I intended, you know, to come here by last Tuesday's Chester mail, but having learnt that it was the custom of that coach to be upset about twice a week, and having *by perfect accident* discovered that there was a daily coach that passed at ½ past nine in the morning by Kinmel to Liverpool … came by this coach last Wednesday … We stopt an hour and a half in Chester …

Those men of legend, the coachmen, would have split their sides laughing if they had been told their days were numbered. What could possibly replace the horse and coach?

But new modes of transport were literally in the air. There were three balloon ascents from Chester in just one year. Vincenzo Lunardi's attempt in August 1785 was only partially successful and he was seriously hurt. The following week, his balloon was successfully piloted by a Chester man, Lt. French, from Chester to Macclesfield. The same balloon was taken up in September by scientist Thomas Baldwin, who later wrote about his adventures in his pioneering book *Airopaidia*.[15]

Mr Sadler's balloon caused a stir in 1812. Fascinated Chester citizens paid a shilling to inspect Sadler's conveyance in a building behind the White Lion Inn on Princess St, 'where an account of his recent ascension from Manchester may be seen'.[16] Sadler visited Chester again twelve years later. On 7 June, he made a 'Grand Ascent' from the esplanade in front of the castle: 'The spectacle was truly sublime.'[17] The balloon was inflated by gas from the gasworks, using leathern pipes. Sadler flew to Utkinton, where he landed. The intrepid aeronaut was 'carried on the shoulders of the peasantry', and, along with his 'car', taken to the Swan Inn at Tarporley, before returning to Chester. Unfortunately, Sadler was killed during an ascent in Lancashire a few months later.

Of course, balloons could only take one or two passengers so they didn't pose any threat to the coaches. But the days of mass transport were approaching – on land rather than by air. When Robert Stephenson's locomotive *Rocket* achieved an amazing twenty-nine miles per hour (unladen) during the Rainhill trials in October 1829, its potential was soon obvious. The Liverpool and Manchester Railway opened to passengers in 1830.

New iron steeds, puffing and snorting steam, replaced the sturdy coach-horses. Names like the *Wonder*, *Telegraph* and *Highflyer* became distant memories. Mail-coaches were redundant by the early 1840s and the great coaching inns fell on hard times. Turnpike roads no longer rang to the jingle of harness and thunder of hooves; they became silent trackways, overgrown with grass. Be-whiskered Victorian gentlemen wept tears of nostalgia, bewailing the long-lost romance of the roads of their youth, but it was too late.

The golden age of coaching had gone for ever.

9

Making a Packet

One of the most surprising things about the era of 'Canal Mania' in Cheshire wasn't how many canals were built, but how many opportunities floated away into oblivion.

Canals were needed to transport heavy goods because of the dire state of the roads during the eighteenth century, which made the transport of goods slow and difficult. The canalization of the River Weaver, so vital for the salt trade, had already shown large profits were possible. The Weaver Navigation was constructed to make it easier for flats (a type of sailing barge) to travel between Winsford Bridge and Weston Point on the Mersey. The first Act to make the river navigable from Frodsham Bridge to Winsford was passed in 1720. However, the Navigation didn't open to canal traffic until January 1732, when the first tolls were collected on the Northwich section; by April that year, it was navigable as far as Winsford.

A three-way trade grew up, nurtured by hard-nosed Liverpool businessmen with interests in coal and salt. The Sankey Navigation, completed by 1757, provided a through route for coal from St Helens to travel to the Cheshire salt-fields via the River Mersey and the Weaver Navigation. The flats were loaded with salt at Winsford and Northwich. They sailed down the Weaver and then along the Mersey to drop off their cargoes at Liverpool for transhipment ready for export. Then, laden with another cargo such as manure, for example, the flats journeyed up the Sankey Navigation to exchange their cargoes for coal, which they carried to the ever-hungry salt pans in Northwich and Winsford. On average 88,640 tons of coal per annum came up the Weaver to Northwich, Witton and Anderton between 1796 and 1806.

Although the Weaver Navigation was a long-established trade route by our time period, the trustees continued to upgrade the waterway. Vessels were towed by sturdy men called bow-hauliers until 1793, when a new towing path for horses was completed. (Men were still used to tow vessels below Frodsham Bridge.) A new basin and canal were cut at Anderton basin in the same year to aid transhipment between the Trent & Mersey Canal and the Weaver, because there was a fifty-foot height difference between the two waterways. The main cargo was salt (both common and rock salt), which was laboriously transhipped by handcart.

More works began in 1799 when a 'railed road' or tramway was constructed to tranship rock salt. Another railed road was added the following year for general goods. It is possible that the two railed roads were used to complement each other, so that trucks trundling down the slope (on one set of rails) to the river basin helped raise trucks going back up (on the other rails) to the canal. In 1808 Henry Holland commented favourably on the 'inclined plane' which gave: 'a greater facility of conveyance down to Liverpool'. Common salt was transhipped using handcarts until after 1800, when chutes were built. Other cargoes included china clay, flints, pots and crates, which were carried up and down the canal to the Potteries.

Low tides often made access difficult to the Weaver at Frodsham lock; there were lengthy delays, which cost the carriers money. The solution was another Act in 1807, which authorized the Navigation trustees to make a new cut or extension from Frodsham Bridge to Weston Point on the Mersey. A new basin opened at Weston in 1810 and it was buzzing with activity by the end of the next decade.

Vessels on the Weaver Navigation paid a toll of 1s per ton at the turn of the nineteenth century and the profits were used to repair bridges in the county. The costs of Harrison's building works at the Chester Castle site, and the new Knutsford Gaol and Sessions House, were defrayed by the Navigation tolls. By Ormerod's day, the trustees' gross income was on average £16,000 annually. The trustees also donated to local charities such as Chester Infirmary and the Northwich National School.

The flatmen who worked the flats carrying salt down the Weaver lived and worked on their boats. Wives and children helped steer the boat, or to load and unload cargoes. There were other women workers on the trustees' wage books: a female lock-keeper at Acton Bridge, Elizabeth Gerrard, earned 12s per week in 1797. Ann Latham was a blacksmith for the trustees; she was paid 5d for each pound of fresh iron worked, and half that amount for re-working old iron. The trustees looked after their workers; they gave their labourers on the Navigation a pay rise during the Napoleonic wars to combat inflation. After the war, they found the flatmen extra work during hard winters when there was a downturn in trade. There was no statutory sick pay at that time, so workers clubbed together. Friendly Societies paid their funeral expenses, or looked after them if they were injured or ill. The Northwich flatmen formed a Friendly Society as early as 1792.

The other major river navigation was the Mersey & Irwell, first authorized in 1721. It linked the towns of Liverpool and Manchester via Warrington; its route just skimmed across Cheshire's northern end. The Navigation took over three decades to begin making a profit and its main traffic was coal.

The first 'true' canal through the county was constructed by James Brindley and James Gilbert. The 'Canal Duke', Francis Egerton, 3rd Duke of Bridgewater (1736–1803), built the canal to provide cheaper carriage for the coal from his Worsley mines to the coal-hungry towns of Manchester and Salford. The Bridgewater Canal was authorized by Parliament in 1760 and opened to boat traffic a year later.

The next logical step was to provide a through route for the Duke's coal from Manchester to the growing port of Liverpool. The roads between the two towns were 'execrable'; land carriage cost an extortionate £2 per ton of goods. The alternative route via the Mersey & Irwell Navigation was 'tedious and difficult' and it depended on the state of the tides. Carriage by this route was somewhat cheaper than by land, but was still 12s per ton of raw materials.[1]

When the Canal Duke decided to extend the Bridgewater Canal from Manchester to Runcorn, his scheme met huge opposition from local landlords, and of course the proprietors of the Mersey & Irwell Navigation, who didn't want to lose their monopoly. However, the traders and merchants who used the Navigation and had suffered for years at the proprietors' high-handed business methods petitioned Parliament in favour of the Duke. The new extension for the Bridgewater Canal began at Longford Bridge in Manchester, crossed the Mersey by aqueduct, bypassed Altrincham, then crossed the Bollin river. The Bridgewater Canal now terminated at Runcorn with a series of ten locks, first opened in 1773.

Runcorn was formerly a tiny village. In the early 1800s, it became popular for sea-water bathing with visitors from the Manchester area, helped by its fine air and pleasant neighbourhood. Traffic from the Bridgewater Canal transformed Runcorn into a busy industrial complex. The Canal at Runcorn:

> ... communicates with the Mersey, descending precipitously through a grand series of all the locks on his canal. These are supplied with vast basons, or reservoirs; and from the attendance they require, occasion a great conflux of workmen, and the consequent increase of dwelling-houses, inns, shops, etc. A vast warehouse has likewise been erected on a new plan, and various wharfs built for the accommodation of traders.[2]

An extra flight of locks was added in the late 1820s to improve access between the Bridgewater Canal and the Mersey. But the Duke's new enterprise hit a snag while under construction. The canal's projected route ran through land belonging to Sir Richard Brooke of Norton Priory. Engineering problems meant the route required an alteration. The new route would come uncomfortably close to Sir Richard's property. He refused point-blank to sell his land to the Duke and there was deadlock for a couple of years. The canal was completed on either side of the disputed section but the Duke was forced to pay for land carriage across the missing mile of canal. At last, Sir Richard, mollified by a hefty cash payment, agreed to sell the land. The canal was finally completely open in 1776. The cost of goods sent by the new waterway was just 6s per ton.

The Canal Duke also had to contend with competition from the Mersey & Irwell Navigation. The Mersey & Irwell trustees, in their turn, were forced to pull up their socks. They kept a weather eye on the Duke's tolls, which was good news for customers as it forced prices down. But because the Navigation was tidal, and full of sandbanks, it wasn't a speedy route for freight. Boats often met with delays while travelling from Warrington to the Runcorn Gap if the tides weren't right. To circumvent tidal delays, the Mersey & Irwell trustees cut a new waterway, the Runcorn & Latchford Canal, from just north of

Warrington to Runcorn. It trimmed three miles from the journey, and greatly shortened travelling times. Work began in 1799 and the project was finally completed in 1804. The boat captains were on a bonus system: the master who gave the best service received some extra cash. The company was now making a handsome profit and it had sufficient funds to build a new lock and basin at Runcorn in 1822 to speed up the boat traffic joining the Mersey. The basin had sufficient capacity for over a hundred boats to wait for the tide.

Although the Duke had invested vast sums in the Bridgewater Canal, the gamble paid off and it brought him huge profits. Even more markets were open to the Duke's collieries after the Grand Trunk Canal (later known as the Trent & Mersey) was authorized in 1766. The Grand Trunk connected with the Bridgewater Canal at Preston Brook. It then meandered past Northwich and Middlewich, leaving the county at Church Lawton. The new canal became a busy thoroughfare for Cheshire salt and trade from the Potteries.

The success of the Bridgewater Canal and the wealth it brought to the Canal Duke naturally concentrated Cheshire landowners' minds on getting a slice of the pie for themselves. The next grandiose scheme in Cheshire was the Chester Canal, first authorized in 1772. The original plan was to connect Chester with the Grand Trunk Canal at Middlewich. The *Chester Chronicle* (2 May 1775) published news of a special meeting of the proprietors of the Chester Canal on 4 May to decide on the best methods of making and completing the 'said navigation'. The plan caused huge excitement: 'the good folks of Chester … thought that their fortunes were about to be made … almost everyone that could by any means scrape together a hundred pounds, was anxious to embark in this golden scheme, by purchasing a share in it.'[3] The city was illuminated when the first sod of the canal was cut on 4 May 1771. The canal's construction costs were £80,000 – a vast sum. But there was a catch. When the plan was mooted, the Grand Trunk proprietors and the Canal Duke, seeing a threat to their profits, kicked up a fuss. Parliament only granted permission for the Act provided the Chester Canal *didn't* join the Grand Trunk at Middlewich. As a result, the canal was only completed as far as Nantwich. This meant that commercially, it was dead in the water. The canal shares were virtually worthless.

This wasn't the first time Nantwich had missed out on a commercial opportunity. Thomas Pennant, writing in 1780, commented that years ago the inhabitants of Nantwich had created an Act to make the River Weaver navigable between the town and Winsford Bridge, but the work was never carried out. Now history had repeated itself.

> The Chester Canal is now completed from that city, and finishes in a handsome broad bason (*sic*), near the road between Acton and the town; but at this time it remains an almost useless ornament to the country; nor has it, as might have been expected, given the least increase to the salt-trade, for which this ancient town was most distinguished. Unfortunately, the other salt towns lie more conveniently for commerce, and abound almost to excess with that useful article.

In spite of the Chester Canal's problems, canal mania was still rife. There was a rush to subscribe to the Ellesmere Canal, first authorized in 1793. Thomas Telford (1757–1834) was the engineer in charge. The *Chronicle* editor John Fletcher was instrumental in raising funds for the canal and he also had a hand in the engineering works.

The first section of the Ellesmere Canal to open was the Wirral branch from the Dee to Ellesmere Port (Netherpool) on the Mersey. This marked the beginning of Ellesmere Port's success. John Fletcher's new boat service on the canal for freight and passengers began on 1 July 1795. The canal could accommodate boats seventy feet long and fourteen feet wide. The *Chronicle* (9 October 1795) listed prices for goods sent to Manchester and Liverpool (via Ellesmere Port) by this 'perfectly safe' conveyance. Freight charges cost 10d per cwt between Manchester and Chester, and 5d per cwt from Chester to Liverpool – much cheaper than by land. (Land carriage was 2s 2d between Manchester and Chester, and 8d from Chester to Liverpool.) Goods left at John Fletcher's office in Chester were 'delivered the same day they are received'.

At Chester, an extension was cut from the Ellesmere Canal to the moribund Chester Canal. Major works were needed to create one junction with the Chester Canal, plus another to the nearby River Dee and they were completed in 1797. This vital link saved the Chester Canal as cargoes could now reach Manchester and Liverpool. The Ellesmere and Chester Canal companies' interests were now so intertwined that it made commercial sense for the two firms to join forces and the merger took place in 1813.

Chester's commercial reach was extended to the Welsh coalfields when another section of canal was built. This waterway, later known as the Llangollen Canal, started from Hurleston (Nantwich) on the Chester Canal, went through Whitchurch, and then along Llangollen Vale. It terminated at Llangollen, where it joined the River Dee. Telford's magnificent Pontcysyllte Aqueduct, which spanned the Dee, was a major engineering feat – one of the wonders of the world. The canal was carried across the valley in a cast iron trough supported by a nineteen-arch aqueduct over 1000 feet long and over 120 feet high. The aqueduct was eight years in the making and was completed in 1803.

Telford also made ingenious use of cast iron at Beeston, where the locks on the Ellesmere Canal kept sinking because there was a layer of quicksand under their foundations. The problem was cured when Telford rebuilt the locks in cast iron. Cast iron was less affected by extremes of wet and dry conditions than timber.

Nantwich had to wait for years before it got its link to Middlewich. The 'New Cut' ran from the Ellesmere & Chester Canal at Wardle Green (near Nantwich) to the Trent & Mersey at Middlewich. Joseph Priestley, writing in 1831, said the work on the new cut was being carried out 'under the skilful direction of Mr Telford; and it is expected shortly to be opened'.

Although the many new canal works brought some extra trade to Chester, traders still found the Mersey more convenient and Liverpool's success was unstoppable.

That redoubtable rider, John Mytton, exhibited a different kind of 'canal mania' when he tried to jump his horse over the Ellesmere Canal. Horse and rider inevitably ended up in the cut. On his way back to his mansion at Halston, Mytton suddenly felt very cold as well as wet. He spotted a flannel petticoat drying on a garden hedge. He swapped it for his wet coat, and continued his journey home, much to the amusement of passers-by; the petticoat's owner had the privilege of bringing Mytton's coat home for him.

Mill-owners and businessmen in the industrial Cheshire towns were keen to promote improved communications so they could cut down on transport costs. But their schemes were often foiled by the Canal Duke, the 'rottweiler' of north-west canals. The Duke wanted to monopolize canal carriage for his coal so he could undercut his competitors.

In the Stockport area, plans were set in motion by the Duke for a branch to the Bridgewater Canal as early as 1761 and James Brindley surveyed the land between Sale Moor and Stockport. But the canal stayed on the drawing board for some time, perhaps because the Duke had enough financial outlay to keep him busy for the present. The plan was resurrected, however, when the Duke got wind of a project in Macclesfield which threatened his interests.

Macclesfield businessmen had caught 'canal mania'. In 1765, they tried to get permission from Parliament to cut a canal linking Macclesfield with the Weaver Navigation (hence providing an easy route to Manchester and Liverpool). Charles Roe of Macclesfield wanted inexpensive carriage for copper ore used in his smelting works. Sir George Warren at Stockport had coal interests at Norbury, and of course the silk manufacturers were interested. The planned route went through the towns of Mottram St Andrew and Knutsford, terminating at Witton Bridge. The plan was supported by the Weaver trustees, who saw a chance to increase their profits. Another branch of the canal would begin at Mottram, then go on to Stockport and Manchester. But this scheme was blocked by the Duke of Bridgewater, still guarding his canal 'bone'. To circumvent the Roe and Warren scheme, the Duke promised to start work on his Sale Moor to Stockport plan, which he claimed would have cheaper tolls for transporting lime (highly prized as a fertilizer). Although the Macclesfield project passed the House of Commons, it foundered in the House of Lords, where of course the Duke, being a peer, could raise objections to it. It is difficult to estimate how much trade and industry which could have enriched the town went elsewhere because of this lost opportunity.

The navvies were set to work cutting the Duke's canal from Stockport to Sale Moor in 1772, but for some reason it was never completed. An attempt by the Duke's competitors to revive this plan briefly materialized in 1790, but never got off the ground.

Interest in a canal link for Stockport was renewed by news of the Ashton-under-Lyne Canal, first authorized in 1792. The pits in the Ashton-under-Lyne, Oldham and Dukinfield areas supplied Manchester with coal. The canal company soon realized the potential for extra profits if they forged a link to Stockport, which also had industries hungry for coal. Permission was given by Parliament for a branch to the town the following year. This canal was only suitable for narrow boats seven feet wide by seventy feet long. The cut ran from Clayton and terminated at the turnpike road on the summit of Lancashire Hill. It was first opened in 1797. A branch of this canal from Reddish to Beat Bank, which would have given Stockport access to the coal mines at Haughton Green, was left unfinished when the canal company ran out of money that year.

The Peak Forest Canal was originally intended to form part of the Ashton Canal, but high cost estimates caused a rethink by the Ashton canal shareholders. A fresh company was formed to carry out the project. The canal company planned to carry limestone from the Peak District, and coal for the Hyde and Dukinfield mills and other industries. Limestone was burned to produce lime, which was used in mortar for building work as well as in agriculture.

Cotton magnate Samuel Oldknow was a major shareholder in the canal, first authorized in 1794. Oldknow wanted to begin a lime kiln business at Marple and the planned canal would provide easy access to the quarries in Dove Dale and Barmoor. When finished, the waterway ran from the Dukinfield aqueduct (on the Ashton-under-Lyne Canal) to Bugsworth, with a short branch to Whaley Bridge. The principal engineer was Benjamin Outram, builder of the Cromford Canal. Oldknow's kilns began manufacturing lime in July 1797, when the canal was partially open. By 1800 the kilns were producing over 70,000 horse loads of lime in one year. The lime was taken by cart to Heaton Norris. The canal, another narrow waterway, was also used by Oldknow to carry nightsoil from Manchester to use as manure on his farm at Mellor.

The engineers needed to overcome some formidable obstacles. Three tunnels were built and the Hyde tunnel was the biggest, at over 300 yards long. The section across the River Goyt near Marple caused some headaches. The original plan included an impressive flight of sixteen locks which linked to a splendid hundred-foot high aqueduct. But the shareholders' funds were running low, so although the aqueduct was finished, a tramway was built instead of the locks between the upper and lower canal stretches.

The canal company briefly considered a suggestion from famous American engineer Robert Fulton that the aqueduct should be constructed from cast iron. But stone was finally chosen as the building material and the 'Grand Aqueduct' took seven years to construct.

> The great Marple Aqueduct ... consists of three equal semi-circular arches of sixty feet span each; the middle one is seventy-eight feet high, and the whole structure has an elevation of one hundred feet. The river, except in times of floods, is confined to the middle arch. The lower halves of the piers are constructed from rough red masonry, from Hyde-bank quarry; the upper part is of handsome white masonry.[4]

Ormerod was very impressed by the aqueduct. He called it: 'the noblest architectural work of the kind in Cheshire, and a distinguished ornament of the romantic scenery in the neighbourhood'.

The Peak Forest Canal and tramroad were fully opened to traffic in May 1800. As its traffic increased, however, the tramway caused major problems, because the freight had to be transhipped off the canal boats onto wagons, then loaded back onto boats at the end of the tramway. Night shifts were introduced, and a second tramway built, but there were still lengthy delays. Richard Arkwright (the famous cotton spinner) and Oldknow stumped up the money needed for the locks, which were built under the supervision of Thomas Brown. Although the locks were completed in 1804, the tramway was in use until early 1807.

It is said that Oldknow desperately wanted one of his lime barges to have first go on the canal when the locks were finished. His workmen were busy building a bridge where the canal linked to his lime kilns and to spur them on, he rewarded them with ale posset; the bridge was christened 'Posset Bridge'. Oldknow's treats did the trick and his boat *Perseverance* made the first trip along the completed canal. A boat-building yard to maintain Oldknow's fleet of barges was constructed near the lime kilns.

In the meantime, Macclesfield's businessmen were still pining for a canal. A proposal in 1796 to cut a canal between the Peak Forest and Trent & Mersey Canals failed to generate enough financial backing. Several more proposals surfaced during the following years, but all of them came to nothing. The Macclesfield Canal Bill was finally pushed through Parliament in 1826. The waterway was surveyed by the ubiquitous Thomas Telford and built by William Crossley. It provided a link to Manchester via a junction with the Peak Forest Canal at Marple, and to the Midlands via the Trent & Mersey Canal at Talke.

Macclesfield Canal eventually opened in 1831, just as the railway age was dawning. To mark the opening ceremony, two cavalcades of boats carrying local dignitaries sailed along the waterway. The canal carried coal, stone, goods from Birmingham and beer from Burton's breweries. Pickford's, the carrying firm, had a base at High Lane. But the canal's investors, rather than making their fortunes, didn't even cover their original investments. Macclesfield Canal was only really in use for about two decades; the railway killed off its trade.

Passengers as well as goods were carried by canal companies. The Canal Duke made a packet on passenger traffic as well as coal. Packet boats had right of way on the canals. His boats had a sickle painted on the bow and the unspoken threat was that any boat impeding their passage would have its towline slashed. On the Bridgewater Canal, packet boats sailed from Runcorn to Manchester via Altrincham. Refreshments were served en route. Coach passengers from Liverpool met the barges at Stockton and Chester passengers disembarked at Preston Brook.

The Mersey & Irwell (also known as the Old Quay Company) began a packet service from Manchester to Runcorn in 1807, in competition with the Bridgewater packets. Passengers disembarking at Runcorn could board sailings across the Mersey to Liverpool. In 1817 a steam packet service was launched to meet the Old Quay's passengers. The Runcorn boats moored very close to where the Mersey packet docked and this gave them an advantage over the Duke's passengers, who had to find a porter for their luggage, then clamber up past the staircase of locks to meet the packet. George Head paid 3s 6d in 1835 to travel on one of the Old Quay's boats. The company on board wasn't to his taste. His fellow passengers were a 'rough set of people ... All classes were jumbled together; groups of men and women dirtily dressed, and noisy. The former smoked tobacco, and guzzled beer; so did the latter, besides occasionally picking periwinkles out of their shells with pins.'

The Ellesmere Canal carried human cargo from Chester to Liverpool by canal and sea. An advertisement in the *Courant* (30 June 1795) announced the opening of passenger services 'with every accommodation for the safety and convenience of passengers', beginning on 1 July 1795. Another advertisement in the *Chronicle* (20 November 1795) gives more details. Boats left from the canal basin near the Water Tower two and a half hours before high tide. Seats in the 'best apartment' of the packet, under the capable direction of Captain Samuel Ackerley, were 1s 6d for the Ellesmere Canal leg of the journey. The River Mersey stretch was captained by Patrick Coffield and seats for this section cost 1s. Seats in the 'other apartment' cost a total of 1s 6d for the whole journey, which took about three hours; passengers' luggage was included in the price. In the 1820s, the Liverpool packets left from the Ellesmere Canal Tavern, at the end of Canal St.

Livestock and dairy produce were also transported to Ellesmere Port on the Chester packet. George Head and his fellow passengers on the Chester packet were inconvenienced by baskets of live chickens. The breeze covered people with dust and feathers, and the hens' 'cackling extended to every corner of the vessel'.

Robert Southey much preferred the 'silent and imperceptible motion' of a canal boat to being 'jolted over rough roads in a crowded and noisy coach'. But the poet endured an uncomfortable voyage on the Chester packet boat after it ventured out into the Mersey:

> We left Chester yesterday at noon ... The canal reached the Mersey, a huge river ... across which we had three leagues to sail in a slant direction. A vessel was ready to receive us, on board of which we embarked, and set sail with a slack wind. At first it was pleasant sailing, – the day fair, a castellated hill in full view up the river, and Liverpool at a distance near its mouth, upon the northern shore. But the wind rose, the water became rough, there came on a gale from the west with heavy rain, which drove us below deck, and then we were driven up again by the stench of a close cabin, and the sickness of women and children. The gale was so strong that we had reason to be thankful for reaching the town in safety.

Even the relatively short journey between Liverpool and Ellesmere Port could prove perilous, as passengers on the *Prince Regent* steam packet discovered. On the night of 5 December 1822 a terrific storm swept through Cheshire. Many buildings were damaged by gales. In Chester, the cathedral, Blue Coat Hospital and Royal Hotel all suffered and many citizens had a narrow escape from falling chimneys. Meanwhile, out on the Mersey, the *Prince Regent* faced a battle for survival.

The wind was just a fresh breeze when the vessel left Liverpool pier head at 3 p.m. with over twenty people on board, including the crew. But by the time it reached Eastham, the gales were terrifically strong and the passengers grew alarmed. However, the ship's captain, James Dimond, had confidence in his vessel and he refused to go back and find calmer waters. At about midnight the boat struck a flat and began taking on water. Some of the crew and passengers, including Mr Burt, an artist, managed to reach the deck of the flat. Suddenly the two vessels lurched apart, leaving the captain and most of the passengers, including Mr Burt's 9-year-old son, still on the packet boat. The *Prince Regent*'s cable was cut and its engine was stone dead. The ship drifted helplessly towards Ellesmere. At about 4 a.m., still with fourteen people on board, the packet struck a sandbank near Stanlow House. The shore lay tantalizingly close, about seventy yards away, across a morass of mud and sinking sand. Three passengers managed to scramble to safety ashore, but all the others perished. Captain Dimond was washed overboard with his infant son clasped tightly in his arms. Among the dead were Mr Burt's little boy, a stonemason's wife and her two children, and the blind fiddler who attended the boat. However, the captain's faith in his boat proved eerily correct: the packet was hardly damaged.

Another steam packet service, the *St David*, was introduced between Chester and Bagillt in 1825, but made a loss, despite attempts to increase revenue with trips to Bangor and Liverpool.

Intrepid Georgian travellers ventured even further afield, at considerable risk. Parkgate had been a point of departure for passengers to Ireland (such as John Wesley) since the late seventeenth century. The port was also used by the Royal Yachts, which sailed on the Lord Lieutenant of Ireland's official business. The Royal Yachts carried passengers for the Lord Lieutenant and this encouraged the formation of extra passenger services to Dublin. The R.Y. *Dorset* was on station at Dublin between 1771 and 1813 and was commanded by Alexander Schomberg until 1804. The Royal Yachts were increasingly rare visitors during our time period, however; the R.Y. *Dorset*'s final visit to

Parkgate was in the autumn of 1812, under the command of Andrew Sproule.

Parkgate's chief claim to fame was as a fashionable bathing-place. The neat, modern brick buildings of the town were arranged along one side of the banks of the Dee, which inspired the old Cheshire saying 'all on one side, like Parkgate'. Although it was double the distance by sea from Parkgate to Dublin than the alternative route via Holyhead, the port was a popular terminus because of its good coach links with Chester. One visitor to Parkgate was Emma Hart (later to become famous as Nelson's lover, Lady Hamilton) who stayed there on holiday in 1784.

Passengers for Dublin caught a 'new and elegant coach', the *Mercury*, which left the White Lion Inn, Chester for Parkgate every morning at eight, except for Mondays, and returned the same evening.[5] The shifting sands of the River Dee meant sea access to Chester was fraught with problems, so a large part of its freight business came through Parkgate.

The reputation of Parkgate and Neston as tourist hotspots was greatly enhanced by 'the extensive and brilliant patronage shewn to the Parkgate packets, which, from the regularity of their sailing, the excellence of their accommodations, and every other advantage, seem to have a decided ascendancy over all others; and in consequence, Parkgate is become the resort of elegance and fashion'.[6]

The Parkgate Packet Company was formed in September 1785. The company started out with just three ships, patriotically named the *King*, *Queen* and *Prince of Wales*. The *Princess Royal* joined the fleet two years later and another two vessels were added in 1792. The company's ships sailed to Dublin at least four times a week at the turn of the century. But the firm faced a setback when the *Queen* packet, whose master was Captain Miller, was 'totally lost on the Lancashire coast near Formby – The passengers and crew, we are happy to hear, were saved, though not without great difficulty…'.[7]

A sensational incident in October 1804 was reported in the *Chester Chronicle*. A crew member from one of the packets was captured by a naval press-gang, and taken on board the H.M. *Favourite*. The crews of four of the Parkgate packets, all armed to the teeth, stormed the *Favourite* and rescued their shipmate.

The company hit more trouble when a rival firm was set up by one of its former captains. Captain Brown evidently quarrelled with his employers, because he left to form his own business after twenty years' service at sea. He bought two second-hand ships, the *Bessborough* and *Loftus*.

The Parkgate Packet Company already faced growing competition from the port of Liverpool. But worse was to come. Because the Packet Company was now reduced to three ships, another vessel, the *King George* (formerly a privateer), was bought, but it was an unlucky purchase. The ship's design was unsuitable for the treacherous sand-banks in the Dee estuary and it was wrecked off Hoylake during its second voyage to Dublin in September 1806. Most of the ship's passengers were poor Irish workers going home after working on the harvest. When the *King George* struck the Salisbury sandbank, it was undamaged at first. Her crew waited patiently for several hours on the sand for the next tide. But when the tide returned, the vessel hit the bank again and began taking on water. One newspaper report claimed that as the water rose in the hold, the terrified Irishmen used their large harvest knives to hack their way onto the deck. Contemporary accounts disagree about the number of casualties. *The Times* (22 September) claimed that over 120 people perished and only five or six people were saved.

The loss of the *King George* sounded the death knell for the Parkgate Packet Company. By 1815 the passenger packet trade from Parkgate to Ireland was virtually extinct. The village was still popular as a seaside resort, however. The Georgians certainly liked to holiday in style. A house with a sea view in Parkgate was advertised for let in the *Chester Courant* (5 May 1812). It was 'elegantly furnished and fitted up with every possible convenience', with three parlours, a drawing room, eight bedrooms with ten beds, together with garden, stable and coach-house.

Even by the late 1820s, a local guidebook declared Parkgate was still 'much resorted to during the bathing season … with all the advantages to be derived from salt water bathing'.[8] There were two ferry boat services, one to Flint and one to Bagillt, with timings determined by the tide. A coach waited for arrivals from Wales who wanted to travel to Liverpool.

The loss of the Parkgate packets led to plans in 1822 to establish a steam packet service from Dawpool for a 'safe and speedy passage to Ireland'. Thomas Telford was called in, but when his plans were submitted for an artificial harbour and floating roadway, the estimated

£30,000 cost was too steep for the citizens of Chester to swallow. Liverpool merchants, too, were very unhappy with the scheme. They made it difficult for the plan's supporters to hire a steam packet to prove Dawpool's merits. At last, the *Mountaineer* was hired at a cost of £110. On 3 August 1823, many people from Chester and the surrounding area paid £1 5s for a return trip to Dublin. 'At twenty minutes before eight in the evening, the paddles were set in motion, and the vessel proceeded majestically' on its journey. After encountering heavy gales during its voyage, the packet reached Howth at 2.30 p.m. on Monday. The travellers continued their journey by post-chaise and they arrived in Dublin at 3.15 p.m. The jaunt shaved four hours off the time from Holyhead; the captain believed the total time saved would have been nearly seven hours if the weather had been calmer. But the high cost of the proposed harbour, and opposition from the 'leviathans of Liverpool', who didn't want to lose any passenger traffic, meant the plan sank without trace.[9]

The fever of 'canal mania' had scarcely died down in Cheshire when it was replaced by 'railway mania'. The new technology met great resistance from the canal and landed interests. The peace and tranquillity of the landscape was under attack from the new iron steeds, as we saw at the close of the last chapter. But no matter what their mode of transport, visitors to the county were struck by the county's fertile soil and lush green countryside.

10

Country Living

Farming was the mainstay of Cheshire industry at the beginning of the nineteenth century. The county was still largely rural in character but over half of the population lived in the towns. Approximately 38,000 people worked in agriculture, compared with a total of 67,000 in factories, other trades and handicrafts.

Travellers through the county commented on its beauty. Frenchman Louis Simond wrote: '… the country here is cultivated like a garden'. Southey found Cheshire a delightful contrast with the Black Country, which he had just passed through:

> We were now entering Cheshire, the great cheese country, and the difference between a land of manufactures and a land of pasturage was delightful. The houses of the labourers were clean cottages; those of the old, rich mansions with old trees about them in sight of the village church, where generation after generation, for ages back, the heirs of the family had been baptised in the same font, and buried in the same vault; not newly erected brick buildings with shrubs and saplings round them, in hearing of the mill-wheels and hammer, by which the fortune of the owner had been fabricated …

Henry Holland, who wrote an overview of the county's agriculture in 1808, believed Cheshire's climate was one of the reasons why farming was so successful. 'Mild and temperate', with plenty of rainfall, Cheshire had 'one of the most productive grass-land districts in the kingdom'.

The type of soil in the county varied greatly: clay, sand, peat, marl and gravel, mixed in various proportions. The fertile soil of the Cheshire plain gave a special sweetness to the pasture, which in turn encouraged bountiful milk production.

Most farms were, on average, between 50 and 100 acres, although some were over 400 acres in extent. The great county families such as the Grosvenors of Eaton Hall and Lord Crewe of Crewe Hall, as might be expected, owned the lion's share. Holland estimated there were fifty noblemen and gentlemen with property of £3,000 to £10,000 per annum, with as many again in the £1,000 to £3,000 bracket.

It was unusual for an estate to be concentrated in one area; more often than not, a landowner's holdings were scattered across the countryside. (The Dorfold estate, owned by the Tomkinson family, is a good example. The Tomkinsons owned farms at Acton, Wetenhall, Hurleston, Swanlow and so on.) As a consequence, landowners such as Lord Cholmondeley of Cholmondeley Castle kept a weather eye open for land coming up for sale which could augment or rationalize the shape of their estate. Sometimes landowners would swap pieces of land of mutual benefit to their estates, or they would sell plots of land too tiny to be economic.

As land holdings became consolidated over time, the number of tenants in an area was likely to reduce as a number of small farms were amalgamated into one, as the authors of *The Beauties of England and Wales* commented: 'The evil of congregating farms ... has ... in a limited degree, extended into Cheshire; and the possessions that furnished support, and gave independence, to several families, have been confined to one.'

Although some common land in Cheshire had already been enclosed, open heath and commons still remained in the 1770s, especially in Delamere Forest and west Cheshire. Thomas Wedge estimated the amount of arable land, meadows and pasture in the county as 615,000 acres in 1794. This included roughly 30,000 acres in total of waste heath and commons. Peat bogs and mosses covered about 20,000 acres and the sandy lands within the Dee estuary around 10,000 acres. Very little – less than 1000 acres – of open arable fields remained; they had been enclosed bit by bit over the previous two centuries. The pace of enclosure, which had been proceeding in a piecemeal fashion for many years, began to quicken after 1750. The idea behind enclosing open fields and common land was to increase the profitability of agriculture by making farming more efficient (because land was formerly divided into tiny fields), bring more land under the plough and make more land available for pasture.

Common land was constantly under threat. Tenants, either with or without their landlord's permission, encroached onto the common. It was also 'nibbled' away by the spread of industry. At Macclesfield, silk mills, dye-houses, bleachworks and smaller industrial buildings were built on common land. Sometimes land was enclosed to provide building land and an income for schools, chapels or workhouses, such as the new workhouse at Daw Bank, Stockport (1812). A parcel of common land was leased at Acton in 1818 to help meet a school's running costs.

Because enclosure made more land available for cultivation, it increased the amount of rent landlords could earn. The landed gentry, who had most to gain from enclosure, were keen supporters. Forty Acts of Parliament were approved for enclosing land in the county between 1790 and 1820. There were some initial costs involved as the newly enclosed land needed fences and hedges and the enclosure commissioners normally required new roads and public footpaths to be built at the landowner's expense.

Holland was doubtful of the benefits of enclosure in Cheshire. He felt that time and labour enclosing waste land might be better spent improving and draining land already partly cultivated. Among the areas he believed would require 'great expense' to enclose, providing 'little profit to the undertakers', was Delamere Forest. The Forest, an area of 8750 acres, was the largest waste in Cheshire to be enclosed by order of Parliament. It was Crown land. The Forest, a 'bleak and dreary waste' was mostly inhabited by rabbits and a few black terns which skimmed across its lakes and stagnant pools.[1] But the Forest was of great utility to the locals. They used it for pasturing sheep, cattle and pigs, and collected brushwood and cut turf for fuel. Several thousand sheep roamed there.

The first attempt to enclose Delamere was in 1796 and it took years to complete the process. The scheme suffered a setback when landowners in over fifty different townships, including Budworth, Eddisbury and Kingsley, claimed they had rights over the land. After much negotiation an Act of Parliament to enclose the Forest was passed on 9 June 1812. Two commissioners were appointed to allot the waste lands and enclosure was to be completed within three years. All common rights in the Forest were to cease, except for forest rents belonging to the Crown, and those belonging to John Arden, chief forester, bow bearer and forest bailiff. Oakmere and the quarries at Eddisbury were reserved for the use of Thomas Cholmondeley of Vale Royal, and Fish Pool and Hatchmere were reserved for John Egerton of Oulton Park. Some Delamere land, the Old and New Pale farms, had already been enclosed many years earlier. They were leased to the Earl of Cholmondeley. A portion of Crown land was used to create a new parish of Delamere with a church and parsonage.

This award also hit trouble when court cases disputing land rents and rights were filed. More Acts to amend the original enclosure award were passed in 1814 and 1818. While the lawsuits were being settled, the Crown lands (about 3850 acres) were enclosed and planted with timber but some sheep and cattle were still allowed to graze the land in places where plantations hadn't yet been established.

At Macclesfield, an Act to enclose the common was passed in 1796; over 850 acres were up for grabs. As at Delamere, the commissioners were faced by a baffling variety of conflicting claims on the land and the award took eight years to complete. The corporation and local manufacturing families, such as the Ryles and Roes, were awarded land, as well as the Earls of Derby and Cholmondeley and other local proprietors.

Two years later, all the waste lands and commons belonging to Congleton corporation, including Mossley Moss, Lower Heath and West Heath, were enclosed following an Act of Parliament in 1795. The money gained from the enclosure was invested and used to reduce the town rates.

After enclosure, chunks of the old common land were often parcelled up and sold, sometimes in a package with farming land. A freehold estate in 'the capital market town' of Frodsham was put up for sale in July 1794. Its twelve lots, totalling forty-four Cheshire acres, brought in rents of £185 per annum. The new proprietor was guaranteed a pew in the church, and 'an allotment of the common and waste land'.[2]

Enclosures didn't always pass without protest. The proposal to enclose Beam Heath at Nantwich in 1801 met with such prolonged and virulent hostility that enclosure wasn't completed for another seventy years. At Tarporley, a labourer, 53-year-old Samuel Lloyd, was sentenced to twelve months' hard labour in 1809 for knocking down a stone wall erected by 'victualler' John White for 'inclosing a part of the wastelands in that township'.[3]

Although common land was slowly disappearing, families living in or near the countryside could still glean a hedgerow harvest. George Slater, who enjoyed a rural childhood at Gawsworth, collected sap or 'birch water' from birch trees. George and his friends sold the sap at Macclesfield; it was used to make birch wine. He also cut turf from the 'moss room' on his father's farm, and sold it for 7s per one horse load.

Adam Rushton remembered 'blackberry, raspberry and bilberry bushes' growing near the lanes in Hurdsfield. But the common land, where 'people's fowls, donkey, ponies and cows' found food and shelter, and children and cattle roamed, was gradually 'levelled, enclosed, and joined on to rich men's estates'. When Rushton was about five years old, the family moved from Hurdsfield to Lower Fold Farm. Their new house, an old, dilapidated building, had a garden and three fields. Here a life of 'hard work' began. Adam's father George worked as a farm labourer and carter, taking coal and stone to Macclesfield. Adam's mother Martha looked after their three cows, did the milking, and made butter to sell. The family grew their own vegetables such as potatoes in the garden and Adam helped battle the weeds.

The Rushtons' story shows how, through no fault of their own, a family could descend into poverty. George Rushton was owed money by the builders and silk men in Macclesfield for whom he'd been carting. An economic downturn meant the townsmen delayed payment, then went bankrupt and Rushton in his turn became bankrupt. The farm and all its stock, except for one cow and its calf, was sold off to pay his debts. The family moved from their farmhouse to a croft at Cliff Lane End; the four-roomed house had no cellar or back door. George got work farming for John Broome of Shores Clough. His wages were 7s per week in winter and 9s in summer, including his meals, except at weekends, when he ate at home. Broome's wages were said to be the best in the neighbourhood: '... no better wages could then be obtained anywhere about'. To make ends meet, country-loving

Adam was sent to work in the silk mills. When the mill closed, Adam dug and harvested potatoes to eat and sell to the neighbours at 6d for 20lb, a welcome addition to the family's income. But it wasn't enough and when another factory place became available, Rushton bid a sad farewell to all the familiar birds and wildlife he knew so well.

A bewildering variety of tenancy agreements were in force on farms. It was previously the custom for land to be leased for lives (that is, the life of the tenant plus other family members), but by the 1790s it was more usual for leases to run for a set number of years. On the Tollemache estate, a mixture of systems was in operation: some farms were leased for lives, others for a term of years, and others 'at will'. On farms near gentlemen's residences, leases were becoming much shorter; the Stanley family of Alderley had seven-year and one-year tenancies on their lands.

The covenants attached to a tenancy varied according to the landlord. Commonly, the tenant paid his rent half-yearly; he was expected to keep buildings and fences in good repair, and pay any relevant taxes. There were restrictions on how much land he was allowed to till and plough for grain, because dairy farming was considered the most profitable use of the land. (When choosing a new tenant, it was considered an asset if his wife was a good cheesemaker.) No hay, straw or manure excess to requirements was to be sold and potato planting was normally limited to the amount needed to feed the tenant's family. The land was to be kept manured with lime, marl or dung as required and timber lopping and cropping was usually forbidden. The landlord reserved any mineral or mining rights. In some cases, as on the Cholmondeley and Stanley estates, the tenant was required to plant a certain number of trees each year, or face a fine. Typically, the tenant was required to provide a couple of days' teamwork (from his horses) at harvest time. Depending on the lease, part of the rent, especially for small farms, was sometimes paid in kind with a cheese or perhaps some capons.

New tenants normally took possession at Candlemas in early February. The outgoing tenant was allowed to use the farm buildings and a field of pasture for his cows until 1 May; by custom, he was entitled to three-quarters of the wheat growing there at the time he left.

Because the top families spent a large part of the year in London, they reposed a great deal of trust in their agents. Some landowners, such as the Earl of Kilmorey (Shropshire), didn't even live in the county. So an agent was necessary to keep an eye on tenants and manage daily life on the landlord's estate. Agents paid bills and servants' wages on the estate, and supervised building work as necessary. As the squire's eyes and ears, the agent had great power; he decided if a tenant behind with his rent should be allowed to stay, perhaps because he was in trouble because of poor health or other difficulties. Perhaps the tenant had lost a valuable cow, and needed financial help to buy a replacement. Or, if a farm was badly run, the agent would recommend looking for a new tenant. Allowances were made if a tenant had had a large expense, such as building work, or paying for fertilizer to improve the land when starting out.

The main crops were oats, barley, wheat, rye, clover and potatoes. Cereals were grown primarily as cattle feed. Few turnips (the winter fodder crop popularized in Norfolk and Suffolk) were grown, even as late as 1800. Turnip and swede production gradually expanded after this date, although these crops were less popular in the Wirral. Just eight years later, Holland commented: '... in the middle and southern parts of the county ... every farmer has now his field of turnips and cabbages, which he uses for his milch cows, during the winter and spring months.'[4] Cabbages were much favoured by Cheshire farmers as a green fodder and the county was renowned for its potatoes. Potatoes were greatly in demand after the end of the Napoleonic wars, when there was a food shortage. Frodsham was an important potato-growing district; in the 1790s, 100,000 bushels (each of 90lb weight) were grown yearly in this area alone. Chester, Manchester and Liverpool were good markets for this lucrative crop.

Cheshire's main (and most famous) product was, of course, cheese. The prime dairies were near Nantwich. The Weaver valley had some of the 'finest dairy land in the county', which produced a 'fine, rich cheese'.[5] A typical dairy farm of one hundred acres was usually divided up into ten to fourteen acres of oats, twelve acres of hay, with six to eight acres of fallow wheat, a similar area of summer fallow, and the rest given over to pasture.

About 92,000 cows were kept for dairy production in the first decade of the nineteenth century and approximately 11,500 tons of cheese were produced every year. A typical herd contained twelve cows or fewer. No particular breed was favoured. Cheshire farmers knew their own business best and they used their own judgement when choosing dairy cattle, rather than following the new-fangled breeding methods coming into vogue at that time.

Cows were put out to pasture in early May, where they stayed all summer. As autumn approached, they were pastured during daylight hours, then tucked up in the cowsheds at night. As the cold weather intensified, they were kept indoors until spring, as James Higginson, who farmed near Great Barrow, recorded in his diary: 'Saturday 15 November, 1817. We removeing the oats out of the shiping [shippon] into the Barne for to Tye the Cows up wich we completed ...'

Cows were milked twice a day at six o'clock in the morning and evening. The annual yield of cheese from each cow varied hugely, from 50lb to over 500lb, depending on the season, quality of the soil and pasture, time of year, and how well the stock was over-wintered. About eight quarts of milk were needed to produce one pound of cheese.

Cheese-making methods varied from dairy to dairy; some dairies made cheese twice per day, others just once. The following description is only a broad outline of this careful, time-consuming process.

The evening's milk was kept in a cool place until the following morning. The cream was skimmed off and heated to about 55°C (the dairymaid guessed the correct temperature by touch). Some of the frothy cream was saved to make butter. The heated cream was mixed with that morning's fresh milk. The dairymaid next added rennet and colouring. The best colouring was Spanish 'arnotta' or annato, derived from plants, but this was very expensive, so it was sometimes adulterated with cheaper substitutes. The mixture was left to curdle.

After the cheese had 'come', i.e. properly separated into curds and whey, it was cut into large chunks with a knife. The dairymaid put her hands into the cheese tub and broke the curd into smaller pieces, which were left to settle, and the whey was poured off. The process was repeated until almost all the whey was removed. Then the drained curds were mixed with salt, placed in a vat, and weighted down. When as much whey as possible had been expelled, the cheese was put in a press lined with a cloth. If a hard coating was required, the cheese was immersed in hot whey.

After spending a couple of days in the press, the cheese was placed in a salting tub for three days. Then it rested on a bench for eight days, where it was turned every day, and well salted again. 'After this process it is turned twice daily for six or seven days, and then washed in warm water, and wiped dry with a cloth; and when dry, smeared over with whey-butter, and placed in the warmest part of the cheese-room' where it was left to mature.[6]

Nothing was wasted in the cheese-making process. A mixture of whey and buttermilk called 'fleetings' was drunk by indoor servants and day labourers. Leftover whey was used to feed calves weaned from their mothers and for fattening pigs.

When the cheese was ready for sale, it was either taken to market by the farmer, or sold to a cheese factor or middleman. Large dairies in the middle and southern end of the county supplied the cheese factors for London markets. Farmers delivered cheese to Chester for shipment to London, or to Frodsham, where it went by packet boat to Liverpool before commencing its voyage to London. Some cheese was transported to the Midlands by the Trent & Mersey Canal. The smaller dairies, and those in the northern end of the county, sold their cheese to factors supplying the Stockport, Manchester and west Yorkshire markets.

The average size of a Cheshire cheese was 60lb but some were up to 140lb in weight. Huge cheeses were given as presents or as marks of respect. The largest Cheshire cheese ever made (before 1800) was a present for George III, made in May 1792 by Thomas Heath, a Nantwich farmer. It weighed 192lb, was 12 inches thick, and measured 2 feet 4 inches in diameter.

The chief dairymaid (if the farmer's wife didn't superintend the dairy) earned £8 to £10 per year in the 1790s. An assistant dairymaid was paid about £5 5s per year.

Cheshire butter-making differed from other counties because the whole of the milk, including the cream, was churned together. It was sold by the 'dish' of twenty-four ounces.

An advertisement by Mrs Jones, a farmer at Poulton (near Chester) who was retiring, gives us an insight into the livestock and equipment on a dairy farm. Mrs Jones's cheese-making equipment, including three stone cheese presses, was included in the sale. Among the 'valuable farming stock' were twenty-nine dairy cows, calved and in calf, three yearling heifers, two yearling bulls, waggon horses, a brown mare, and two 'in-pig' sows.[7]

The end of the Napoleonic wars and the trade slump led to hard times for farmers. Henry Tomkinson at Dorfold found it difficult to sell his cheese. The price of cattle and horses fell and some farmers got in arrears with their rent. 'Times were bad, and hard work a necessity … Milking cows at that time cost six or seven pounds each,' George Slater recalled. 'The very best cow that my father bought in 1823 cost eight pounds. This was considered a very extravagant price.'

The breed of pigs kept on Cheshire farms, according to Wedge, was a mixture of long-eared and short-eared breeds. The pigs were fattened from ten to twenty score in weight (a score was 20lb). Many labouring families kept their own pig, which they fattened and killed at Christmas.

Few sheep were kept on the Cheshire plain. The sheep roaming in Delamere Forest had to find other homes after its enclosure. After turnips became more popular as a crop, the number of sheep kept in the county increased. Some were kept in the great Cheshire parks of Tatton and Lyme, and on the Dorfold and Cholmondeley estates.

With so much of the farmer's wealth tied up in his animals, it was in his own interests to look after them. Unfortunately veterinary care, like human medicine, was in its infancy and blood-letting was used on animals as well as humans. The blacksmith was sent for to treat common ailments such as 'foul in the foot', 'garget' (a diseased udder), or for tasks such as castration. Infected areas were cut away and dressed with poultices.

One lucky cow was spared these 'remedies' because of its owner's belief in the power of prayer. Sometime in 1817, the only cow of a Northwich widow became ill. The good lady didn't want a vet's services, or any kind of medicine for her cow. She was convinced the only way her cow would recover was if the popular Methodist preacher, the Rev. Jonathan Crowther, came and prayed for it. Crowther good-naturedly agreed and the cow duly recovered. The story doesn't end there, however. When Crowther became dangerously ill, the widow returned the favour, and prayed by him. The preacher, who wasn't expected to survive, made a miraculous recovery.

Cheshire was the market garden of Manchester and Liverpool. Fruit and vegetables, hay, corn, flour and meat all made their way by canal, river or horse and cart to the hungry towns. Thomas Pennant noticed that farmers' market women in the Beeston area used the Chester Canal to take their produce into the city.

Fourteen weekly markets took place across the county during the first decade of the nineteenth century. Wednesday and Saturday were market days in Chester for: 'flesh meat, fish, poultry, vegetables and fruits of all kinds'.[8] Fish and vegetables were sold in an open area near the Exchange and there were three 'Flesh-shambles' or meat markets nearby.

Six livestock fairs were held throughout the year at Chester. The February 'Horn and Hoof' fair was mainly for cattle and horses. Horses, cattle and tanned leather were also sold on the first day of the July and October fairs for Irish linen.

New markets for farm produce opened in the summer of 1830 at the Union and Commercial Halls, which were suffering from a decline in the general wholesale trade. Cheese, bacon, butter and other products were sold on the same days as the livestock fairs. The new markets were a great success. Dairy farmers sold their produce direct to shopkeepers and Chester townsfolk without going through the big factors and dealers, and everyone benefited, except the middlemen. The farmers got a better price (and ready cash) for their cheese and customers paid lower prices for their provisions.

Corn dealing had moved away from the public markets and grain was now bought and sold privately, usually at inns. 'Little corn or grain of any kind is now brought into the markets, being generally sold by samples to the dealers.'[9]

The smaller towns, including Knutsford, Nantwich, Northwich and Frodsham, held markets on one day a week. Stockport's market was on Friday and the town also had four annual fairs: two in March, one in May and another in October. Macclesfield held five fairs each year. The largest fair was held on 22 June and it lasted for three or four days. On sale were cattle, Yorkshire cloth, shawls, ribbons and handkerchiefs, toys and cutlery.

Nantwich was famous for its cattle market, which began in February. A toll was paid to Earl Cholmondeley on all the cattle, roots and fruits sold at Nantwich fair. The church patron, Mr Crewe, also received a tithe from the corn and fish sold in the town. Under the tithes system, the church (or some lay persons as at Nantwich) received a cut of farm produce, either in money or as a payment in kind. Tithes were 'regarded with much dislike'. If anything, this is an understatement by Holland; tithes were massively unpopular, especially among farmers with nonconformist beliefs. Tithes paid in kind were believed to slow down agricultural improvements, because they reduced the farmer's profits. The system was overhauled in the mid-1830s by the Tithes Commutation Act.

Farm work, then as now, was governed by the seasons. James Higginson and his workers were busy all year round. Higginson had a small dairy herd, and grew crops: potatoes, wheat, oats and barley. During November, wheat was sown, the 'flooding guttars' in the 'little Meadow' repaired, and gooseberry bushes in the farm's kitchen garden trimmed. (Higginson's gooseberries were probably for home consumption, although there was increasing interest in growing giant gooseberries for show in Cheshire at this time.) Barley and oats were threshed and winnowed throughout the winter months. Christmas Day brought an unwelcome visitor: '25 December 1817. Being Christmas Day Samuel Cropper came with Catherine Norton's bill wich was 15s 7d ...'

Ploughing for barley began in April and work began on the potato crop in May: '23 May 1818. Setting and plowing for potatoes all Day.' The June days were hectic: '1 June 1818. We all Imployd in Scutching and Cleaning our Turnip fallow in the afternoon. William and Edward getting the last of our hay in and getting the horse shod the weather still Dry.' The following week, Higginson was worried by a drought; his pasture was 'burning up'. Potatoes were lifted and sold during July.

Higginson and his wife fed and bought clothes for their labourers. They paid 5s for a 'smock frock' for 'Charles' in December 1817. There were broadly two different types of farm labourer. The 'indoor farm servants' lived in the farmhouse. They formed the largest body of labourers. Day labourers, who didn't live with the farmer and were taken on for odd jobs as needed, formed rather fewer than 2000 of the 9000 agricultural labourers recorded in the 1831 census.

'Indoor' servants earned £6 to £9 per year in the 1790s, plus their food and lodging. In the summertime, working hours were six in the morning till six at night, with an hour for dinner. In wintertime, the normal working day was confined to daylight hours. Wages for day labourers varied with the season; a labourer might earn 7–8s per week during the winter months, 8–9s in spring. Harvest-time was the most lucrative time of year for them, at 9–15s per week. Farmers commonly worked fifteen hours a day during the harvest months. Workers received a beer allowance during harvest, and perhaps some bread and cheese. Mowing and threshing, both skilled tasks, were paid by piecework. Grass mowing was paid at 18d to 2s per acre, reaping from 6s per acre. Threshing wheat was paid at 3d or 4d per measure of thirty-eight quarts.

Day labourers included boys and girls, who were paid for odd jobs according to the season: weeding, picking up stones, or assisting with haymaking. Young girls earned 6d per day for scattering mole hills. Moles were regarded as a pest, despite a plea from poet James Hogg (the Ettrick Shepherd) for tolerance towards the 'innocent and blessed little pioneer who enriches our pasture'.[10] Farmer James Higginson paid 'Nathan' two payments of 3s and 2s for killing moles.

Vermin were a constant problem on farms. Poison was a common solution, such as 'Dr Hamilton's Infallible Ratpills', and 'Atkins' Composition'.[11] The latter was allegedly so tasty that rats and mice queued up to feast on it: '… such are the extraordinary and attracting powers it possesses, that the Inventor has frequently known them to take it from his hand with the greatest avidity'.

Several contemporaries noted an increase in agricultural wages during our time period. The spread of industry had the effect of putting up farm labourers' wages near towns. Workers could potentially earn higher wages in the factories, so there were fewer hands to work on the land. Wedge commented that in harvest time in 1792, farmers were forced to raise wages to 3s and upwards *per day*, as well as giving their labourers food and drink, in order to have enough hands. At Macclesfield, Stockport and other manufacturing districts, Holland reported: 'few are now brought up to husbandry, and it is there as difficult to find a boy to drive the plough, as a man to hold it'. Industry also had the side-effect of reducing dairy sizes. Because oats and corn were needed to feed Lancashire cotton workers, these crops became more profitable.

Day labourers' livelihoods, however, were less secure than those of 'indoor' servants. They were unlikely to be able to put money by for times of hardship, perhaps through accident or illness. Families who faced real hardship were given food, clothes, and financial or medical help by the parish overseers.

In Wedge's day, agricultural labourers mostly lived on potatoes, barley bread, butter and buttermilk, whey and 'fleetings'. They ate very little cheese, presumably because as much as possible was sold. Holland, writing a couple of decades later, said their diet was supplemented with a little bacon. Small farmers ate much the same foods, but their bread was made from wheat, or a mixture of wheat and barley; oatcakes were regular fare. Tea was the favourite drink, enjoyed with at least one meal every day.

Older farm buildings had thatched roofs and were mostly timber-framed, with brick walls. Some old properties had walls made from twisted hazel wood daubed with clay. Newer buildings were stone or brick, with slate roofs. Dairymaids were said to prefer thatched roofs because they helped maintain an even temperature for the milk. Workers' housing left a lot to be desired, particularly in the Wirral area. The rent of a farm labourer's cottage with sufficient land to keep a cow was £7 to £9 in 1808.

As already noted, landlords were keen to ensure land was improved. Covenants on leases often specified the types of manure to be used and frequency of application. The principal fertilizers used were muck, marl, lime and peat depending on the type of soil. Lime was in general use particularly in east Cheshire, which had access to cheap supplies from Derbyshire. There were lime kilns at Marple and Newbold-Astbury near Congleton, which supplied a large part of south-east Cheshire. The new wonder fertilizer of bone dust was scarce when Holland wrote his report, but quickly grew in popularity. Bone grinding mills like the one in Northwich (1818) were set up in Cheshire to meet the demand.

Henry Holland called marl 'the most important of the Cheshire manures'; there were 'numerous marl pits ... on every farm'. Marl was a special type of soil found naturally, composed of clay and lime; it was used as fertilizer, except on clay soils. Because marl was a very bulky, heavy material, it was usually dug out of the ground close to the site where it was needed, then carted to the fields and spread over the soil as a top-dressing. The marl pits which littered the landscape filled up with water over time and were used as watering holes for cattle.

Marling took place during the summer months; the gangs began work in May, once ploughing was over, and continued until the beginning of the harvest. If the farmer wanted to grow oats, marl was sometimes applied to the land during wintertime, then ploughed in when spring arrived. It was a huge operation; James Higginson hired seven teams to marl his land.

The 'marling' gangs had their own special language, songs and customs. On warm summer evenings, the shouts and cries of the marlers could be heard echoing for miles across the fields. The marling gangs in Bucklow and the western hundreds of Cheshire would elect a 'Lord of the Pit'. They would ask for money from the local landowners as they passed by. When money was forthcoming, if it was less than sixpence, the men formed a ring and joined hands, then shouted and chanted: 'Oyez! Oyez! Oyez! Mr – of – has been with us today and given us part of a hundred pounds!' If the donation was more than sixpence, the words were changed to 'part of a thousand pounds!' The proclamation was accompanied by repeated shouts and long whoops. Every day, the marlers shouted out how much they had been given and, on Saturday, the ceremony was repeated at the village ale-house, where they put their bounty to good use.

A lack of drainage was a particular problem in Cheshire, which had large tracts of low-lying marshy areas as well as moss-rooms. Several factors held back progress. Because land holdings were often mixed up together, general agreement was needed before drainage could take place. Tenants on short leases were unlikely to go to the bother and expense of draining the land. Another problem was the tax on bricks, which made drainage works expensive.

Farmers' livelihoods were at risk from floods. Nearly 700 acres of land in the Frodsham area were in danger from flooding by the Mersey. The embankments meant to protect the town were overwhelmed by the tide in 1793 and 1802; the floodwaters swirled up to within a hundred yards of the town centre.

The 1828 flooding of the River Dane caused 'tremendous devastation through the whole line of its course'; many small farmers were said to be 'irretrievably ruined'.[12] Thomas Williams of Croxton Hall, who had regularly suffered crop damage because of the Dane flooding, never recovered from his losses from this deluge. He left Croxton in 1833 to farm at Mobberley.

As we have seen, the smaller farmers enjoyed only a little meat as part of their diet. The countryside around them abounded with game, but it was reserved for their 'betters'.

Shooting parties were an important part of estate life for families like the Grosvenors, Cholmondeleys and Egertons. Game preservation provided a source of income for the estate as well as supplying entertainment. Wildfowl, rabbits and pheasants were shot during these parties. The estate gamekeepers faced a constant battle of wits to protect the estates from poachers' unwelcome attentions. Poachers faced the hidden menace of man-traps and spring-guns. Unfortunately, these instruments of torture didn't discriminate between their victims. The setting of spring-guns was made an offence in 1827 after a number of accidents to law-abiding folk.

The game laws were bitterly resented. No doubt some poaching was down to men who just enjoyed the sport, but many hard-up men and boys took 'one for the pot' to feed their families, or to make some money. There was a huge black market for game.

The laws were tightened up to levels of unprecedented harshness. The Act of 1800 said that suspected poachers faced imprisonment with hard labour; for a second offence the penalty was seven years' transportation. Offenders over twelve years old could be pressed into the army or navy. Three years later, a new Act upped the stakes even further: armed poaching became a capital offence. Following another Act in 1817, anyone caught with a net for poaching, even if unarmed, faced seven years' transportation. It must be borne in mind that the JPs trying poaching cases were usually landowners themselves, who were unlikely to entertain clemency to poachers.

The sheer savagery of the laws, far from discouraging poachers, meant they had everything to lose if caught. The poachers organized themselves into gangs for self-protection, and to make it less likely they would be captured and arrested. The game laws weren't just unpopular, they were flagrantly flouted. In Nantwich, incidents occurred more akin to the American Wild West than rural Cheshire.

At the 1829 spring Assizes, the Chester courtroom was packed with a huge crowd, with many 'elegantly dressed females', for the case of the 'Nantwich Poachers'.[13] Twenty-eight men faced trial, some for poaching and malicious shooting, some for riot and rescue. All pleaded 'not guilty'.

The story began the previous December, when a gamekeeper spotted four men in the grounds of Edwin Corbett of Darnhall Grange, Winsford. Moments later, he heard shouts. He discovered twenty to thirty men, many clad in flannel jackets, approaching him. Some were armed. He ran back to Corbett's mansion, and rounded up the coachman and several other manservants to help. The keeper and his companions ventured forth again but, far from being scared, the gang made a fight of it, and fired at them. Corbett's men ran back into the house. The gang marched victoriously round the building, and shot all the pheasants they could see.

On 9 February, the gang of poachers was caught, and imprisoned in the lock-ups at Nantwich. The prisoners were taken out of the lock-ups so they could be examined before the magistrates at the solicitor's office. The men were chained together, two by two, connected by one long chain. As the poachers were being taken through Nantwich, guarded by constables, a mob of two to three thousand men attacked, hooting and shouting as they surrounded the constables. The men were rescued. The freed prisoners ran towards the canal smithy, where they hoped to find tools to strike off their iron fetters. But before they could reach the smithy, Waterloo veteran Major William Tomkinson of Dorfold took action. He sprang onto a horse he found in the street and gave chase. The major overtook the escapees, and read the Riot Act. During the mêlée, he hit rescuer John Stringer with a stick and knocked him unconscious. With the help of the other magistrates and constables, 'with some difficulty the fugitives were recaptured and taken back to the round-house'.[14] The alarmed magistrates then sent a messenger galloping to Chester to request military aid to calm down the town.

At the 1829 spring Assizes, Stringer and seven other men were found guilty of riot, assault of a constable, and rescuing the poachers. They were sentenced to hard labour (of various durations) in the House of Correction. Another six men were found guilty of carrying arms and firing at Corbett's gamekeeper; they were given fourteen years' transportation. When sentence was passed, a lady in the crowd (perhaps a poacher's loved one) screamed hysterically and was carried out of the courtroom. Another fourteen men changed their plea to 'guilty'. The judge warned them that if they offended again, they would be transported like the others. The men were discharged upon payment of a £100 bond each.

The story had a final twist. While the men sentenced to transportation were cooped up in prison hulks, waiting to begin their voyage to Australia, a crafty solicitor spotted an error in the original indictment against them. The men were set free and allowed to return to their families.

At the same Assizes, seven men (one, Enoch Cooke, was only nineteen years old) were sentenced to two years in the House of Correction after being caught in Sir J. B. Broughton's grounds the previous December. The men were armed with guns, pistols and bludgeons when the gamekeepers discovered them.

Yet another serious poaching incident took place in December 1828. The gamekeeper at Dunham Massey asked for help from his neighbours after hearing gunshots. A posse of gamekeepers including Thomas Foster (a gamekeeper employed by the Earl of Stamford and Warrington) went to investigate. The keepers found a gang of poachers near Ashley Bridge and gave chase. Several shots were fired and Foster was injured, though not seriously. John Henshall, aged twenty, was tried for the shooting at Chester Assizes the following September. Judge Thomas Jervis felt he had no choice but to sentence Henshall to death but he wept as he gave judgement. Henshall wept too; he was hanged on 26 September 1829.

The game laws were amended in 1831; one reason was that juries had become reluctant to convict. The qualification for killing game was broadened, and the sale of game legalized. But the terrible consequences for poaching remained on the statute books.

Thefts of livestock and produce were also treated with severity. Thomas Hough, a Macclesfield brewer, was given twelve months' hard labour at Knutsford House of Correction in January 1820 for stealing a cheese. At the same county sessions, Nathaniel Perry, a 32-year-old joiner at Macclesfield, was given six months' hard labour for stealing a hen.

Three of the 'Rudheath Gang', long 'the terror of that part of the country' were found guilty at the 1828 midsummer Sessions in Knutsford of stealing wheat and wool from Clement Swetenham of Somerfood Booths. John Kirkman (fifty-eight) and Samuel Shingley (eighteen) were each sentenced to be transported for seven years; Kirkman's 27-year-old son, John, was sentenced to fourteen years' transportation.[15]

Country living had its own special customs whose origins are lost in the mists of time. The lower classes had great fun with ancient custom of 'lifting', which took place on Easter Monday and the next day. On the first day, men carried a chair decked with flowers around the houses in each village. The chair was used to lift the ladies one at a time and the men were paid with money or kisses. On Tuesday it was the ladies' turn to lift the men, and receive payment in return.

'Lifting' was also performed in many of the great Cheshire houses. (Some of the upper classes frowned on the custom; they felt it was too rowdy.) Servants placed a chair covered in garlands and ribbons in the breakfast room. The master and mistress of the house were 'lifted' on the appropriate day and the servants were rewarded with gifts.

On May Day, houses were decorated with may-flowers and coaches were decked out in lilac and green boughs. Maypoles were set up in Chester and other places. Weaverham had two maypoles, lovingly decorated according to ancient custom: 'the sides hung with garlands, and the top terminated by a birch or other tall slender tree with its leaves on, the bark being peeled, and the stem sliced to the pole, so as to give the appearance of one tree from the summit'.[16]

Harvest-time was the high point of the year. The fun began when the final field was cut; a small amount of corn was left in the field, fastened up with ribbon. The shearers hurled their sickles at the sheaf and the man who cut the ribbon was given a gift by the farmer. A huge feast was given to ravenous workers when all was safely gathered in, whether corn or potatoes. George Slater recalled Mr Crabtree, the friendly, chubby vicar of Gawsworth (who was also a kindly schoolmaster) joining in the Harvest Home or 'Shutting of Shearing' as it was known. Crabtree loved to dance an Irish jig or a hornpipe with the servant girls in the farmhouse.

Folk believed their ancestors' souls could return to the family fireside on All Souls' Eve. Special 'soul-cakes' were made to appease the spirits. It was the custom for young children or servant-girls in Cheshire, Staffordshire and Shropshire to knock at household doors, singing a traditional souling song; they received money or soul-cakes in return. There were several different versions of the song.

Soul Day, Soul Day, Saul!
One for Peter, one for Paul,
Three for him who made us all.
An apple or pear, a plum or a cherry,
Any good thing that will make us all merry …[17]

The 'soulers' went from door to door to perform the ancient soul-caking or mummers' play. Mummers' plays were performed in many other parts of England (there was a Lancashire Pace-Egging play performed at Easter). The Cheshire play was performed by men or young lads and was the only one to star the supernatural 'Wild Horse'. (Some counties had a custom known as 'hodening' which featured a horse's head, but this didn't form part of a mummers' play.) The motley crew of colourful characters in the Cheshire play may originally have represented the souls of the dead.

'Wild Horse' looked like an apparition from the Dark Ages. It was a real horse's skull painted black, with wired jaws so it could 'snap' its teeth at the audience in a terrifying manner. A man covered with a blanket or rug worked the skull; his legs formed the rear end of the horse. A short pole supported the skull to suggest the horse's front end.

The words of the play or 'nominy' were hundreds of years old, passed down the generations by word of mouth, often from father to son. The players were paid with drink, money or apples. It's a great pity that Ormerod, who was all set to print an authentic version of the play given to him by a local resident, had a sudden fit of refinement and decided it was too 'barbarous' for his readers. He substituted another version instead, performed at Easter in Lancashire and Cheshire. The play bears a strong resemblance to one that Henry Green saw performed in Knutsford in Victorian times.

The main action of the play was a mock fight. In the nineteenth-century versions of the play, the main combatants were 'St George' and 'Slasher' (King George and the Black Prince in later versions).

I am St George, the noble Champion bold,
And with my glittering sword I've won three crowns of gold;
It's I who fought the fiery dragon,
And brought him to the slaughter,
And by that means I won fair Sabra,
The King of Egypt's daughter ...[18]

The villain, 'Slasher', was killed by St George, then magically brought back to life by another character, the 'Doctor'. The finale was the arrival of the 'Wild Horse' with his 'Groom' or 'Driver', dressed in hunting livery. The horse capered for the audience, who were expected to show their appreciation. (The soul-caking play almost died out in World War I, but survived in Antrobus and Comberbach; it has enjoyed a revival in recent years.)

Towns and villages had their own special customs. At Peover, to check if a young woman was sturdy enough to be a farmer's wife, she had to be strong enough to lift the heavy oaken lid of the chest in the parish church.

When a couple from Knutsford got married, their friends and family celebrated with: '... the very singular custom of strewing their doorways in brown sand; and on this they figure various fanciful and emblematical devices, with diamond squares, scallops, etc., in white sand; and over the whole are occasionally strewed the flowers of the season'. The sand was sprinkled using a funnel. Sanding wasn't confined to weddings and the streets were sanded for George III's Royal Jubilee in 1809, and for the victory celebrations for the Battle of Salamanca in 1812.

Of course, couples didn't always live happily ever after. An old custom, if one's neighbours felt a matrimonial dispute had got out of hand (especially if a man had beaten his wife), was to make a tumultuous protest: 'Riding the Stang'. A procession went through the village streets banging pots, pans, tooting horns, and so on. The 'Stang' was a pole, suspended across the shoulders of a couple of men or boys; their leader perched on the pole, banging a kettle with a stick, and chanting a rhyme appropriate for the alleged misdemeanour outside the victim's house. Although this 'punishment' was normally reserved for wife-beating, it was sometimes used if neighbours fell out, or when a community uncovered unseemly behaviour. Sometimes the person being held up to ridicule was made to 'Ride the Stang' through the streets accompanied by a noisy mob, as happened to a Rainow lady of alleged doubtful virtue during the 1820s.

Chester Assizes heard a case in 1820 when a young woman, Mary Dutton, claimed her character had been defamed. She was said to have enjoyed an 'improper connexion' with Thomas Percival, an 'infirm old man of 70'. Some lads allegedly paraded through the streets, 'riding the stang' with 'tin pans, kettles, files, sheep bells' and so on, making a hideous noise.[19] Dutton's case against the boys was dismissed because of a lack of evidence.

'Riding the Stang' sometimes reared its head during industrial disputes. It was used to punish 'knobsticks', as black-legs were called. And the Regency period was a time of great unrest in the textile industries.

11

Smooth as Silk

The silk industry was well established in east Cheshire by the end of the eighteenth century. But because silk was a luxury item, it was highly fashion-dependent. Work wasn't guaranteed for the large numbers of Cheshire folk who relied on silk for their livelihoods. Trouble with the trade led to 'trouble at t'mill' and confrontation, sometimes violent, between masters and workers.

'Tram', a lower quality silk thread, was made in England (possibly in east Cheshire as well as London) early in the seventeenth century. Silk isn't a vegetable fibre like cotton, it's a filament used by the silkworm to build a protective cocoon around itself in preparation for its metamorphosis into a silk moth. The silk fibre is incredibly light, fine and long: the filament in one tiny cocoon is hundreds of metres in length. It is extracted by boiling the cocoon with the hapless silkworm inside, so it doesn't munch its way out and damage the fibre. The filament is then unwound or 'reeled' to form a skein of raw silk. To make it easier to weave the silk thread, it is first wound onto bobbins, then made stronger by twisting it ('throwing'). Two or more threads of thrown yarn are twisted together ('doubling') to create different grades of thread.

The lucrative secret of throwing the very best quality thread, called 'organzine', was first discovered in Italy during the seventeenth century. English silk weavers were forced to import expensive Italian silk yarn. There was an obvious business opportunity here for anyone who could unravel the secret of its manufacture. Thomas Cotchett of Derby made the first attempt in Britain to build a water-

Part of the ancient refectory and cloisters at Chester Cathedral (*A Visit to the Cathedral*)

Wesleyan Chapel (1825) at Tiviot Dale, Stockport. The 'castle' shaped building in the background on the right is the old Castle Mill (From *Lancashire Illustrated*, H. Fisher, Son, and Jackson, 1831)

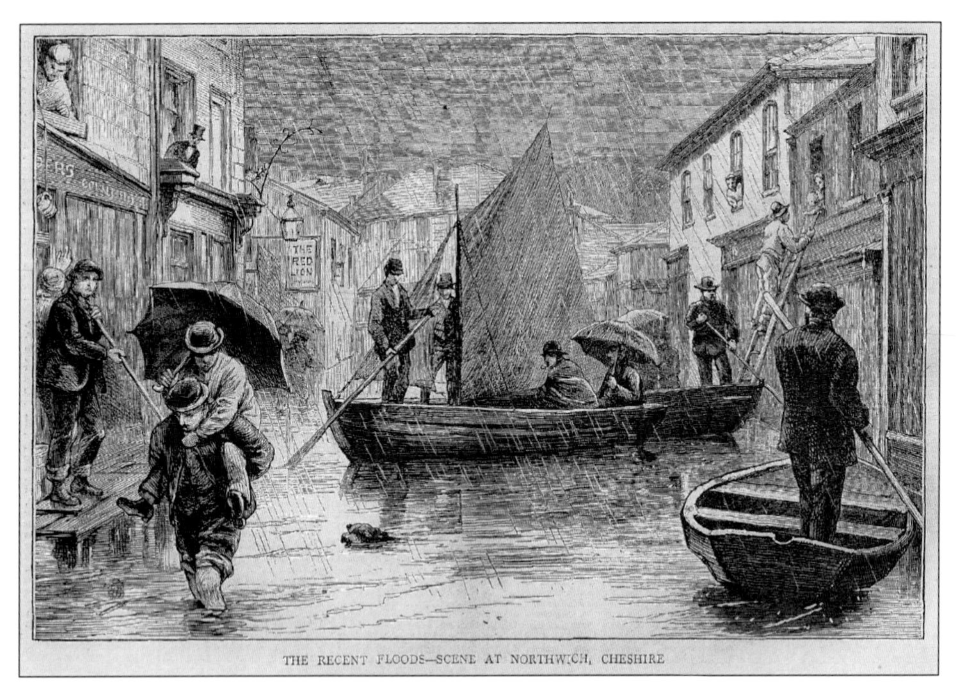

THE RECENT FLOODS—SCENE AT NORTHWICH, CHESHIRE

Northwich floods, 1872. There were similar scenes in the floods of 1798, 1799, and 1828 (*Daily Graphic*)

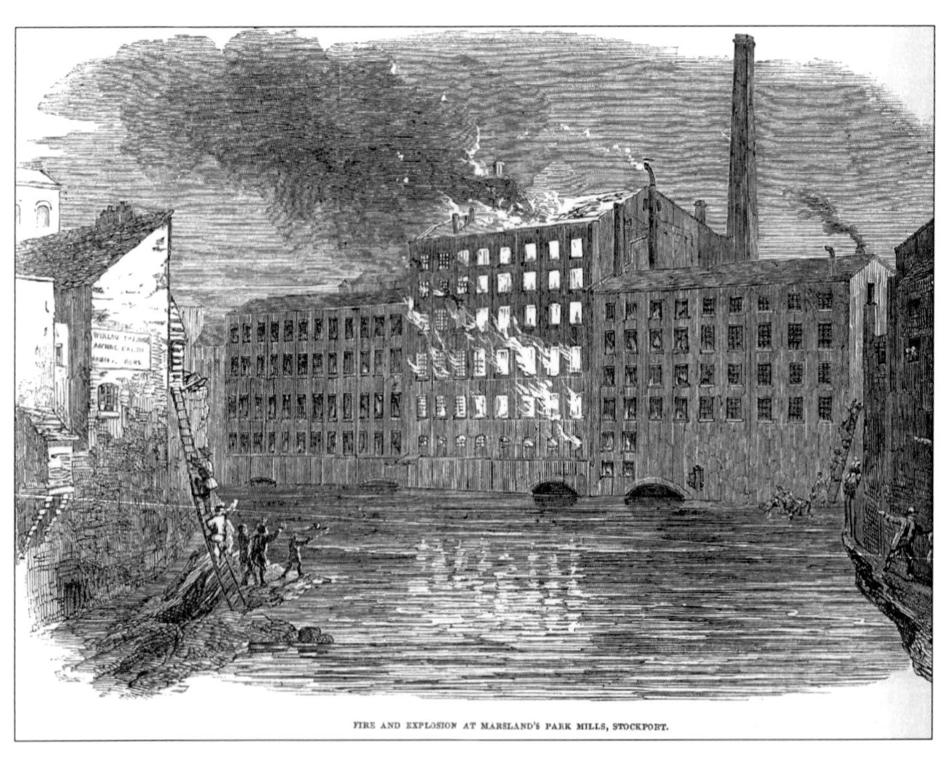

FIRE AND EXPLOSION AT MARSLAND'S PARK MILLS, STOCKPORT.

The fatal fire and boiler explosion at Henry Marsland's mill, Stockport, 17 March 1851. This engraving is thought to be one of the earliest depictions of the Park Mill site (*Illustrated London News*, 29 March 1851)

George IV, 1822. While Prince of Wales, he stayed in Congleton during the autumn of 1806 (Engraving by William Darton)

Sir Walter Scott, 1822. The famous novelist passed through Macclesfield during the trade slump of 1826 (Engraving by William Darton)

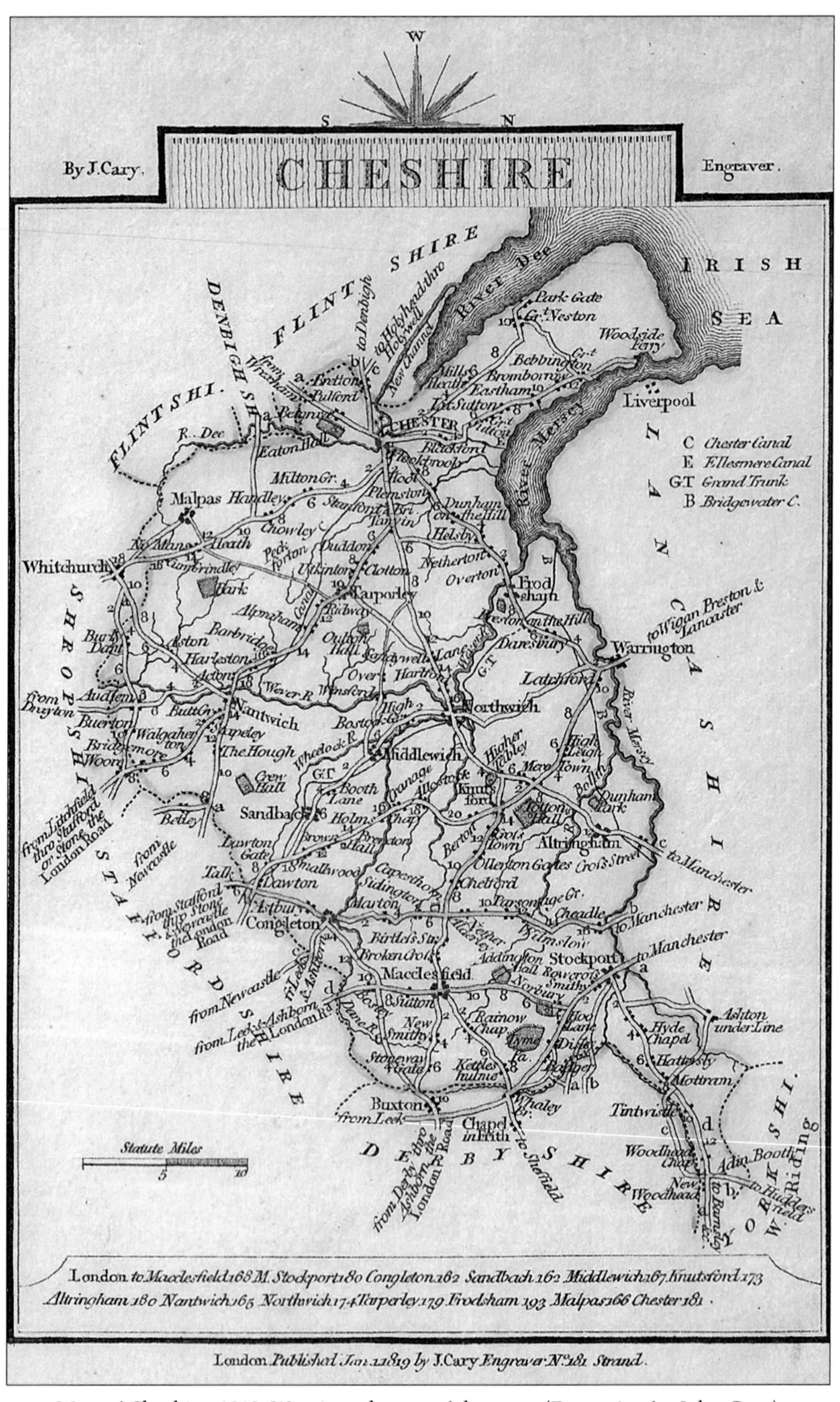

Map of Cheshire, 1819. West is at the top of the map. (Engraving by John Cary)

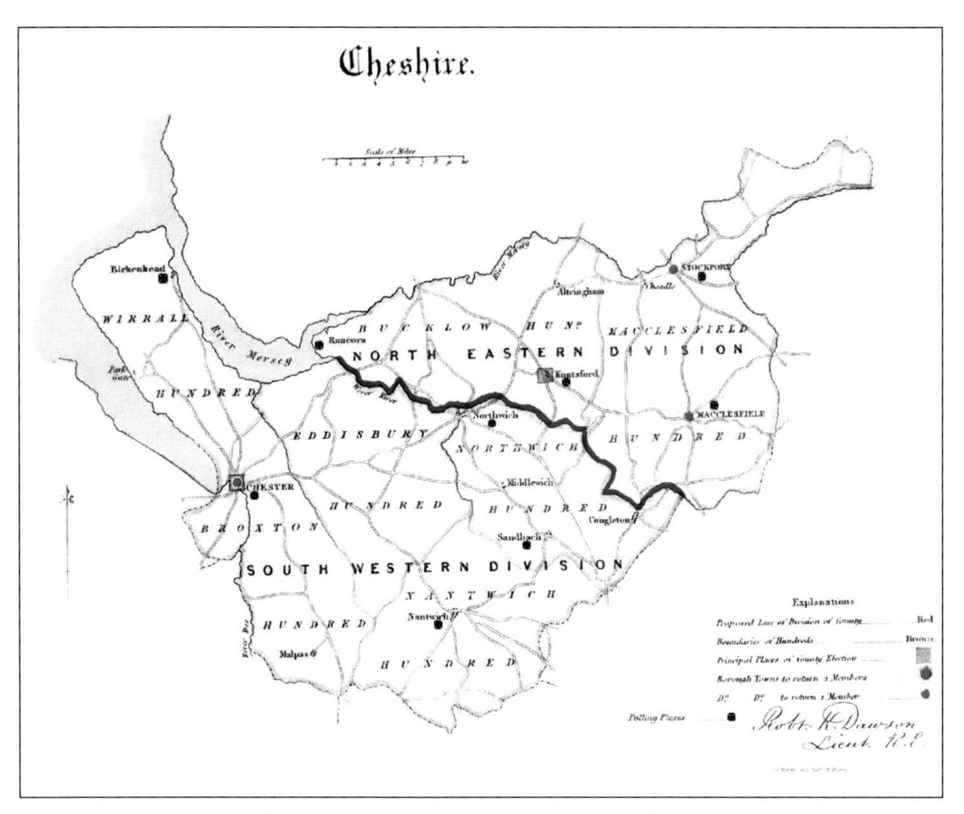

Map of planned Parliamentary Divisions for Chester in 1832
(Engraving by Lt. Robert K. Dawson)

Lieutenant John Shipp of the Cheshire Regiment
Memoirs of the Military Career of John Shipp
(Engraving by an unknown artist for T. Fisher Unwin, 1890)

Tabley House, near Knutsford.
Home of Sir John Fleming Leicester, commander of the Cheshire Yeomanry

Dukinfield Lodge, 1809 (Engraving by T. Bonner for the *Beauties of England and Wales*)

St Michael's Church, Macclesfield, 1810 (Engraving by J. Neagle)

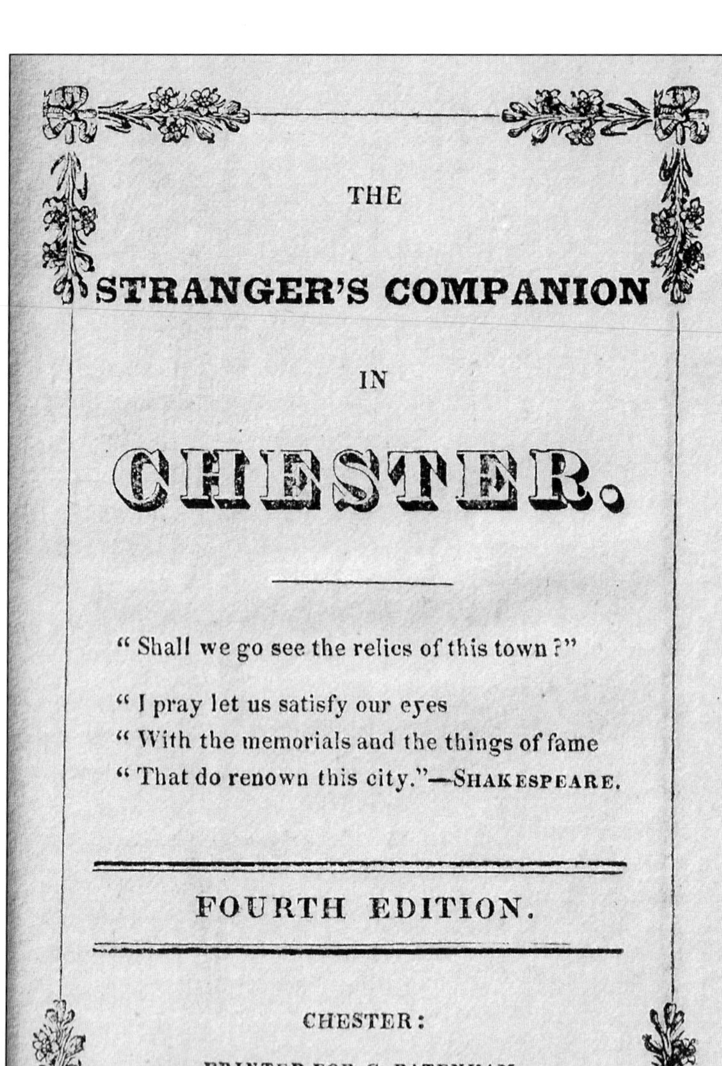

THE

STRANGER'S COMPANION

IN

CHESTER.

" Shall we go see the relics of this town ?"

" I pray let us satisfy our eyes
" With the memorials and the things of fame
" That do renown this city."—SHAKESPEARE.

FOURTH EDITION.

CHESTER:

PRINTED FOR G. BATENHAM,

BY R. EVANS, FOREGATE-STREET.

Title Page of *The Stranger's Companion* (*c*.1828), a popular guide book

powered silk mill to make organzine, some time between 1702 and 1704 but he failed.

The technique for creating organzine didn't reach Britain until about 1717. Norwich man John Lombe travelled to Italy and spied on the Italian machinery, which used water power. He returned with the vital designs for the machines which wound, spun and twisted the thread. Lombe's relative, Sir Thomas Lombe (1685–1739), patented the designs, and built a mill for throwing organzine at Derby in 1721. The new mill still required a large workforce, however, because the machinery for doubling the thread was worked by hand. John Lombe died the following year.

Thomas Lombe's patent was only granted for fourteen years although he tried to renew it before it expired. Textile manufacturers from Stockport and silk manufacturers from Macclesfield, anxious to use the designs themselves, petitioned against the renewal. Parliament decided the country as a whole would benefit from the throwing machinery. They ordered Lombe to put an exact model of the machinery on show in the Tower of London, and compensated him with a £14,000 payment.

When the patent ended in 1732, some Stockport and Lancashire gentlemen (Thomas Eyre, Talbot Warren, Thomas Hadfield and others) quickly exploited the new technology. 'In Stockport were erected some of the first mills for winding and throwing silk, on a plan procured from Italy ...'[1] 'Procured' seems a very polite way of describing cloak and dagger espionage!

The Park silk mill (1732) in Stockport was the first in Cheshire. It was constructed over four decades before Richard Arkwright's cotton mill at Chorley (1777), often thought of as the 'first' water-powered textile mill in the northwest. The Park Mill was built on land next to a corn mill and a logwood mill (logwood was used for dyeing textiles). Italian John Guardivaglio, who had worked for Lombe, brought some of the Derby workforce to Stockport, and helped with the mill's construction. The Carrs Mill was established in the town shortly afterwards. Joseph Dale built a water-powered silk mill at Adlington Square in 1775.

However, the silk industry only enjoyed a few decades of success in Stockport. Cowdroy includes silk manufacture in his description of Stockport in 1789, but John Aikin, writing around the same time, asserted that the silk industry there had fallen into decline. Stockport's future prosperity lay with cotton.

Silk manufacture had the biggest impact on Macclesfield. The town's 'bread and butter' was originally the manufacture of: 'wrought buttons in silk, mohair, and twist. ... Macclesfield was always considered as the centre of this trade; and mills were erected long ago, both here and at Stockport, for winding silk, and making twist, and trimming, suitable to the buttons ...'[2]

Charles Roe was a Derbyshire man who started out as a button merchant and manufacturer. He built the first silk mill at Macclesfield (*c.*1743) which used the new water-powered throwing machinery, at the northern end of Park Green. Despite Charles Roe's huge investment in silk, it obviously didn't pay well enough, because after less than two decades he sold off his interests in the industry and concentrated on his copper business.

It is possible that James Brindley (the Bridgewater Canal engineer) installed Roe's silk mill machinery for him. Samuel Smiles says Brindley was in the area fitting up water-powered silk throwing mills at roughly the right date for the construction of Roe's mill.

While Brindley was still an apprentice, his first successful piece of work was to repair fire damage to machinery at Michael Daintry's 'small silk mill' in Macclesfield in 1735. (The term 'mill' was used to mean a workshop with machinery, or any ordinary factory, or a 'Double Dutch' mill, which was a more efficient method of throwing tram by hand power.) No one knows exactly what type of machinery Brindley was working on in Daintry's mill.

Early silk mills, such as the Pearsons' Sunderland St Mill in Macclesfield, were usually water powered, although some used horse gins. Macclesfield was poorly supplied with water and water rights were jealously guarded. Steam engines were used to complement or replace water power if a mill's water supply was unreliable. Daintry & Ryle installed the first steam engine in Macclesfield: a 32 h.p. engine supplied by Boulton and Watt to the Park Green silk mill in the spring of 1801. Steam engines, though more dependable, brought unwelcome pollution to the silk towns.

Congleton's main silk manufactures included broad silks, handkerchiefs and ribbons. 'This place was formerly celebrated for the manufacture of tagged leather laces, called Congleton points; but the chief employment of the poor is now derived from a very capital silk mill, erected on the river; and from the ribbon manufactory ...'[3]

The first silk mill in Congleton for throwing organzine was the Old Mill, powered by water from the Dane, a reliable power source. The Old Mill was built by Stockport man John Clayton, 'an active and successful manufacturer', and his business partner Nathaniel Pattison in the early 1750s.[4] James Brindley worked as a millwright for Pattison & Clayton.

Clayton, who became Mayor of Congleton, leased the garden of the town workhouse and erected a silk doubling mill on the site. He next leased the Corn Mills, spending £2000 on mill buildings and machinery.

Over four hundred people were employed in silk at Congleton at the turn of the nineteenth century. By Corry's time (1817) there were seventeen silk mills in the town and surrounding area and the number of people employed in silk and cotton had expanded to almost 3000 men, women and children. Ormerod commented on Congleton's many elegant mansions with their own pleasure grounds, owned by merchants and manufacturers.

Macclesfield and Congleton were on major turnpike routes to the cotton towns of Stockport and Manchester by the 1760s. Surprisingly, the two silk towns had to wait until 1796 for a turnpike trust to take over the road linking them. Macclesfield manufacturers and merchants had easy access to London via the Leek road and Macclesfield was linked to Buxton via a road over the Pennines; the turnpike route via the Cat & Fiddle Inn was completed in 1821. Another important trade route was from Congleton to Derby (via Ashbourne). Derby was home to a silk and hosiery industry and was a good market for Cheshire yarn.

Macclesfield grew hand-in-hand with silk's success. By the 1790s the town's population was two-thirds the size of Chester's. Byng found the silk and copper trades in: 'a most flourishing state ... they seem in prosperity from their trade, and are building away'. The population spiralled upwards, reaching almost 12,300 by 1811.

New terraced houses were built to accommodate the influx of workers. The more genteel folk gradually 'upped sticks' to the suburbs, abandoning the town centre to the workforce. The worst-quality housing was extremely cramped and overcrowded.

In the 1770s, men in the silk throwing mills earned a low wage, around 7s per week; doublers (usually women) earned 3s 6d. (For comparison, food prices in the town were: brown bread, 1¼d per lb.

butter, 4d per lb. and milk was 1d per quart.) After 1785, the advent of cotton manufacture, with its fantastic profits, meant some silk mills switched to cotton. The higher wages on offer tempted many workers to move to the cotton mills. The silk throwsters were forced to raise their wages to match. Men in the silk mills earned an average of 16s per week in the late 1780s and doublers earned between 8s 6d and 10s.

By the beginning of the nineteenth century, half the silk mills in England were based in Cheshire. Macclesfield alone had thirty mills specializing in silk throwing, and making sewing silk.

The secret of silk weaving added a new strand to the complex tapestry of industry in Macclesfield. The technique was brought to the town in about 1790 by weavers from London and Dublin. These weavers were members of Huguenot communities, descended from immigrants who settled in Britain during the seventeenth century after being persecuted for their faith. The Spitalfields weavers in London were especially renowned for their skill.

The first silk weaving workshop in Macclesfield was owned by Leigh and Voce in Back who paid high wages. Despite the firm's efforts to keep their new industry under wraps, others in the town smelt a chance to make extra profit. Silk throwsters George Pearson and his sons James and George, who had premises in Sunderland St, joined the fray. James Pearson enticed Margaret Moburn, a silk weaver at Leigh and Voce's, away from her employment there. James and Margaret lived together for a number of years. Margaret taught James and his factory hands the secret of the complex, skilled method of warping and weaving silk. Word quickly spread, and 'the manufacture of Silk handkerchiefs, shawls, and other kinds of broad silk became … a new impetus to the population and prosperity of the town.'[5]

As silk weaving grew in importance, garret houses three storeys high were constructed for the handloom weavers. The garrets on Paradise St in Macclesfield are a good example of those still surviving. The top floors were used as workshops; they had large windows to let in the daylight.

The success of silk weaving rippled outwards, bringing wealth in its wake. The trade embargo on Continental silk because of the Napoleonic wars stimulated the market yet further: '… war is more advantageous to this town than peace'. Silk manufacturers had 'never had it so good' and the whole town benefited. In addition to the 'handsome modern mansions, built and furnished in a very elegant style, by opulent manufacturers', the tradesmen had enough money to rebuild their shops and houses.

Growing numbers of silk throwsters were encouraged to set up business in Macclesfield. Dyehouses were erected, new banks opened, and the housing boom continued.

Workers made the most of the good times 'Nothing was thought too good for the industrious weaver, and the advance of rent kept pace with his prosperity.' Corry disapproved of the workers' pernicious habit of enjoying their earnings: '… the weavers earned high wages which they improvidently wasted; nothing that the market could afford was too good for them; and house-rent and provisions were raised to an extortionate height. Many of the weavers who settled here were profligate characters; equally destitute of religion and morality …' A typical weaver's wage was about 18s net per week in 1815.

The townspeople became smarter and more elegant as profits and wages rose. 'The females employed in silk mills … are really well and handsomely clad, and present an appearance of outward respectability, equal if not superior to that of hundreds in the middle walk of life …'[6]

Even manners were said to have improved. Corry noted approvingly that the 'ill-mannered and uncouth habits of the preceding age, were superseded by the adoption of more fashionable modes of life'. There were ten coaches kept by wealthy Macclesfield families – a sure sign folk had disposable income.

The manufacturers' wealth was built on cheap labour. Children's wages started at sixpence per week in the 1770s. Child workers were normally hired for three years, with their wages rising to 1s in the third year, although they were sometimes apprenticed for longer periods. If trade was slack, the master reserved the right to sack his small workers, regardless of any hiring agreement.

Like the adults, children's wages rose over the next decade. They were paid on a sliding scale: 2s 6d, 3s, 4s and 5s, according to their skill. Children worked in the mills as 'piecers', joining broken threads, or as 'winders', winding the thread onto bobbins. Teenagers also worked as 'doublers'. The children who worked as apprentices included the offspring of families living nearby as well as pauper apprentices bound to masters by the parish overseers.

Some apprentices 'lived in' with their masters and received board and lodging. On 25 September 1827, Joseph Bowker, a Macclesfield butcher, bound his 13-year-old son Joseph to silk weaver Robert Woodfall for seven years as an apprentice. The parish paid £10 from William Acton's bequest as an apprenticeship fee to Woodfall. Young Joseph was to be instructed in the 'Art, Trade, Mystery, Business or Employment of a Silk Weaver'. He promised to 'diligently faithfully punctually and honestly serve' the weaver. In return, Woodfall was to give his apprentice 'good sufficient and wholesome Meat Drink Washing and Lodging and also Cloaths (*sic*)…' However, local children bound to manufacturers by their parents often lived at home.

Child workers helped throwsters in workshops or 'shades'. For certain grades of silk thread, 'throwing' was still done by hand. Silk threads were attached to hooks around the circumference of a wheel or 'gate' situated at one end of a long room. The throwster's helper, usually a boy, then ran to the other end of the room, carrying the other ends of the silk threads on bobbins. He hooked the threads onto a fixed framework, then ran back to the gate (rather like fixing several lengths of washing line). The throwster twisted the silk threads by spinning the wheel. Their young helpers ran miles barefoot every day.

Contemporaries considered the atmosphere in the silk mills was healthier and more temperate than the cotton factories, where the operatives worked in 70-degree heat, breathing in cotton dust or 'fly'. Nevertheless, conditions were far from pleasant.

John Wright, a steward at Brinsley & Shatwell's silk mill in Macclesfield, was interviewed by an inspector for the 1833 Factories Inquiries Commission. Wright had worked at the mill for over thirty years. His working life there began when he was only five years old, around the turn of the nineteenth century. Wright testified that the hours in 1833 were exactly the same as when he started work: 'Eleven hours per day and two over-hours: over-hours are working after six in the evening till eight. The regular hours are from six in the morning till six in the evening, and two others are over-hours: about fifty years ago they began working over-hours.' The workers stopped for twenty minutes at 8 a.m. to have breakfast; they had an hour for lunch at 2 p.m., and had a short break for tea at 5 p.m. The Saturday shift was ten hours and forty minutes. 'Learners' had a shorter working day: they worked two hours less. The mills were kept at an 'agreeable' temperature and were heated by steam during the winter.

The workplaces were lit by gas, candles or lamps; the workers toiled 'amid the smoke and soot of the same; and also a large portion of oil and grease is used in the mills'. Wright also complained: '... the privy is in the factory, which frequently emits an unwholesome smell'. But the silk mills were, of necessity, kept reasonably clean; they were swept daily and white-washed once a year.

The steward painted a black picture of the monotony of mill work, and the silk operatives' physical and mental condition. There were a 'great number of hands congregated together ... The tediousness and the everlasting sameness preys much on the spirits, and makes the hands spiritless.' Some child workers were crippled by the long hours and close confinement within the factory walls:

> From my earliest recollection, I have found the effects to be awfully detrimental to the well-being of the operative; I have observed frequently children carried to factories, unable to walk ... two of my sisters (have) been obliged to be assisted to the factory and home again, until by-and-by they could go no longer, being totally crippled in their legs.

However, Samuel Higginbotham, manager of Samuel Pearson's silk mill, said that hardly any children in his mill were crippled.

Country boy Adam Rushton had unhappy memories of his time as a child factory worker. He vividly recalled his first day at Green's silk mill on Commercial Rd in 1829. Mill life came as a shock to the 8-year-old after the fresh air in the fields: 'The close, impure air seemed to be stifling me. The clangour of machinery deafened me ...' The working day at Green's sounds very similar to that at Brinsley & Shatwell's mill. At first, Rushton earned 6d per week, working from 6 a.m. to 6 p.m. as a piecer on silk 'swifts'. (A swift was a rotating frame which wound the thread onto bobbins.) As Adam became more skilled, his wages were increased to 1s 6d, but his working day was extended to 8 p.m., with an hour and forty minutes for meals: 'This was a murderous length of time to work.'

Rushton likened factory work to 'imprisonment' and 'crushing slavery'. His healthy country glow faded and he lost his appetite; his growth was retarded, and his limbs became chronically weak. He believed the 'half-time' system would have prevented his health from deteriorating, and he would also have enjoyed a better education. (The 'half-time' system, in which children worked for half a day and spent the other half at school, didn't come into force until 1844.) Sunday school was the only bright spot in his whole week.

Despite the limited educational opportunities available, some silk workers were highly literate. Silk winder James Hall was 'an ardent student of the writings of Flavius Josephus'.[7]

The young operatives' unceasing toil had consequences as they grew up. The poor health of the adult hands meant they were often unfit to serve in the army. Wright commented: 'I remember some ten or twelve years ago working in one of the largest firms in Macclesfield (Messrs Baker & Pearson), with about twenty-five men, where they were scarce one half fit for His Majesty's service. Those that are straight in their limbs are stunted in their growth: much inferior to their fathers in point of strength.' Unguarded machinery was a daily hazard: 'I have seen some that would have been killed on the spot if had it not been for the prompt exertion of some person at hand to stop the whole machinery.' On the positive side, when Wright visited several families who had children working in the silk mills, he was told none of the children were usually beaten (unlike cotton mills of the same era).

Waterloo brought an end to the long wars with France and with it came a sudden slump in trade for textiles. The door was now wide open to foreign competitors, especially those on the Continent. Cloth goods were no longer in such demand to clothe the army, so manufacturers were left with a surplus and prices fell sharply.

Macclesfield and Congleton suffered during the trade depression. Manufacturers went bust, jobs were lost and wages slashed. Corry claimed the cost of provisions also fell, which helped to offset the reduction in pay packets. He admitted the workers endured 'a few privations'. This was a rather rose-tinted view, however; the price of bread rose sharply. A very poor growing season and the impact of the controversial Corn Laws combined to push the price of wheat from 52s 6d per quarter (8 bushels) in January 1816 to 76s 4d in May the same year.

Macclesfield cotton operatives who lost their jobs tried to find work in the silk mills. The cotton handloom weavers, too, switched to silk, which had the effect of depressing wages further in the silk trade. The most skilled weavers (who owned their own looms) wove four 'cuts' of silk each week on average; a cut measured seven yards. Gross earnings fell to 14s per week in 1817. However, 3s of this was deducted for 'pin-winding', rent of the workshop and wear and tear of the loom. Take-home pay was now 11s, a savage drop from the days of plenty just a couple of years earlier. Their apprentices earned around 1s 9d per cut – barely enough to scrape a living. Journeymen weavers in the factories had their production curtailed to three cuts per week, for which they earned a net wage of 8s after deductions: hard times.

Despite the slump, two years after Waterloo there were 10,000 people – almost two-thirds of Macclesfield's population – employed in silk and cotton together. Twenty-eight throwsters and twelve manufacturers employed silk weavers. Different kinds of silk goods were made: 'fancy' work, broad silk such as bandanas, and small wares such as hatbands and ribbons. Altogether about 400 skilled journeymen weavers were employed, plus up to 600 apprentices. The size of firms ranged from S. Pearson & Co., with 240 weavers on its books, down to Wadsworth's, who employed six.

The Jacquard loom was probably introduced to the silk towns very early in the 1820s. The looms, patented by the eponymous Frenchman in 1801, created beautiful, intricately patterned cloth using a complex system of perforated cards; the weaver still worked the loom by hand. Most Jacquard weaving took place in weavers' garrets. The looms were too expensive for ordinary workers to buy so they were rented from the master manufacturers.

Valuable silk goods were a temptation to dishonest mill hands. For years a black market, known as the 'Turkey Trade', flourished in stolen raw and processed silk. Joseph Jackson (thirty-two), a silk throwster from Congleton, was sentenced to seven years' transportation: 'for stealing out of the silk manufactory of Messrs Pattison, in Congleton, several parcels of organzine and thrown silk'.[8]

Isaac Moors was a 27-year-old cotton spinner from Chorlton. This 'most notorious character' was sentenced to death in April 1818 for stealing silk and linen from Mrs Smith of Cheadle Bulkeley. He was executed a few weeks later.[9] 'Turkey merchant' James Okell (again from Congleton), was transported for seven years in May 1829 for organizing the theft of 10lb of silk from Richard Hall.

Wealthy silk manufacturing families such as the Brocklehursts helped provide a steadying influence through the vicissitudes of trade. The Brocklehursts worked their way up from small beginnings. John Brocklehurst, who started out as a chapman in the 1740s, lived at Pear Tree House (later Jordangate House). His son John joined forces with some button makers on Hurdsfield Rd and the firm of Brocklehurst, Acton and Street became throwsters. The second John's sons, John and Thomas, ventured into the silk-weaving business during the Napoleonic wars. The Brocklehursts served as mayors and were on the town council. The third John Brocklehurst (1788–1870) became the town's first MP after the Reform Act was introduced in 1832.

The Brocklehursts' business was so profitable that they could afford to take over Critchley & Turner's bank in Macclesfield when it ceased payments in 1816. The Brocklehursts' bank, which traded under the imaginative title of the Macclesfield Bank, prospered for many years. Another silk firm which ventured into banking was Daintry & Ryle. They took over the bank of Hawkins, Mills & Co. (on Jordangate) after it went to the wall in 1800. (Daintry & Ryle's bank didn't enjoy the same success as the Brocklehursts. Much later in the century, their bank, cotton and silk mills suffered a calamitous financial collapse in 1842. This was a catastrophe for their employees and the town.)

Meanwhile, the depressing cycle of boom and bust continued throughout the 1820s. The prosperous early years of the decade were followed by an abrupt crash, exacerbated by the banking crisis of 1826. In the past, the silk industry had been cushioned by protective tariffs, and also by an embargo on imported foreign silk. Trouble began in 1824 with ominous news. The President of the Board of Trade, William Huskisson (1770–1830), was an advocate of free trade. He proposed measures which would have a massive impact on the Cheshire silk towns. He demanded an end to the ban on imported foreign silk goods, and a reduction of the duties on 'raw' (unprocessed) silk and thrown silk. Although the latter was good news for silk manufacture, the lifting of the imports ban meant silk manufacturers suddenly faced a much more competitive market. They needed to increase their profitability and in April 1824, the masters of the Macclesfield mills attempted to increase the working day. They wanted to bring their factories into line with those in Congleton and Stockport and they asked the men to work twelve-hour shifts instead of eleven hours. The silk spinners refused, even though they regularly worked overtime anyway. They objected to the principle of a compulsory twelve-hour shift.

The men 'turned out', including those at Mr Knight's and Mr Powell's mills. Powell's factory at Sutton was attacked; workers 'crowded' the marketplace, and some windows were broken. Mayor Thomas Allen took no chances; he 'dispatched expresses to Stockport and Manchester for Troops'. An extra force of special constables was sworn in. In an attempt to defuse the situation, the silk masters called a meeting with the workers at the Macclesfield Arms, but no agreement could be reached and the meeting was adjourned until the evening. The atmosphere in the town grew increasingly tense.

'At six o'clock in the evening the Committees of Masters and Workmen assembled at the Macclesfield Arms, and about half past seven o'clock a mob of more than 12,000 persons filled the Market Place, and the space opposite the Hotel, and several stones were thrown into the room where the Masters were sitting.' The local magistrates asked the Stockport and Adlington troops of Yeomanry to rendezvous in front of the hotel and disperse the mob, aided by the special constables.

> The Bugle sounded, and several of the Yeomanry appeared, each of whom was greeted individually by a volley of stones, and loud shouts of disapprobation and defiance, but such was the density of the crowd, and the violence of the people assembled, that only about eight or nine of the Yeomanry, including Captain Barra, the Adjutant of the Regiment, and two other officers, could reach the appointed place of rendezvous.

The mayor addressed the crowd. He ordered them to be calm and peaceable, but to no effect. It must have been terrifying for the masters and workers sitting inside the pub, listening to the roaring of the crowd outside and the whinnying of the Yeomanry's horses.

The Yeomanry was ordered to clear the streets. The marketplace soon emptied of protestors, but about 300 rioters made a stand in the churchyard, where they defended themselves, 'protected by Iron Gates, and a strong and lofty wall, and supplied with an infinity of paving stones'. They repulsed two attacks from the cavalry and several attempts by the constables to dislodge them. The Yeomanry took a real beating and all its men were hurt. Lt. Thomas Grimsditch (the solicitor) and Cornet Daintry were badly injured. At about 8.30 that evening, another troop arrived, and the mob was finally moved on. But the men won their point and the masters backed down.[10]

It seems probable that workers only took to the streets if they felt they had no alternative. They looked to the law to protect them if they felt they had been unfairly treated, even though the courts viewed strikes as disputes between masters and servants.

A Macclesfield mother sought redress for her son through the legal system. In April 1825, Chester court heard a case where a Macclesfield magistrate, Mr Ward, was charged with false imprisonment by Mrs Hunt, mother of a young silk worker. During the previous August, the silk workers had another general 'turn-out' for higher wages and any strike-breakers faced real social stigma. Mrs Hunt's son, a 13-year-old boy, came out on strike with the other workers. His master, Mr Braddock, charged him and some other boys with deserting their work. He asked Mr Ward, also a silk master, to issue a warrant for their arrest. Ward not only arrested the boy, but sent him to prison for three months; he had to work on the treadmill for the whole of his sentence. The boy's mother, Mrs Hunt, was present in court when her son was convicted. She was very angry, and told Ward: 'Sir, you have no right to commit these boys; you are in the same trade.' Mrs Hunt took her son's case to court. The jury found in favour of the boy and they awarded him £20 damages.[11]

Congleton mill workers went on strike during this month. The courts issued warrants for their arrest 'for leaving their service before their hirings were expired'. When constables tried to take one striker, Stephen Dale, to Knutsford House of Correction, he was 'forcibly rescued from the constables by a mob of 1300 people before he left Congleton'. The authorities cracked down hard on the workers: a reward was offered for Dale and several people were arrested. The magistrates promised not to take any further proceedings against the 'deluded men' after they 'expressed their contrition' and surrendered Dale to the authorities.[12]

Even before the new laws on silk duties came into force, the proposed legislation had a knock-on effect in the silk towns. Merchants reduced their orders towards the end of 1825 because they knew they would soon be able to order cheaper foreign silk. Wages were slashed, workers were put on 'short time' and many mills locked their gates for good.

Huskisson's free trade measures on silk became law in 1826. This caused great anguish in the already distressed silk towns. The bad news of the Bill's passage through Parliament caused more 'riotous proceedings' in February that year. On Monday 27 February, thousands of men and women gathered in Macclesfield. They marched through the town, arms linked together, jeering and hooting. The Angel Inn suffered a 'general attack' and stones were thrown at shop windows and the gas lamps. An eyewitness described the scene at Mr Johnson's bread shop: 'I was standing close by the shop window; it was about nine o'clock. There was (*sic*) a great number of people there. A Macclesfield lad ... was pulling the loaves out of the window. There were many more than 100 people present; they were kicking out the windows, and getting the bread out.'

A widow, Mrs Wrigg, also had her shop attacked: bread rolls, ham, beef and pies were taken by the angry mob. An Irish labourer, Valentine O'Brian, was accused of stealing beef and pies from the shop but he indignantly told the mayor: '... it's not true, your honour – I only took a piece of beef!'[13]

Special constables routed the mob and dragoons arrived that evening to prevent further trouble. Three of the rioters were later sentenced to two months in the House of Correction. There were more disturbances in early May. Three young lads – John Lennard, William Worthington and Daniel Morrall – were committed to Chester Castle to await trial for riotous behaviour. Two of the boys were only twelve years old.

With little work available, the outlook was bleak for unemployed workers with hungry mouths to feed. The *Chester Chronicle* (28 April 1826) pitied the 'miserable, half-famished creatures' at Macclesfield. At Congleton, the Old Mill and others closed down for four years – a terrible blow when most of the town's 9,300 inhabitants worked in the silk mills.

The county's wealthier inhabitants attempted to provide some relief. A charitable fund was set up for starving silk workers and their families. George IV donated £1000, Earl Grosvenor gave £100, and Lord and Lady Belgrave gave £50. A Grand Ball was held at the Exchange Rooms in Chester; mayor John Fletcher provided all the refreshments, and paid for the lighting and musicians. The *Macclesfield Courier* (22 April 1826) commented: 'We hope an intimation may go forth, that it is expected that Ladies and Gentlemen may make silk a prominent feature in their costume.' More than half Macclesfield's workers were totally dependent on this charity. The ball raised £340 11s 8d for the Macclesfield workers, and £170 5s 10d for Congleton.

Sir Walter Scott passed through Cheshire that autumn on his way up north:

> … slept at Macclesfield. As we came in between ten and eleven, the people of the inn expressed surprise at our travelling so late as the general distress of the manufacturers has rendered many of the lower class desperately outrageous. The inn was guarded by a special watchman, who alarmed us by giving his signal of turn out, but it proved to be a poor deserter who had taken refuge among the carriages, and who was reclaimed by his sergeant. The people talk gloomily of winter, when the distress of the poor will be increased.

Hard-up silk throwsters and dyers in Macclesfield petitioned Parliament to reinstate the ban on imported silk and raise protective tariffs to their former levels, but to no avail. By the spring of 1829, 14,000 workers were unemployed. Thousands of families relied on charity handouts and they subsisted on potatoes and oatmeal.

The Brocklehurst family exacerbated an already bad situation by reducing wages, which workers claimed were already very low – about 30 per cent below other manufacturers. The Brocklehursts admitted that their weavers at Hurdsfield were paid less than elsewhere, but said they gave them regular employment, and better quality materials to work with. The *Macclesfield Courier* editor, who was 'on the spot', couldn't reconcile the 'contradictory statements' on wages by both sides. At Hurdsfield, the Brocklehursts paid 6s per dozen for 34-inch 'black banddanoes' (*sic*); other mills paid 7s. The workers said the 'soft silk piecers' (who joined broken threads) earned 5s at Brocklehursts', but 5s 6d elsewhere; the family claimed they paid 6s 4d.[14] A difficult thread to untangle.

An angry mob assembled in the marketplace on Monday 26 April. They marched to the Brocklehursts' mill, demolishing gas lamps in the street on their way. All the mill windows were smashed. The crowd was eventually dispersed by the authorities. Thousands of silk weavers in neighbouring mills, worried their own wages would follow suit, voted to strike. The Mayor sent for troops yet again to keep the peace.

On Wednesday 29 April, thousands of people paraded through the streets dressed as mourners, carrying black crepe flags and other emblems. One banner read: 'We only want to work for our living.' Another worker carried a loaf at the end of a pole, decorated with knives, forks and shuttles. There were similar processions over the next two days. A handcart was used to carry a loom, bearing the inscription: 'Silk machinery to be sold by auction, by W. Huskisson.' On a more macabre note, several teeth dangled from the end of a pole, with the message: 'To let, the owners having no further use for them.'[15]

Conditions were no better at Congleton and twenty-eight mills were forced to close by early 1829. In March, loaves and soup were distributed to over 1,200 people. The following month, the town was still in a 'very distressed state'; 6,270 people were being fed by a 'soup shop'. A sad procession of 7,000 people made its way through the town, hoping to draw attention to their plight; there was 'a deep sense of calamity visible on every countenance'.[16] Rumours of more mill closures led to vandalism in May and windows were smashed. A procession of weavers marched to Buglawton, where they burnt an effigy of an unpopular manufacturer.

Trade revived towards the end of 1830. The Old Mill at Congleton was bought by Samuel Pearson. The new owner signalled new hope for the town by ringing the factory bell himself to call the operatives to work on the morning the gates opened again.

New technology provided fresh opportunities: silk 'spinning' and powered silk weaving. Silk spinning was a method of utilizing damaged cocoons or waste silk. Silk thread manufacture was a terribly inefficient process; large quantities of short strands were left over, too short for early machinery to weave into cloth. Valuable leftover silk was painstakingly spun by hand until the invention of mechanized silk spinning in the mid-1830s. The yarn produced by the new technique was used for the cheapest silk shawls and handkerchiefs. Firms such as Reades of Congleton invested in the very heavy equipment needed for silk spinning. Ribbon manufacture also became important in Congleton after 1830.

During the slump, the Brocklehurst family in Macclesfield took advantage of plummeting property prices to buy up mills on the cheap. Their shrewd investment meant they could expand into silk spinning and powered silk weaving during the 1830s. As in the cotton industry, the introduction of powered weaving in silk sparked riots by angry handloom weavers. But powered silk weaving only produced extremely coarse, plain fabric; it couldn't compete with hand weaving for quality. As a consequence, powerlooms for silk only slowly gained ground. Even by the middle of the nineteenth century, most silk weaving was still done by hand.

Stockport had a brief flirtation with silk spinning. It had seven mills involved in the trade by 1827, but was given the *coup de grace* by Huskisson's legislation. Silk weaving had more success in the district; hundreds of handloom weavers worked at Bullock Smithy under the 'putting-out' system. Silk yarn from Macclesfield was woven into cloth in the weavers' homes, and returned by carrier. The 1826 crisis led to the same hardships there as in the main silk towns. But silk wasn't the biggest employer in Stockport; there, cotton was king.

12

Spinning a Yarn

Cotton was the silk industry's younger sister. Although cotton is indelibly associated with Lancashire, it played an important part in Cheshire's economy. Cotton re-shaped the county's landscape, especially in its north-eastern corner. And just like its sister industry, if relations between masters and workers didn't run smoothly, riot and disorder flared.

For centuries, the spinning and weaving of cotton fibre to make cloth took place in workers' homes: the domestic system. The technological advances of the Industrial Revolution – Kay's flying shuttle, Hargreaves's spinning jenny, Arkwright's water-frame, and Crompton's mule – changed workers' lives forever. It became more economic to process cotton under one roof. (Briefly, cotton wool fibres are first 'carded' to untangle the fibres, then combed out into a long, fluffy rope or 'slubbing', which is then twisted slightly into a 'roving'. Spinning machinery rolls and twists the roving into yarn ready for weaving.)

Some contemporary observers looked back to the days before factories as a golden age. The domestic worker, although not as productive as a mill hand, '… worked by the rule of his strength and convenience'. His labour was 'sufficient to feed and clothe himself and family decently … to lay by a penny for an evil day, and to enjoy those amusements and bodily recreations then in being. He was a respectable member of society; a good father, a good husband and a good son.'[1]

The new regime of factory life meant workers became machine minders, their days regulated by the factory whistle. The Industrial Revolution also impacted on the other end of the social scale: cotton masters made (and lost) fortunes. Successful entrepreneurs muscled their way up the social ladder. As they grew richer, they bought estates, built elegant villas, and married into respectable families. The family of ironmaster John Wilkinson became linked to the Leghs of Lyme Hall at Disley when his daughter Mary Anne married William Legh in May 1821.

Cotton spinning was the first major focus for investment. In 1785, after a series of legal battles, Lancashire's Richard Arkwright (1732–92) lost the patents for his roving and spinning machinery. Some time during the 1780s, a Stockport man (possibly John Swindells) invented a device called a 'billy', a cheaper and more efficient way of processing carded cotton into rovings ready for spinning. The Stockport jenny spinners had a whip-round to reward him.

Around the same time, Samuel Crompton introduced his spinning 'mule', but he couldn't afford to patent it. After trying in vain to keep his invention 'under wraps', Crompton was persuaded to hand it over to Bolton manufacturers; he died in poverty. The mule, a hybrid of the spinning jenny and water-frame, produced incredibly fine yarn strong enough to be woven into fashionable muslin.

Mule spinning was hand powered at first, but was converted to water power in the 1790s and the technology was later adapted for steam power. Spinning, traditionally a woman's occupation, was now done by men, as a man's strength was needed to operate the machinery, especially for fine spinning. The highly skilled fine spinners earned high wages: 30s per week in 1812 at Manchester. Women working on small mules and 'throstle' spinning machines (which made a noise like a thrush) only earned about 15s 7d per week.

As each technical innovation improved efficiency (and hence profits) a free-for-all followed as canny entrepreneurs such as Samuel Greg, Samuel Oldknow and Henry Marsland hurried to put their money in cotton.

As in the silk mills, child labour was a key factor in profitability. Before the advent of steam, water rights (to power the mill wheels) were a frequent source of disputes between mill-owners. This may be why Samuel Greg (1758–1834) built his new cotton spinning mill at Styal by the River Bollin in 1783, away from the towns, where there was plenty of labour available. Luckily, a cheap workforce was easy to find. Parish poorhouses all over the country, with hundreds of children on their books needing food and clothing, were desperate to reduce their costs. They offloaded (even advertised) surplus children by apprenticing them to employers for years at a time, often many miles away from 'home'. Parish overseers paid manufacturers a couple of guineas for each child apprenticed (this was still more economic than maintaining them for years at the parish's expense). The overseers provided each child with a set of clothes. Approximately half of Greg's workforce were pauper apprentices. They came from places close by like Wilmslow and Macclesfield, or far away like Hackney and Chelsea.

Samuel Greg was considered a 'model' employer by contemporaries; he treated his apprentices comparatively well. The children earned a couple of pennies per week, as well as their food and lodging. They worked a six-day week, 6 a.m. till 7 p.m., with half an hour for breakfast and an hour for lunch. Children slept two to a bed in the purpose-built Apprentice House and they had plenty of fresh local produce to eat. Dr Peter Holland cared for children who became poorly, such as Mary Chadwick and William Topping. After work, the boys learnt to read and write and the girls had sewing lessons, and made their own clothes and shirts for the boys. Although the girls learnt to read, too, they weren't as proficient as the boys at writing because their sewing was considered more important.

But apprentices in other mills weren't as fortunate as those at Styal. A series of scandals relating to overcrowded conditions and the cruel treatment of parish apprentices led to Sir Robert Peel's Health and Morals of Apprentices Act in 1802. The children's working hours were limited to twelve per day and night work was phased out. Apprentices were to receive some education and have a suit of clothes each year; no more than two children were to share a bed. The sexes were to have separate sleeping arrangements. Many of the Act's provisions, however, didn't apply to free labour children, even if they were working in the same factory as apprentices. And in practice, the Act had little effect; children were still at the mercy of their masters. In September 1806, Frodsham weaver Jonathan Roberts was fined £10 and imprisoned in Chester Castle for three months for 'having ill-treated and neglected children as his apprentices'.[2]

The advent of steam power reduced the need for parish apprentices in the mills. Mills could now be built where labour was plentiful, even if water power was limited. In one Stockport spinning mill, 145 of the 418 operatives employed in 1816 were under the age of eighteen. The 250 children who worked at Daintry & Ryle's cotton spinning mill at Park Green in Macclesfield early in the nineteenth century probably lived locally. Increasingly strict factory legislation made apprentice labour more expensive and less convenient so free labour children were employed instead. However, child apprentices were still employed at Styal until the 1840s.

Cotton spinning turned Stockport into a boom town, as John Aikin explained: 'The people of Stockport first engaged in the spinning of reeled weft, then in weaving checks, and lastly in fustians; and they were so ingenious as to attempt muslins … besides a large number of cotton spinning-shops, here are twenty-three spacious cotton factories, some of them worked by steam engines.'

A very early water-powered mill was built by Sir George Warren in Stockport (*c.*1778) on the site of the ancient medieval castle. Warren gave the building an appropriately medieval-style appearance, noticed by John Byng in 1790. 'Where the old castle stood, are cotton works built in a castellated stile, with battlements, etc, looking like one of the grandest prisons in the world.' He marvelled at the pace of change, noting how the town 'increases hourly; and in every field adjoining is land to be let for building'.

Stockport's rapid growth appeared 'almost incredible' to other contemporaries. It expanded from 'an obscure and miserable place' into a thriving new town 'erected as if by inchantment (*sic*)'.[3] The town's access to coalfields via a branch of the Ashton Canal helped industries take permanent root.

Cowdroy confirmed that Stockport was, at this time: 'a town of great and growing population … the residence of many spirited and opulent manufacturers who, in the articles of silk, cotton, and check, give employment and bread to many hundred industrious families'.

One of these 'spirited' manufacturers was Samuel Oldknow (1756–1828), a Lancashire man. He produced the best fine muslins in England. Oldknow bought a house at Higher Hillgate in Stockport in 1784 and constructed a huge works next door. His brother Thomas, a bleacher at Heaton Mersey, was joint purchaser of the plot. Oldknow kept 300 handloom weavers in work and his wage bill just for weaving was £1,000 per month. His weavers, who produced calico as well as muslin, collected raw materials from his warehouse, took them home and brought back the finished cloth. Samuel obtained fine yarn for muslin from cotton spinner Richard Arkwright. In addition, Oldknow occupied one of the Carrs mill sites, where he spun his own yarn, and also employed local spinners in their own homes. But he struggled to get material in sufficient quantities to satisfy the demand for muslin from London warehouses. So he invested in a new mule spinning mill at Hillgate. He also constructed a new cotton spinning mill, said to be the largest in the country, at nearby Mellor in Derbyshire.

In 1791 Oldknow installed an 8 h.p. Boulton and Watt engine for carding, roving and spinning cotton in his Hillgate mill – the first steam engine in Stockport. Tradition says Oldknow's engine was so famous, the drivers of the London coaches slowed whenever they passed the mill so they could tell their passengers about the wonders inside.

Oldknow's sphere of operations was huge. Together with his Mellor works, his factories produced enough yarn to keep nearly 2,000 weavers busy. He had bleaching and printing premises at Heaton Mersey, and finishing works at Bullock Smithy and Disley. Despite being bankrolled by the Arkwrights, his 'empire building', coupled with a downturn in trade, left him deeply in debt. By the mid-1790s, he had abandoned his Cheshire mills and retreated to Mellor.

One of the most important cotton men was Henry Marsland (1733–95), who played a key role in Stockport's future prosperity. Marsland already had cotton mills on the outskirts of the town at Bosden (Cheadle). The Park silk mill at Stockport was purchased by Marsland in 1783 and he switched its operations over to cotton spinning. Henry's sons Samuel and Peter also went into the cotton business and their father transferred his business to them in 1792. Three years later, Samuel, the eldest, joined a Manchester firm, so Peter became sole owner of the Park Mills. Peter Marsland (1770–1829) was a great man in Stockport. By 1812, his mule spinning business alone had over 80,000 spindles at work.

Stockport's flourishing industries attracted workers and by 1811 the town's population reached 17,545. Four years later, Stockport and its environs was home to forty large cotton spinning mills, fifty-five cotton manufactories (making checks, fustian and muslins) and eighteen large hat factories. The Wellington Mill, near Wellington Bridge in Stockport, had a special fireproof construction. At seven storeys high, it formed an eye-catching addition to the Stockport skyline. It was built for Thomas Marsland (no relation to the Park Mills family) in about 1826 and housed cotton spinning and weaving machinery.

Even the little village of Mottram in Longdendale benefited from cotton: '... there being no fewer than twelve large cotton machines worked by water, and many lesser ones turned by horses, within a very small part of the surrounding district; the principal source of the employment of the labouring inhabitants is the cotton trade.'[4] Northwich and Nantwich also had cotton factories.

In East Cheshire, mills were built at Bollington, Kettleshulme and Rainow. Congleton's first cotton spinning mill was erected by Richard Martin in 1785 and by 1817 the town had five cotton mills. Mills were notoriously high fire risks. Fogg & Co.'s 'new cotton manufactory' at Nantwich was burnt to the ground in 1798.[5] Lowerhouse Mill (1818) at Bollington is an early example of a 'fireproofing' design in the county.

The first cotton mill in Macclesfield was opened in about 1785 by some Lancashire businessmen. Very soon there were nine cotton spinning mills in the Macclesfield district, all powered by water at first, some being situated on the banks of the Bollin. Handloom weavers made calicoes, fine muslins and fustian at home or in workshops, using rented looms. (Fustian was a hard-wearing fabric.) Although the cotton industry thrived at first, its success in Macclesfield was short-lived. The masters paid good wages, which forced up the silk workers' earnings, as we saw in the previous chapter. But the post-Waterloo trade depression led to cotton's decline and the Macclesfield factory hands were thrown out of work.

Corry believed the introduction of cotton spinning had a negative influence on the health and morals of the Macclesfield townspeople. In earlier times the silk workers, although paid only 'moderate' wages, lived in 'general contentment'; (no doubt Corry himself didn't have to try living on a silk-worker's wage). The changeover to cotton changed this cosy picture. Large numbers of strangers flocked to Macclesfield to work in the cotton mills. Mill life was particularly hard on young people: 'The close confinement' and unremitting toil was 'prejudicial to their health', causing 'deformity of limb, and debility of constitution, which were irremediable'. But conditions may have been better in the factories than for handloom weavers working in damp cellars.

The government made an attempt to limit children's working hours in 1819. Peel's Act, which only applied to cotton mills (silk and other textiles were excluded), banned the employment of children under nine years old. Children under the age of sixteen were limited to a twelve-hour day, plus mealtimes. John Cam Hobhouse's amending Bill of 1825 limited children's Saturday work to nine hours, that is, a sixty-nine-hour working week (not including meals). Even then, children were often made to clean and oil the machinery during their mealtimes.

The textile finishing trades were also well represented in Cheshire. The Stockport area had bleaching, dyeing and calico printing works. There were bleachworks owned by Mr Sykes (Edgeley), Peter Marsland (of Park Mills), Robert Parker (Heaton Mersey) and James Heald (Disley). Thomas Marsland & Son had a huge dyeing and calico printing works at Daw Bank and Chestergate – the Daw Bank factory was said to be the largest in Europe. Thomas was Mayor of Stockport in 1825 and went on to become the town's MP.

As in the silk mills, health and safety were low on the agenda. Ralph Pendlebury, whose father ran Peter Marsland's bleachworks, was very badly injured when his arm got caught in some machinery. (Pendlebury survived and later became Mayor of Stockport.) In February 1822 'a young woman of the name of Lee, lost her life by her clothes being caught in the machinery in a factory at Stockport in which she was at work'. She was so badly crushed, she only lived for a quarter of an hour after the accident.[6] The *Courier* reported another case in the spring of 1829. A young lad, Joseph Mellor, was killed after falling four storeys from a doorway in a cotton mill while trying to hoist up a skip of cotton. It wasn't until 1844 that manufacturers were compelled to fence off machinery safely.

The success of powered cotton spinning meant weavers couldn't keep pace with the amount of yarn produced. This led to efforts to speed up the weaving process. The first power looms in Cheshire were introduced in the Stockport area. The power loom or 'steam' loom, as it was known, was first patented by Edmund Cartwright in 1785. Cartwright's invention had many teething problems and several technical difficulties needed to be overcome to make it economically viable.

The first breakthrough came from Stockport manufacturer William Radcliffe, aided by Thomas Johnson of Bredbury. Their invention of a 'dressing' machine, in about 1803–4, was intended for use on handlooms. It 'dressed' warp threads with a starchy solution so they wouldn't break during weaving. Radcliffe bought Oldknow's empty mill in 1801. Another innovation was the 'dandyloom', a more efficient type of handloom for plain woven cloth; Radcliffe had devised a way of 'taking up' the cloth as it was completed. The firm of Radcliffe and Ross had 200 dandylooms in the Hillgate Mill and they owned another mill in Adlington Square. Radcliffe was a captain in the Volunteers and became Mayor of Stockport in 1804. Unfortunately, he went bankrupt three years later. But Radcliffe's innovations paved the way for powerlooms.

Another Stockport man, William Horrocks, successfully used powerlooms; his design was swiftly pirated by other manufacturers. He came to Stockport with his father Thomas in 1790. Little is known about Horrocks senior's Muslin Hall factory because his operatives had to swear not to divulge any of his trade secrets. William took out patents in 1803 and 1805 for improvements to powerloom technology. His relatives had a spinning and weaving factory which used powerlooms in Stockport in 1806.

Peter Marsland patented a powerloom during the same year. His patent, however, wasn't taken up by other manufacturers, as it was extremely complicated to use. Marsland also tried to introduce the woollen trade in Stockport, using a powerloom which wove with wool yarn. He sent samples of his high quality, soft woollen cloth to George IV, who wore a suit of it which was greatly admired.

Cheshire manufacturers who installed powerlooms were taking a real physical risk as well as a financial one. Lancashire Luddites had already made short work of powerlooms at Manchester in 1790, when a mill was razed to the ground. Nevertheless, by 1812 there were powerlooms installed at mills owned by Marsland, Hindley and Goodair at Stockport.

At around the same time, the Ashton family introduced powerlooms at Hyde. The Ashtons were a powerful cotton family. Samuel Ashton had started out as a farmer. Of his six sons, three went into the hatting trade, the others into cotton. In 1810, Samuel went into the cotton spinning business and around a decade later he began weaving, too. He owned a cotton mill at Woodley, Stockport (built in 1828), and another at Apethorn Lane, Werneth. His son Benjamin built a calico printing works, specializing in brown, black and purple styles, at Newton Bank in 1816. Benjamin's brothers John, James and Thomas were partners in the print works until the 1820s. The Ashtons' switch to powerlooms encouraged industrial growth in the neighbouring towns of Dukinfield and Stalybridge.

The powerloom took a long time to catch on, however. By 1813 there were still only 2,400 in the whole of Great Britain. In this year, Horrocks took out another important powerloom patent. However, because he spent a great deal of time and money protecting his work from patent infringements, he didn't make any profit from his inventions. Manchester firm Sharp and Roberts built on Horrocks's work and produced the first really 'accomplished mechanism' in 1822.[7] Early powerlooms were usually tended by women, girls or young lads.

Powerlooms became more widespread during the boom years of the mid-1820s and early 1830s, when there was more money around to invest in the new technology. Manufacturers who spun and wove cotton in-house acquired greater quality control over their products and reduced costs. The Andrew family's mills at Compstall (c.1823) had spinning and weaving machinery on the same site, as did Thomas Marsland's massive Wellington Mill.

Because powerlooms were only slowly introduced, the clacking of handlooms could still be heard in weavers' garrets, or in cotton workshops with several looms under one roof. The handloom weavers' slow, painful descent into obsolescence is a huge blot on the story of early industrial history. Handloom weavers had prospered for a brief spell because of the abundance of yarn created by Arkwright's waterframe. When they found wages weren't keeping step with rising prices, they began pressing for a minimum wage. Journeymen weavers from Chester joined an association with workers from Stockport and Lancashire and published an address to the people in 1799. They humbly detailed their increasing poverty, and denied they were dangerous agitators. Parliament was not only unmoved, but responded by passing the Combination Act in July that year, outlawing combinations of workers (and, in theory, their masters were banned from combining as well). Despite this setback, workers continued to petition Parliament for a minimum wage like the silk weavers.

It wasn't a simple case of 'class war'. The handloom weavers had some allies among the cotton masters, gentry and middle classes. Like the workers, their 'betters' faced jail sentences for their trouble. When Lancashire and Cheshire weavers held a mass meeting at Heaton Norris during the trade slump of 1808, Mr Dawson, a master spinner from Stockport, was arrested for encouraging the weavers to persevere with their demands, even though he advocated peaceful protest.

A mass meeting of 70,000 workers was held at St George's Fields (Manchester) in May the same year; the Riot Act was read, and dragoons ordered to clear the field. One man was killed, and many others wounded. One of the speakers was Joseph Hanson of Strangeways Hall, a colonel in the volunteers. Hanson supported the weavers' campaign for a minimum wage. The authorities took a dim view of this independence of mind shown by 'one of their own'. Hanson was arrested, and imprisoned for six months. As a token of their gratitude for his efforts on their behalf, each weaver gave a penny to help pay his fine. Hanson refused the money, so the weavers used the 39,500 pennies collected to buy a huge gold cup. When Hanson was released from jail, an immense crowd of workers met him at Heaviley near Stockport, unyoked his horses from his carriage, and drew it themselves as far as Heaton Norris. The workers presented the gold cup to Hanson at Strangeways Hall.

The weavers, unable to support themselves and their families on their meagre wages, became increasingly bitter and militant as the price of grain and potatoes sky-rocketed. Wheat rose from 112s per quarter in 1810 to 152s 3d in 1812, and potatoes tripled in price, to a penny per pound. Potatoes were the biggest food staple, along with oatmeal and bread. Meat and bacon formed only a small part of the diet. Within the same time period, handloom weavers' wages plummeted. A weaver of 'fancy' goods with a complex pattern (which took longer to produce), received wages in 1810 of 21s (after deductions) for a six-day week, working twelve hours a day. By 1819, wages for weavers of fancy goods fell to 10s 3d and were still decreasing. A weaver making 'nankeens' earned 9s 6d.[8] A typical working-class family of six people would spend 18s 7¼d in total each week on basic foodstuffs, rent, coal, candles, soap, etc. Obviously a weaver with a family didn't have enough income to pay the bills so his wife or children needed to find work. If no work was available then, predictably, people starved. Even more predictably, the famished weavers sought a scapegoat for their misery. In Stockport, the new powerlooms seemed the obvious culprits.

When powerlooms were first introduced, the hard-pressed Stockport weavers tried to negotiate. They visited Charles Prescott, the rector and local magistrate, and explained their worries that the new steam looms were depriving them of work. Prescott suggested they approach the Secretary of State. The men tried, and were rebuffed; they were told the new technology was too important to the country's economy. Their next step, early in 1812, was to try and negotiate higher wages with the manufacturers, once again with the rector's help. The masters agreed to a wage increase, but almost immediately went back on their word. The workers' anger grew.

Meanwhile, news that a Westhoughton factory had been torched by Lancashire Luddites, along with lurid and alarming reports from *agents provocateurs*, convinced the government that a mass uprising was imminent. Alarm spread to the local authorities, who looked for sedition everywhere. John Lloyd, the local magistrates' clerk, and officer in the Yeomanry Cavalry at Stockport, was well known for his dogged pursuit of conspirators.

It is most unlikely that the Cheshire Luddites were part of a larger conspiracy; the strikes and riots which broke out were probably symptoms of dissatisfaction with local conditions rather than a precursor to armed insurrection. But their desperate measures were widely reported, stoking up people's terror.

The workers decided on direct action. Peter Marsland's steam loom factory at Stockport was attacked by arsonists in February 1812 and there was an unsuccessful attempt to burn down William Radcliffe's steam loom factory in March. Manufacturers weren't even safe in their own homes. At the beginning of April, Peter Marsland's house windows were broken (which led him to move out of town, as noted in an earlier chapter). Homes belonging to manufacturers William Radcliffe and Mr Hindley were also attacked.

There was more rioting by cotton workers at Macclesfield on 13 April. Trouble began when a crowd gathered outside the town. Next, they went to the marketplace, and asked the current price of potatoes. When they received an unfavourable answer, they began throwing the offending vegetables about. One man was arrested by the authorities and put in gaol. The mob broke into the gaol, rescued the prisoner, then carried him in triumph back to the market. By this time hundreds of people were swarming all over the streets, shops were smashed open, and cheeses and other goods rolled down the street.

The town's magistrates, hoping to frighten the men into going home quietly, called in the Royal Cumberland militia and read the Riot Act, but they were wasting their breath. At last the magistrates sent for the Macclesfield Volunteer Cavalry, commanded by Captain Daintry. The Yeomanry made short work of the rioters, in spite of a hail of stones and brickbats thrown at them. In the confusion two of the cavalrymen, Alderman Higginbotham and our old friend Thomas Grimsditch, were hurt. One of the rioters, William Stubbs, received a head wound from Grimsditch's sabre and a woman rioter was trampled on and had her arm broken. Stubbs and two other rioters were arrested and taken to Chester Castle.

At Stockport the following day, steam loom mills and shops were attacked. Reinforcements were sent for, and order restored by the six troops of the Chester Yeomanry and the Scots Greys, who were quartered in the town.

The next day, hundreds of people met in a 'disorderly manner' and the Riot Act was read.[9] Luddites smashed steam looms at Goodair's Edgeley Mill works. Goodair's home in Castle St was next; his house was set ablaze, and his furniture used to make a bonfire in the garden. The riots were suppressed with the aid of the Cheshire Yeomanry. The magistrates also took drastic action; all the pubs were closed that evening. Captured rioters, weighted down with irons, were later escorted by the Ashton Hayes Troop to Chester Castle to await trial.

A Special Commission to try the rioters was held at Chester in the last week in May, presided over by Justices Dallas and Burton. Over forty people were awaiting trial for disturbances across the county and the local militia were stationed in the city during the trials. James Radcliffe was charged with rioting, stealing and destroying flour at Bredbury. William Walker had been arrested for rioting and seizing flour and other goods at Gee Cross, at Hyde. Walker, a 59-year-old collier from Werneth, Stockport, was dubbed 'the General Ludd' for Cheshire: 'having frequently signalised himself at the head of the multitude, which placed themselves under his orders. A large cocked hat formed part of his dress.'[10]

Among those found guilty of rioting at Bredbury, and of attacking Joseph Clay's mill, were Radcliffe, Samuel Lees and Thomas Brunt, alias Etchells. Fourteen prisoners were sentenced to death, but only two were actually executed; the rest were reprieved.

John Ellis, who had been capitally convicted of destroying machinery at Tintwistle, was spared. Eight workers were transported for seven years, including the Luddite 'General' William Walker, Radcliffe and Brunt, who were also fined a shilling each. Six people were imprisoned for rioting at Macclesfield; they included cotton spinner William Stubbs, and 19-year-old colliers John Jackson and Thomas Livesley.

Joseph Thompson, a 34-year-old weaver, was found guilty of breaking into John Goodair's house and stealing a silver soup ladle, spoons and other goods. John Temple, a 27-year-old Irishman, was convicted of stealing five silver teaspoons 'and a great variety of wearing apparel' from the house of Samuel Wagstaffe of Adlington.[11] Thompson and Temple were 'launched into eternity' at the 'New Drop' behind the city gaol on 15 June.

It is hard to imagine romance blossoming under these circumstances. But one female rioter, nicknamed 'Mrs Ludd', so bewitched her gaoler while she was held prisoner in the Stockport lock-up, that he proposed when she was released. The two were married, and the wife helped run the prison where she had been held captive.

The post-Waterloo depression and sky-high food prices led to more misery in 1816. Stockport handloom weavers, who were badly affected, petitioned the Prince Regent for help. They still hoped for a guaranteed minimum wage and they also believed a ban on the export of cotton yarn would provide them with more work. Their plea was endorsed by many of the better-off citizens in the town, who wrote to the Prince Regent on their behalf. Their requests fell on deaf ears. This was good news for the Stockport spinners, at any rate, who would have been badly hit by such a ban. The following year saw the Blanketeers' march; John Lloyd took an active part in arresting the marchers when they reached Stockport.

The mule spinners had realized the benefits of banding together very early on: the Stockport spinners had formed a friendly society in 1792. An attempt was made to form a large union from groups in the Manchester area in 1810. The newly formed body brought Stalybridge and Preston workers out on strike that year; they wanted pay parity with Manchester spinners. The ensuing lock-out lasted for several months but the men were forced back to work when their strike pay ran out.

There were several different industrial disputes in the cotton trade in 1818. Hundreds of jenny spinners at Stockport turned out for six weeks. These workers were employed on hand-powered spinning jennies (first patented by James Hargreaves in 1770). They had seen a real erosion in their earning power: from 24s per week for a fourteen-hour shift in 1814 to roughly 15s per week. The masters refused to raise wages back to their former level, but the jenny spinners eventually won a wage increase of 4s.

There was a separate strike by Stockport powerloom weavers in July, the first time these workers flexed their industrial muscles. The weavers earned 15s per week; they wanted a pay rise of up to 5s. Thomas Garside of Hope Carr Mills employed about 300 hands, both spinners and weavers. He brought in 'blackleg' labour (known locally as 'knobsticks') from Burton on Trent to break the strike and housed them nearby. These workers were teenage girls; they earned 12–15s per week, depending on their age. Their youth didn't save them from a rough reception from angry workers. The cotton workers sang the 'knobstick song' when the new girls began work. The factory and house where the 'knobsticks' were staying was attacked. The terrified girls said their prayers, convinced they were going to be murdered. Garside told them that if they left he would get fresh workers and never employ them again. He left some men in the house to protect the girls from the workers, but one of them gallantly ran away when rioters tried to force the door.

The riots lasted for three nights. The Cheshire Yeomanry were in action again and there were casualties among the Stockport Troop when missiles were thrown at them. Their comrades from Tabley, Knutsford and Mere came to their aid the next day and stayed for a few days until the town was quiescent. There was much local sympathy for the strikers: it appears that even the town's special constables, and some of the middle classes, felt that Garside's actions were impolitic.

The local doctor, Thomas Cheetham, who supported the strikers, complained that the Yeomanry had attacked him and his house. Cheetham tried to bring charges against the Yeomanry, but John Lloyd got the case quashed. The rioters weren't so lucky. Twenty-one rioters were arrested, of whom sixteen were tried at the summer Assizes in Chester.

Two rioters, Jacob Hinchcliffe and Joseph Baker, were found guilty of breaking into a dwelling-house with intent to cause injury. The judge sentenced Hinchcliffe to three years in prison, and Baker to one year. Both men were also fined one shilling. They had a narrow escape, because their offence was a capital crime.

The indefatigable John Lloyd finally broke the strike by making use of the Combination Act which forbade workers to 'combine', that is, join a trade union. When Lloyd discovered the strikers were doling out strike pay in a local pub, he arrested them. The three-month jail sentence handed out to the strikers, and loss of strike pay, meant the strike was doomed; the weavers returned to work without anything to show for their efforts.

An upsurge in Radical activity kept the authorities on their toes. Three of the authorities' 'most wanted' men were John Bagguley, Samuel Drummond and John Johnston. With the exception of Drummond, who had relatives in Stockport, these activists weren't locals. They held meetings at places such as Sandy Brow in Stockport. Bagguley and Drummond were prime movers in the ill-fated Blanketeers march. The trio were arrested for sedition and conspiracy on 7 September 1818. They couldn't afford the bail set by the judge, so they were locked up in Chester Castle until the following spring Assizes.

The working classes still had friends. The Reverend Joseph Harrison, a Methodist preacher and schoolmaster at Stockport, was a self-styled 'chaplain to the poor and needy'. He campaigned for the cotton workers and was an advocate of reform. Harrison tried to raise bail for the three imprisoned Radicals, but John Lloyd quickly nipped that scheme in the bud by charging Harrison for attending an unlawful meeting.

The handloom weavers at Stockport, too, attempted to better their lot by going on strike in September 1818. These weavers don't appear to have taken part in the reform movement at this time, because while one Sandy Brow meeting was going on, men and women weavers were parading peaceably through the streets of the town. The strike ended when the masters gave the weavers a wage increase, but it wasn't long before they went back on their word, and the weavers were back in the same boat.

Handloom weavers became increasingly desperate as their wages shrank and living conditions worsened. By 1825, a weaver of fancy goods earned just 8s per week. Even though weavers could produce more complex patterns and finer cloth than powerlooms, they simply couldn't compete in terms of output. 'A boy or girl, fourteen or fifteen years of age, can manage two steam looms, and with their help can weave three and a half times as much cloth as the best hand weaver.'[12]

As powerlooms became more widespread, the once proud weavers were consigned to the dustbin of history. By the middle of the 1830s, their wages reached rock-bottom: a shocking 4s 1½d per week.

Impoverished workers who stole cotton cloth to make some extra cash faced the same harsh penalties as silk weavers. Abraham Rosthern, a 30-year-old weaver from Bramhall, was sentenced to death in April 1818 for stealing muslin from Mr Cumberlidge of Edgeley: 'The Judge did not hold out any hope of mercy to the wretched man.'[13] He was executed on the same day as Isaac Moors, the spinner we met in the last chapter. The men were given fresh oranges and white wine before meeting their fate; the unlucky Rosthern took eight minutes to die because of the hangman's incompetence.

The trade depression and associated radical unrest continued into 1819, Peterloo year. Henry Hunt received a warm welcome when he arrived at Hazel Grove in January; a huge crowd unyoked his horses and drew his carriage through the town. He addressed the people from the window of the Bull's Head Inn.

A badge of freedom, the 'Cap of Liberty', was often displayed at these meetings. To the authorities, it represented Revolution; it was the equivalent of waving a red flag at a bull. Stockport bricklayer Robert Jump carried a pole with a tin cone on top as a 'Cap', which was put to good use after the meetings; it was filled with beer while the men drank toasts and sang songs.

One confrontation long remembered in local folklore was the 'battle' at Sandy Brow on 15 February 1819. A large crowd had assembled at a Radical meeting. Rector Charles Prescott read the Riot Act after a 'Cap of Liberty' was waved. He ordered the local Yeomanry and constables to clear the ground and seize the people's flags and the gathering developed into a riot. The Yeomanry, commanded by Captain Newton, were met by a hostile volley of stones and missiles and were beaten back. The incident was commemorated in verse, containing stirring lines such as:

Hail! sacred spot, where freedom's standard waved
And all the force of proud oppression braved
Let ages yet unborn hear when, and how
The sons of freedom fought on Sandy Brow.[14]

This victory had repercussions in August that year at Peterloo. The Stockport Troop, including John Lloyd, remembered their humiliation at Sandy Brow. When asked to disperse the crowd, they used their sabres with great gusto.

Another flashpoint came in April, when Bagguley, Drummond and Johnston were found guilty of inciting sedition and jailed for two years. The Reverend Harrison led a huge protest meeting at Sandy Brow and over 4,500 people signed a petition to complain that the three imprisoned Radicals hadn't had a fair trial. They demanded a re-trial. When this tack failed, an even bigger rally was held on 28 June 1819. Harrison was again present, but the star turn was Sir Charles Wolseley, of Wolseley Hall in Staffordshire, who made an impassioned speech.

The authorities reacted swiftly. Harrison and Wolseley were indicted at Chester for plotting to cause riots and insurrection. In July, Sir Charles was arrested at his family seat. Harrison was arrested in London after addressing a rally at Smithfield led by Henry Hunt. He was brought back to Stockport on 23 July, accompanied by two special constables: one was William Birch. That same evening, Birch was shot in Loyalty Place. The shooting, which Birch survived, caused a sensation and a reward was offered to find his assailants. The Prince Regent granted Constable Birch a pension of £100 for his injury.

Because the surgeons couldn't extract the bullet, some Radicals even claimed no gun was fired. The poor constable received a chilling anonymous letter: 'The shot unfortunately took an improper direction, but the next shall be sure. Prepare yourself for your fate is fixed. Your life is determined on the very first opportunity. The Decree is irrevocable ...'[15]

Eyewitness William Pearson, who saw the shooting, identified the constable's would-be assassin as Jacob McGhinness, a silk weaver from Edgeley. McGhinness fled to Ireland, but was caught several months later. He was tried in April 1820, when Birch's bloodied waistcoat was shown in evidence to the court. McGhinness said his intended target was John Lloyd. He was sentenced to death for the attack, and was executed on 15 April 1820. His last words were 'Farewell, gentlemen!' One of his accomplices, James George Bruce, was also found guilty, but his death sentence was commuted to transportation for life.

The story has a macabre postscript. After Birch's death in May 1834, a post-mortem was conducted. The missing bullet was found wedged in his breastbone. Much later in the century, when historian Henry Heginbotham was researching his mammoth history of Stockport, he was shown Birch's breastbone by the surgeon at the infirmary. So the constable didn't rest in one piece after his sterling service.

Reformers Wolseley and Harrison were dealt with during the same Assizes in 1820. Each man was sentenced to eighteen months in prison, and ordered to find bail for five years' good behaviour after their sentences had expired. After an additional trial, the Reverend Harrison notched up another two years in prison, because he had made speeches at other Radical meetings while out on bail. The day before Peterloo, Harrison said: '… the Government had starved the people, and it was only right that the people should starve the government … when people asked for their rights, they threatened to make war on them.' Harrison received a total of three and a half years for speaking his mind. While in prison, he was given eight days and nights of solitary confinement for smuggling in a copy of Whig newspaper, the *Chester Guardian*.

The year 1824 was a golden year for the cotton trade. The quest for reform, already weakened by the government's ruthless suppression of Radical agitators in the aftermath of Peterloo, faded away while work was plentiful and mills ran at full capacity. But the panic of 1825–6 in the money markets hit the cotton trade as well as silk.

It was the same old story: mills standing idle led to starving workers venting their wrath on buildings and machinery. Banks stopped payment and the tradesmen and shopkeepers, reliant on the workers' custom, were hard hit.

Relief fund committees bought food and fuel, and soup, potatoes and coal were sold to the operatives at half price. Schemes such as road building were set up so that men could earn a pittance instead of just living on handouts. New Zealand Road, Stockport, was one of these projects. It was originally going to be called Trafalgar Road, but acquired its new name after some men claimed they would rather go to New Zealand (not a transportation colony) instead of working for such tiny wages.

Even the weather added to the misery, with the disastrous floods of July 1828 causing a great deal of damage. One of Peter Marsland's mill buildings at Park Mill in Stockport was undermined by the floodwaters and nearly 1000 pieces of calico were washed away. Bayley's cotton spinning factory was damaged, and the river was polluted by vitriol (used for bleaching cloth).

The most hard-fought 'turn-out' began in the autumn of 1828 when cotton masters slashed wages as a response to shrinking profit margins. The strike, concentrated on Stockport and Hyde, spread throughout the manufacturing districts. It dragged on until the following September and around 10,000 operatives were caught up in the strike action. The cotton masters, who had evidently learned nothing from previous conflicts, caused uproar by importing blackleg labour from out of town.

A dreadful tragedy struck during this industrial dispute. In April 1829, the master spinners at Hyde and the surrounding areas published a handbill. They threatened to dock ten per cent from union members' wages unless they agreed to leave the union. Hundreds of workers attended a protest meeting in the assembly room of the Norfolk Arms Inn, Hyde. Suddenly, the floor collapsed underneath them, and the workers fell into the cellar below. Thirty people died (many from suffocation) and around 200 people were injured. Some workers actually accused the mill-owners of somehow causing the accident: a measure of just how high feelings were running between masters and men. A riot on 5 May was followed by some particularly nasty incidents: acid was thrown at a mill-owner's son, and some strike-breakers were hurt. James Burgess, a 'knobstick' at Jesse Howard's cotton spinning mill, was attacked by four men and stabbed, but survived. After months of hardship, the strikers were forced to admit defeat.

Towards the end of 1830, fifty-two cotton masters in Stalybridge, Ashton-under-Lyne and Dukinfield combined together to deliberately smash the spinners' union. They reneged on a wage agreement brokered just a few weeks previously. In addition, they threatened to close the mills if the men didn't accept a wage reduction. When the workers refused to be bullied, the mill doors were locked shut. Twenty-three thousand men were out of work.

Angry strikers roamed the streets and windows were broken. Workers at Hyde were compelled to join the strike. Vitriol throwing was a feature of this dispute, too. The spinners' union attempted to call out all the spinners nationwide, but other workers, no doubt fearful of losing their jobs, ignored the order.

The masters' intransigence led to a horrific incident which petrified the middle classes and made the national news: the fatal shooting of a mill-owner's son. Samuel Ashton's sons Thomas and James were responsible for the day-to-day running of his mills at Woodley and Werneth. Woodley Mill was in Thomas's charge and he was well known and liked in the district for his kindly nature. The Werneth mill, on Apethorn Lane, was run by James.

On 3 January 1831, a gloomy winter evening, 23-year-old Thomas took his brother's turn doing his usual evening rounds at the mill, as James had a social engagement. James had recently dismissed some workers from the Werneth mill for being union members. In the near darkness, three men lay in wait behind a hedge on Apethorn Lane. They saw a figure approaching and believed it was James Ashton. They pounced, grabbed Thomas, and shot him in the chest at point blank range.

The Ashton family were distraught. A massive reward (£1500 in total) was offered for information leading to the identity of the killer. Conspiracy theories abounded. Was Ashton shot on the orders of the trade union, in order to frighten mill-owners involved in the current dispute, or was it just a personal grudge?

If the murder was on union orders, it didn't bring the conflict to a speedy end. The workers lived on strike pay from the union, but as the long weeks passed their funds dwindled. By March, the starving men were forced to return to work on the masters' terms.

Three years later, while in gaol for a minor offence, James Garside 'confessed' that he had been involved in the murder, along with two brothers, Joseph and William Moseley. Garside said Joseph fired the fatal shot. Garside also claimed he had been offered a pardon if he testified, but an unpleasant surprise was in store for him. William insisted Garside was the murderer, and that the shooting was done on trade union orders. This claim caused great damage to the spinners and their union.

On William's evidence (for which he was pardoned and discharged) at the trial in August 1834, Garside and Joseph Moseley were found guilty of murder. Both men collapsed when sentenced to death. In a bizarre twist, the men had a short but unexpected reprieve. Chester magistrates turned turtle and refused to execute them, in an effort to free the city sheriffs of their long-unwanted responsibility of executing offenders from the whole county. Garside and Moseley were finally hanged at Horsemonger Lane Gaol in London on 25 November 1834.

Ashton's death partly inspired the plot of Elizabeth Gaskell's *Mary Barton* (1848) in which starving worker John Barton shoots the mill-owner's son, Harry Carson. Thomas Ashton's sister is said to have fainted when she read the chapter containing the murder and realized the shocking parallel with her brother's death.

Why was there so much bitterness between the classes? The gulf between masters and workers was self-evident. Working hours were long – usually 6 a.m. till 6 p.m. – and days monotonous. While employers lived in elegant villas out of town, ordinary workers lived in terraced housing, some of extremely poor quality, in the town centres.

In fairness, enlightened employers like the Gregs and the Ashtons took their social responsibilities very seriously. They looked after their workers. The solid, sanitary workers' housing built at Hyde by the Ashtons received glowing commendations by contemporaries. Greg's mill workers at Styal had cottages with gardens where they grew their own vegetables. Each house had a separate privy. Samuel Greg also provided chapels, a school, and a shop which sold wholesome, good quality produce. Wages weren't as high as in Manchester mills, but rents were affordable. However, paternalism evidently wasn't enough to bridge the class divide.

'Boom and bust' and industrial disputes continued to make headlines through the coming decades. Stockport's phenomenal growth simply couldn't be sustained and it ground to a halt. But families such as the Gregs at Styal and the Swindells at Bollington ensured 'king cotton' was here to stay for the foreseeable future.

13

Salt of the Earth

Salt was in great demand before the days of refrigeration. It was used in cheese-making, and to preserve other foods such as meat and fish 'Few articles are more essentially necessary to human comfort, than salt,' commented a writer in 1814. 'Our fisheries for herrings, pilchards, etc.; those of cod on the great banks of Newfoundland; the sea-stores of our navy; our butter, cheese, and a thousand other articles, are dependent on salt for their preservation and extensive usefulness.'[1] Bleachers and tanners also used salt.

Cheshire's brine springs have been exploited since very ancient times – right back to the Iron Age, and possibly even earlier. When the Romans overran the county, they found a thriving salt manufacture, and quickly took advantage of this valuable resource. The 'wich' towns associated with salt-making – Northwich, Nantwich and Middlewich – are mentioned in the Domesday Book. Salt continued to be a vital source of wealth for the county from medieval times. And as the nineteenth century advanced, it acquired even greater importance as a fertile revenue source for the government because it was necessary for certain industrial processes.

Soap-making was a fast-growing industry, especially on Merseyside. Alkaline soda ash (sodium carbonate) was used in this process. Traditionally, soda ash was made from burnt Scottish kelp or imported barilla (derived from a Spanish plant), but suppliers couldn't keep pace with demand. Frenchman Nicholas Leblanc discovered a method of making artificial soda by 'decomposing' salt to produce 'salt-cake'; Leblanc's method was patented in 1791.

In the early 1820s, James Muspratt built an alkali works in Liverpool (and another at St Helens in 1828) which used an improved Leblanc process; salt was the key raw material. The glassmakers of St Helens used soda ash, further increasing demand for salt.

Salt was big business and, despite the questionable environmental effects of brine and rock salt extraction, it was worthy of special notice in the guidebooks of the day: 'The immense trade in this article, and vast revenue derived from its duty, renders it an object of very considerable local and national importance. The principal salt-works are at Nantwich, Middlewich, Winsford, and Northwich.'[2] Although contemporary guidebooks still included Nantwich among the 'principal salt-works', they were often out of date. Nantwich's glory days had long since passed away by the end of the seventeenth century.

Salt was manufactured by evaporating brine in pans over large furnaces. The salt-makers' need for coal decided the fate of the 'wiches'. Salt-makers had previously used wood for their furnaces, but coal gradually became the fuel of choice. Not only could higher temperatures be achieved, but wood, which was also in demand as charcoal for iron foundries, became expensive. Coal fires tended to damage the salt pans, which were made of lead, so salt makers switched to iron pans. Using iron meant larger salt pans could be constructed, so production was more efficient. As we saw in an earlier chapter, a plan to extend the Weaver Navigation from Winsford Bridge to Nantwich was never implemented but Nantwich's salt trade was already moribund because of restrictive policies by the proprietors.

In 1774, Thomas Pennant commented that this proud salt-making town, which in Elizabethan times had hundreds of small lead salt pans, was reduced to just two salt-works. 'The [salt] duty produced from them amounts annually to near five thousand pounds; from the whole district, including the works at Lawton and a small one at Durtwich [Dirtwich], from eighteen to twenty thousand pounds.'[3] Nantwich's salt trade had irreversibly declined, even though its inhabitants claimed the brine springs there 'could be worked so as to yield a sufficiency of salt for the whole kingdom'.[4]

Northwich was now the prime salt-making centre, thanks to the Weaver Navigation. In the early 1790s, over eighty Mersey flats – a 'respectable fleet of small vessels' – busily ferried 58,000 tons of salt to

Liverpool.[5] Other useful transport links which aided Northwich's prosperity were the nearby Grand Trunk Canal (the Trent & Mersey) and the Anderton basin complex. But Winsford was now home to large saltworks and it was catching up Northwich fast.

Salt manufacturers at Lawton, Middlewich and Wheelock found it more convenient to get their coal from Staffordshire collieries via the Trent & Mersey Canal. Most of the salt made at these works was sent down the Trent & Mersey for home consumption. Only a small proportion – about 16,000 tons – of brine salt produced was for home consumption; the export market was far more important. Cheshire salt went all over the world: the Scottish fisheries, the Baltic ports, America, and British colonies on the Continent.

The rights to make salt were usually rented out and brine springs were only rarely exploited by the owners of the land where brine was found. An American, Joshua Gilpin, visited a brine works near Northwich in October 1796. The works was 'supplied by a strong brine from a well sunk to the depth of the salt rock ... it is pumped up by a fire engine. These wells are sunk in a number of places wherever the owner of the land has reason to apprehend there is a salt spring ... the strength of them is very great as a gallon of water will in many cases yield 30 oz of salt ...'[6]

After the brine was pumped up into reservoirs by a steam engine, it was transferred via long troughs to huge, shallow iron pans. 'The process of extracting the salt is accomplished by heating the liquor in iron pans, of 20 to 30 feet square, and about 14 inches deep.'[7] The brine was topped up as the salt crystallized. Depending on the salt grain size required, manufacturers used a wide variety of additives to help clear impurities in the salt: animal jelly, blood (some said this gave the salt an unpleasant taste), wheat flour, linseed, ale or butter.

Several different types of salt were made. The most coarse-grained or 'common' salt, made by 'wallers', was formed by long, slow simmering; salt was 'drawn' from the pans once a day.

Fisheries required crystals of large-grained salt. This was manufactured by very lengthy brine boiling, at a lower temperature: it took five or six days to evaporate the brine. Alum was added to aid the formation of large grains.

Fine table salt was made from 'lump' or 'stoved' salt. The brine was boiled rapidly, and salt 'drawn' from the pan twice in twenty-four hours. Makers of fine salt were highly skilled; they were known as 'lumpmen', and worked from Monday to Saturday. As the brine boiled, the salt formed a crystalline crust on the surface, then sank into the bottom of the pans. Any impurities which rose to the surface of the brine during evaporation were skimmed off by the lumpman. When the lumpman was happy that enough evaporation had taken place for a good pan yield, 'The fires are then slackened, and the salt is drawn to the sides of the pan with iron rakes.' The lumpman scooped up the salt into conical wicker baskets and excess brine was drained off into the pan. The baskets of damp salt were carried to a bench at the side of the pan-house and allowed to finish draining. The lump salt was 'afterwards dried in stoves, heated by a continuation of the same flues which have passed under the evaporating pan …'[8] Another important part of the lumpman's job was using a special pick to remove hard mineral scale which formed on the iron pans; scale reduced the yield and caused damage if left.

Whole families often worked together in the open pan works; young lads aged nine or ten helped their fathers carry lump salt into the stove house for drying. Some of the smaller works were family businesses, and because of the many long hours needed for the salt to evaporate, the wives 'mucked in' and helped, even if they had babies and small children in tow. Women worked in their petticoats because of the heat and steam. They raked the salt from the base of the salt pans with huge iron rakes. When the lump salt had dried out, they broke up the salt by hand ready for packing. Family life and meals were slotted in around the needs of the salt pan, even though twelve-hour shifts were the norm. Workers were forbidden to 'combine' to form trade unions until after the Combination Act was repealed in 1825. However, salt workers didn't have a union until the mid-1840s, when one was formed at Winsford.

Although Barclay's *Dictionary* (1813) lists Northwich as a 'handsome place', it is likely the writer hadn't actually visited the town. The use of low-grade 'burgey' coal for steam engines and brine boiling led to a thick, grimy pall over the 'wich' towns; an early case of industrial blight. Another visitor wrote:

> From the number of steam-engines pumping up brine, or working up rock from the pits, the air was dark with smoke, and the roads to the works black with the falling soot, among which, particles of salt glistened in the sun-beams. The blackness of the salt-houses and lofts, and their age and condition, give the place a rather dismal and ruinous appearance.[9]

Two decades later George Head grumbled that 'a stranger, when arrived, may very reasonably, with being over fastidious, wish himself out of it. The streets are narrow, dark and dirty; some of the inns rather below par.'

Northwich also contained rock salt mines, first discovered in 1670 on William Marbury's land just outside the town. More rock salt was later discovered in nearby Witton, Marston, Wincham and Winnington. There were two main strata of rock salt: the 'upper bed', approximately 30 metres below the surface, resembled: '… brown sugar-candy, perfectly solid, and so hard as to be broke (*sic*) with great difficulty by iron picks and wedges. Latterly the workmen have been accustomed to blast it with gunpowder, by which expedient they loosen and remove many tons together.'[10]

The men arrived for work at 6.30 a.m. It took them about half an hour to descend into the pit before they could begin drilling and blasting. The sound of the blasts echoed loudly round the underground caverns. The men earned 2s 2d for each ton of salt excavated and out of this wage they had to buy their own gunpowder, candles, picks and other tools. They finished work in the middle of the afternoon.

The 'lower bed' of rock salt was discovered at Lawton in 1779, and again at Marston Old Top Mine a couple of years later. This rock salt was crystal clear and white as an iceberg in some places, a brownish colour in others. It was purer than the topmost layer, so after this date any new pits sunk around Northwich were dug low enough to exploit it. The largest rock salt mine was at Witton; it was approximately two acres in extent, and needed twenty-five pillars of salt to support the roof.

The rock salt pits were generally dry, with a comfortable working temperature. When illuminated: 'the crystalline pillars of the roof, pillars and sides … make a glittering and magnificent appearance, which seldom fails to have an impressive effect on the mind of a stranger'.[11]

Gilpin, who visited a Northwich mine (probably Marston) in 1796, likened it to an 'immense cellar or rather a subterranean Cathedral'. The mine cavern was 'dry, spacious and the whole area is kept so clear and neat as to give a comfortable appearance'. Ventilation was provided by a forge bellows pumping air through a tube.

Earlier in the century, horse gins or 'whimseys' were used to raise rock salt in wheeled tubs from the pits, or for pumping brine from the springs. Gilpin noticed a horse gin being used for raising and lowering the workmen. Horses continued in use surprisingly late. Nearly two decades after Gilpin's visit, Henry Holland found them still being used for raising the salt tubs. The workers, carrying candles for light, perched on the edge of the salt tubs as they went up and down the shafts. Each tub held about 10 bushels of salt. (A bushel is 8 gallons or roughly 36.4 litres capacity.)

Workers pulled on a rope, attached to a bell, to let the men above know when they wanted to be hauled up. The salt tubs needed to be very carefully secured to prevent accidents. Louis Simond, a French traveller who visited the mines in 1811, spoke to the bereaved parents of a salt miner who had plummeted down the shaft shortly before Simond's visit. Another Northwich salt-worker was killed and two others badly injured in April 1825 when the tub carrying them on its way down into the mine collided with the ascending tub, and was overturned.

The filled tubs were collected by other workers, who wheeled them to a store-room, emptied and brought them back ready for re-filling. Salt mining was considered clean, healthy work compared with other industries, such as the coal mines. The mines were warm enough for the men to work in their shirts. Small children weren't commonly used below ground, as in the collieries.

During the eighteenth century, some rock salt was shipped to refineries at Frodsham, Dungeon, Warrington and Liverpool, where it was refined into white common salt.

Over 54,000 tons of rock salt was sent from Northwich along the Weaver in 1800; almost 35,000 tons of this was exported to Ireland, the Baltic ports and West Indies. Salt shipping firms included family concerns such as the Okells and the Marshalls, but some firms were owned by women. Emma Jefferies shipped white salt from Northwich from 1797 to 1816, and Ann Worthington from 1809 to 1826.

Although Newcomen engines, which worked by atmospheric pressure, were invented at the beginning of the eighteenth century, they didn't catch on in Cheshire. However, by the late 1770s, steam engines or 'fire' engines were set to work in Cheshire salt-works. The first one in Cheshire was a Boulton and Watt engine (patented 1775) installed in 1778 at the Lawton Salt Works, owned by Edward Salmon and Dr Penlington, near Sandbach. Now tens of thousands of gallons of brine could be pumped up from the underground springs in just a few hours.

Steam engines were also used in rock salt mines. John Gilbert (1724–95), who supervised the boring operations for rock salt at Marston Old Top, part-owned the Marston mines. (Gilbert was the land agent and mining engineer for the Duke of Bridgwater.) Gilbert used a Boulton and Watt engine (c.1788) to raise rock salt from the pit and it did double duty as a pumping engine to remove brine from the shafts.

Brine springs were a source of wealth, but they were also a menace because they sometimes burst through into the rock salt pits. Victorian writer James Stonehouse wrote that: 'in some mines the water can be heard rushing like a torrent'. If the springs dissolved the supporting roof pillars, the whole pit collapsed in on itself, creating a large funnel-shaped hole on the surface. It was the unwelcome appearance of so many 'rock pit holes' at Northwich, especially in the Witton area, which prompted salt proprietors to make trial sinkings elsewhere in the county, and led to the discovery of the lower bed of rock salt at Lawton.

Pit collapses also occurred if the salt pillars left behind to support the mine roof were insufficiently sturdy. John Blackburne's pit at Wincham was in a very precarious state in 1830; after three years the supports gave way and it flooded.

The 'top mines' in the upper bed were gradually abandoned after the purer lower bed was found. As time passed, the old mines filled with fresh water, which dissolved the salt, and huge underground brine reservoirs were formed. These were pumped out by the salt manufacturers for their brine works, leading to catastrophic results later in the nineteenth century.

The salt-works were also in danger from the Weaver, which had a nasty habit of bursting its banks. On 9 October 1798, disaster struck when the River Weaver rose by sixteen to eighteen feet in places and the aqueduct at Wincham collapsed. Northwich's streets were several feet deep under water. The salt-works were flooded and 7000 bushels of salt were destroyed. The following year saw 'the largest flood ever remembered' in August. Bancrofts' works lost over 300 tons of salt, and the Old Rock Pit was partially flooded. Salt proprietors John Marshall and Mr Wakefield saved several lives; the townsfolk were rescued from their houses using Weaver flats.[12]

The Marshalls of Northwich were among the most important salt manufacturers. The family were originally based in Nantwich. The first Thomas Marshall in our story moved to Northwich in the 1720s and, after learning the trade, he began producing brine salt. Father and son Thomas rented a town house at Brine Sheath Brow in Northwich, which they used as a business base as well as a home. They were a hardworking, ambitious and energetic family. The Marshalls leased brine pits at Barons Croft, Anderton and Winnington, and expanded their interests into rock salt at Witton. They edged out longer-established competitors such as the Blackburne family and were quick to take advantage of new technology. In the summer of 1796, one of the new Boulton and Watt engines began winding rock salt at their huge Dunkirk mine underneath Witton.

The first Thomas Marshall built working-class housing at Barons Croft. The houses in his New Street were three storeys high and the top floor could be used as a workshop, so these properties were designed to appeal to craftsmen as well as to the workers who helped create the family's wealth.

Other employers provided housing for their workers, too. An advertisement in the *Chester Courant* (2 June 1818) for a seven-acre salt-works at Winsford listed many desirable features. The site, with direct access to the Weaver, housed eight pans and a range of buildings and warehouses, with 'a capital STEAM ENGINE, of ten horse power, for raising brine, and a spacious Reservoir for supply of the pans … a neat brick-built Manager's Cottage, recently erected, with Garden, etc.; two Labourer's Cottages and Gardens, Blacksmith's Shop …' and so on. The trend continued much later in the century – the Verdin family and Brunner Mond firm built streets of houses for their employees.

We can catch a glimpse of the Marshalls' workers from a visitor who published an account of his expedition down the Dunkirk rock salt mine in *Ackermann's Repository of Arts* in 1814. Before his descent underground, the un-named gentleman was shown some 'flashes' on the surface – deep pools of water where earlier rock-pits had collapsed – which must have concentrated his mind wonderfully.

The intrepid explorer and his lady friends were winched down into the mine in a large bucket hauled by a steam engine. They suffered an anxious moment when the bucket stopped with a sudden jerk. It was drawn up and lowered again several times, then wound back up to the pit entrance. The party was unnerved to discover the rope hauling their tub had slipped off a roller, jammed tight, and was in danger of breaking. The defect was repaired, and the travellers began their descent again, past the upper salt bed and down to the lower bed, 336 feet from the surface.

The author was suitably impressed by the mine: '… we appeared as if in an immense, solemn, and awful temple.' Working hours and conditions appear to have changed little since Gilpin's visit: the men, working by candlelight, still used gunpowder to loosen the rock.

> With a long iron chissel (*sic*) continually worked on the salt, the rock is perforated to the depth of 3 or 4 feet. This is then charged with a few ounces of powder, on which a long straw filled with powder is placed, to serve as a fuse; loose salt fills up the hole, and is rammed hard into it. The men having lit the fuse, retire, and the explosion soon succeeds. It is calculated, that about four tons weight of rock are separated by each 'shot' …

Several charges were 'sprung' for the visitors' gratification. The explosions made a thunderous roar, which echoed from the upper bed. The salt miners worked in 'companies' and they were paid by the amount of rock salt mined rather than a set wage.

The workers, who behaved with 'very great civility', gave the ladies of the party some tools so they could chip out some crystal specimens to take home as souvenirs. The visitors returned to 'the cheering light of the sun' with relief, even though they had enjoyed their visit.

Marshall's son Thomas (1735–97) took over the family business after his father died in 1772. The Marshalls' growing wealth meant the second Thomas could afford a luxurious lifestyle and he and his wife bought a manor house with an estate at Hartford Green Bank. But they kept their town house, with its convenient Northwich location, for business.

Marshall had fingers in many different pies; he invested in houses and commercial properties locally. He bought the Navigation Trustees' warehouses and cranes at Broken Cross in 1784 when they gave up their business as carriers. And, like many other salt proprietors, Thomas owned Weaver flats so he could transport his own cargoes. He cut costs even further by leasing collieries in south Lancashire. A family member worked at Liverpool as his agent, so Thomas could keep abreast of developments at the docks.

Thomas's sons (i.e. grandsons of the first Thomas) maintained the success of the family business. John Marshall (1765–1833) took over the Green Bank house, and his brother Thomas (1767–1831) built a brick house nearby. But this wasn't grand enough, so Thomas constructed Hartford Beach, a spectacular Regency house more appropriate for his rising social status. By 1817, Thomas Marshall (the third) could boast that he owned the largest salt concern in Britain. The house was elegantly furnished, with a huge garden and of course the Marshall family could afford several servants. Their son (yet another Thomas) was well educated and their daughter Elizabeth was an accomplished musician. John and Thomas Marshall also spent money locally – they were the largest benefactors of the new Anglican church built at Hartford in 1822.

Iredale's work[13] has shown that the Marshalls played a key role in controlling salt prices. Over-production was a real problem in the salt industry. From the 1760s onwards, salt proprietors joined forces to try and stabilize the trade. The second Thomas Marshall held meetings with the other salt proprietors and made meticulous records to maintain an informal system of checks and balances which kept prices (and profits) high. But however tightly Marshall tried to control the trade, there was one factor he could do little about: the salt excise.

Salt had been heavily taxed almost continuously since the late seventeenth century. The excise 'clogged' the trade. Because there was so much salt available beneath the county, output was already strictly controlled by producers, but the government's salt excise added an extra burden. The excise duty, already a huge £20 per ton (12s per bushel) in 1796, was raised to £30 per ton (15s per bushel) in 1805. The duty stayed at this shockingly high level for the next two decades.

Pitt's salt tax hike moved a contributor to the *Lady's Monthly Museum* (March, 1805) to pen some verses:

Lines / On Mr Pitt's Additional Duty on Salt

Should our wives, like her of old,*
All suffer transformation,
And not a solitary scold
Be left to cheer the nation,

The loss of sound would sure be great!
But oh! Let Pitt be prais'd,
To serve the purposes of state
What sums would then be rais'd!
(* Lot's wife.)

Salt duty was paid at the salt works but it was waived on exported salt. A permit was needed to move even small quantities of salt and special officers checked the weight of consignments and monitored their movement on the roads. Salt cargoes sent to Liverpool on the flats were re-weighed by excise officers when they reached their destination. If the cargo was under weight, the manufacturer had to make good the shortfall, but if the cargo was heavier than stated, the surplus was seized.

Officers were always on duty at the rock salt mines: William Brooke, John Parland and John Jenkins are listed as salt customs and excise officers at Northwich in Cowdroy's *Directory*. Gilpin noticed that salt workers were searched whenever they came up to the surface and if any salt was found hidden on them, they were very heavily fined – 2s 6d *per ounce*. Unlike coal miners, salt workers didn't get an allowance of the fruits of their labour for their own use; they had to buy their own salt at 6s per bushel.

At the brine works, the excise officer made regular checks on the amount of salt refined and logged whether it was intended for export or home consumption. Sellers and dealers in salt were given printed forms by the excise office. Details of the amount of salt sold, the purchaser and the duty paid were recorded for every transaction. Any salt sold which wasn't recorded in this way could be confiscated and any person involved was fined £50 (a very large sum then). In April 1818, Thomas Albinson was sentenced to seven years' transportation for stealing salt.

The good citizens of Rudheath were said to be particularly averse to paying the salt tax; it was worth their while to smuggle it out of the county. Legend has it that, all too often, a funeral procession of grieving mourners followed a coffin full of salt (instead of a corpse) to evade the excise officer's eagle eyes.

Because salt was so valuable, it was a real temptation to thieves, even though they risked the hangman's noose. One execution which left a nasty aftertaste in Cheshire history was that of George Glover and William Proudlove in 1809. Glover and Proudlove were part of a daring night-time gang raid on the Lawton Salt Works at Odd Rode. Several men had already appropriated bags of salt from the premises and stowed them in a nearby building, when the excise officer on duty, William Stockton, became suspicious. He went for reinforcements. When officers arrived at the scene, the robbery was still in progress and 400lb of salt had already been stolen. In the ensuing mêlée, shots were fired, and Stockton injured. At their trial, Glover and Proudlove: 'acknowledged their guilt of the felony, but persisted in their being innocent of the shooting'.[14] But even though they didn't fire the shots, their presence at the robbery (confirmed by an informant who turned King's Evidence to save his neck) meant they were equally guilty in the eyes of the law.

On 6 May 1809, the condemned men had the privilege of being the first felons to try out the recently erected 'New Drop' at the city gaol. Unfortunately, both ropes broke. Instead of being 'launched into eternity' (as the journalistic cliché of the day went) the hapless men fell only a short distance, and survived. They were taken back into the gaol where they had to wait for nearly two hours while new ropes were installed. They were given a stiff drink while being kept in suspense. Eventually Glover and Proudlove were taken outside and hanged again, successfully, this time. William Whitehead from Northwich and Samuel Johnson from Congleton were later transported for seven years for their part in the robbery, but the actual gunman was never tried and convicted.

The salt excise generated vast revenue for the government: £200,000 in the second decade of the nineteenth century. The government, faced with empty coffers because of the Napoleonic wars, was reluctant to repeal the tax, despite a parliamentary select committee's conclusion in 1818 that: 'a repeal of the salt duties would be productive of the greatest and most important advantages to the kingdom'.[15]

Sir Thomas Bernard, a believer in free trade, also drew attention to the 'impolicy' of the tax two years later. Smugglers kept the excise men on their toes: there were 260 prosecutions and over £1770 of fines imposed for evading salt duties in 1822. But it was a 'top-heavy' system; over 260 excise men were employed in Cheshire in the early 1820s. It cost more than £32,660 to collect the duty in 1824. Roughly half this amount was spent on excise officers' wages and pensions.

Salt had important uses in agriculture, but the tax meant it was too pricey for arable farmers to use as manure. In the 1760s, farmers used refuse or 'soiled' salt (the pan sweepings left over from salt-making) at a lower duty. But because they were so cunning at evading the duty, a new Act was passed in 1785. Refuse salt was banned from being used as manure; the customs men were ordered to dump it in the river. Dairy farmers, who used a lot of salt for cheese-making, also hated paying the duty. After questions were raised in Parliament, the government gradually relaxed duties on salt for agricultural purposes.

There were many learned disputes (some obviously advertisements) in the Cheshire newspapers by correspondents on the efficacy of rock salt as a manure. One author claimed the judicious use of salt increased the yield of wheat, and reduced the ravages of slugs and worms on oat crops. Salt was said to improve turnip crops, grass pasture and potatoes. Cattle and sheep enjoyed salt 'licks'; indeed, sheep were said to be 'uncommonly partial to it'.[16] Hay impregnated with salt helped to prevent sheep 'rot', so rock salt used for feeding to livestock attracted a lower rate of tax.

Rock salt was considered unsuitable for human consumption in its natural form, so it was banned for use with meat, fish or other provisions. But it could be used to produce white table salt if it was first dissolved in water and refined by evaporation. If customs officers discovered that rock salt, which attracted a lower duty, had been used instead of ordinary salt for preserving foodstuffs, they imposed a fine of 40s for every pound of rock salt used.

By 1824, salt excise regulations were bafflingly complex. The trade was 'hampered with restrictions' and 'overwhelmed with prohibitions'.[17] Duties were so punitively high, the retail price bore virtually no relation to production costs. As industrial technology improved, only the bigger proprietors could afford the huge investment needed to construct or maintain a profitable works. Large sums needed to be set aside for salt duties, because duty was paid on site. One salt manufacturer had to pay out £33,000 in salt duties in a six-week period. Smaller salt makers who couldn't keep up with the payments fell by the wayside. In 1818, salt manufacturer John Thompson was declared bankrupt and the Winsford works of Leigh, Thompson & Done, which had fourteen pans, was advertised for sale; salt duties may have been a contributory factor.

The Marshall brothers, John and Thomas, were horrified when some family friends, the Mort-Wakefields, went bankrupt because of their inability to pay salt duties. Their father (the second Thomas Marshall), who wanted to regulate the trade on a more formal basis, had died before he could put his ideas fully into practice. When his sons took over the business in 1797, they were determined to carry on their father's work. In 1805 the Marshalls brokered an agreement between salt proprietors and Liverpool and Cheshire merchants to limit salt output and determine fixed prices and wages. Because brine production was concentrated in a comparatively small geographical area, the Marshalls and other salt proprietors could keep a tight grip on the amount of salt produced and the selling price.

Their newly formed Salt Traders' Association mostly dealt with brine salt shipped down the Weaver, because it was very difficult to police brine salt sent by road or by the Trent & Mersey Canal. A succession of agreements followed and output was slashed to keep prices high. Backsliding firms who tried to undercut the Association were fined, or undercut in their turn by the Association, even though it cost them money and renegades were priced out of the market. The agreement was tightened up in 1808.

The war caused more trading problems, so Thomas Marshall (the third) forged yet another association in 1813 to protect the salt industry. Although the association kept salt prices artificially high for their customers, keeping the trade on an even keel meant salt workers enjoyed good, steady rates of pay, unlike those working in more volatile industries. Marshall was in favour of retaining the salt excise;

he believed its repeal would open the floodgates to lots of new traders, increasing competition and perhaps leading to the demise of older firms.

After Napoleon's defeat in 1815, the salt trade was threatened by the general trade depression affecting the manufacturing industries. The salt proprietors, keen to keep profits up, formed another association two years later to strictly control and limit output and fix prices. Their customers had no option but to pay the prices asked. However, the gradual lifting of salt duties in 1817 encouraged free trade. Salt's growing importance as an industrial chemical and the huge administrative burden of the excise finally led to the tax's complete repeal in 1825. The salt manufacturers sent a last-minute petition against repeal, but the tax had run its course.

Marshall's fears proved correct. Newcomers like Charles William Neumann entered the industry and refused to knuckle down to the association. Customers benefited from new, low prices.

The cosy arrangements of the old salt interests were further disrupted by William Furnival's arrival on the scene. In his *Statement of Facts* written over a decade later, he told the story of his venture into the shark-infested waters of brine manufacture:

> My attention was first drawn to the manufacture of salt in the early part of 1822. I had ... been struck with the very imperfect manner in which it was carried on, and was astonished that, while such rapid improvement was taking place in other branches of manufacture, no attempts were made to effect it in the production of this essential article.

He visited several works in England and Scotland and discovered steam was coming into general use, especially to speed up the evaporation of fluids. Over the following decade, Furnival, James Tilt and others patented processes for using steam to evaporate salt from brine more quickly and efficiently. Furnival began making salt with his new process at Droitwich in 1823 and in the following year he took out a sixty-year lease on land at Anderton in Cheshire. He sunk shafts to look for brine, and made bricks for his planned new buildings. The British Rock and Salt Company bought out his Anderton business in 1825, but three years later Furnival bought land at Wharton, Winsford.

This was followed by another purchase at Marston, where he found 'some of the finest rock salt in the kingdom'. So Furnival now had two strings to his bow: he mined rock salt as well as pumping out brine. The Winsford site alone could produce 130,000 tons per year.

His success 'created a sensation through the whole salt trade … the old proprietors became seriously alarmed … They foresaw that the monopoly they had so long and uninterruptedly enjoyed must inevitably be destroyed, and their truly exorbitant profits abridged …'

Furnival alleged that a 'Coalition' of the major salt interests was formed between 1815 and 1827 to regulate prices and output. But he was determined to remain outside the 'Coalition'. They were equally determined to hold on to their monopoly. Conflict was inevitable.

Given the dates, and that the Marshalls so successfully regulated the trade until 1825, it seems highly likely that Furnival's 'Coalition' had links with, or at the very least shared some of the same members of, the Marshalls' association.

Furnival's account of his troubles must be taken with a pinch of salt. His *Statement of Facts* on the trade was written several years after the events, when an embittered Furnival was languishing in a debtor's prison. But his allegations against the salt trade are set down in great detail, and in view of previous restrictive practices, seem to have more than a grain of truth in them. Even allowing for some exaggeration, the language employed by both sides is more reminiscent of a pirate or gangster war than a disagreement between gentlemen.

The 'Coalition' set quotas for each salt works dependent on the size of the operation. Any proprietor who exceeded his quota had to pay a penalty of 6s per ton of excess production. The members also strictly enforced restrictions on their merchant customers. Manufacturers charged the merchants 3s per ton to convey the salt to Liverpool on their own (the salt owners') flats. Disgruntled salt merchants offered £10,000 to anyone who could break up the proprietors' monopoly.

When the Coalition learned Furnival's business was profitable, they 'viewed with a deadly hatred the man who had broken in upon their hitherto undisturbed monopoly.' In 1824, they slashed salt prices from 20s per ton to 14s. Two years later, prices plummeted to 9s, less than half their original level, even though the old salt men were losing money. Furnival claimed one proprietor swore 'he would lay by £4000 a year to accomplish my ruin'. At a Coalition crisis meeting, the members lamented the shockingly low price of salt, but they were determined not to raise the price again 'until Mr Furnival was disposed of'.

With 'a malignity scarcely to be conceived', the Coalition regulated their salt prices according to Furnival's output, like the rise and fall of a barometer. 'The moment they feared I was making progress, down went the price of salt. When they thought I was crushed by their arbitrary measures, or embarrassed beyond prospect of recovery, they raised the price again.'

The price of rock salt, too, was controlled in much the same way. Furnival even claimed the Coalition tried to 'drown' his mine by stopping their own brine engines from pumping, but he foiled their sabotage by lining the mine shaft with iron cylinders. One salt proprietor told Furnival's miners he wished Furnival 'was stiff at the bottom of it'. The alleged victimization even extended to his employees. An engineer employed by Furnival was a tenant on a farm owned by one of the salt proprietors and he was evicted from his home.

Furnival's new process of salt evaporation using 'the combined action of fire and steam' was a great success. His Winsford works produced four and a half tons of salt by burning one ton of coal; other manufacturers produced just two tons of salt from one of coal. When the Winsford works began production in 1831, the price of common salt fell to 10s per ton.

But the sharks were circling with a vengeance now; Furnival was in serious financial trouble, and going under. He leased out his Wharton and Marston works. However, the Coalition was also out of its depth; its members, deeply unhappy with their shrinking profits, fell out among themselves. Common salt plummeted to a rock-bottom 8s per ton – less than half its price six years earlier.

A combination of unlucky financial speculations in Britain and in Europe, and the machinations of a French con-man, led to Furnival's arrest in 1832. He spent years in the Horsemonger Lane prison in London for debt; the wily salt proprietors must have rubbed their hands with glee when he disappeared from the scene. Furnival himself, now increasingly paranoid, was convinced the salt men not only sent agents to kill off his Continental salt works, but also engineered his arrest. It isn't known what happened to this unlucky entrepreneur – he simply disappears from history.

While salt proprietors fought tooth and nail to maintain their market share, their mine shafts and brine pumping were storing up a sinister legacy for future generations. As more and more rock salt or brine was extracted, more and more subsidences were triggered. Brine pumping dissolved away the land far below the earth's surface. The huge troughs or hollows which appeared in the landscape filled up with rain or surface water to form lakes or 'flashes'. These depressions were on a much larger scale than the rock pit holes. At first, it seems, problems were fairly minor. At Weaverham, some ancient salt-works had caused some slight subsidence between the church and the River Weaver. The Trustees of the Weaver Navigation, who of necessity required a straight and level canal for their vessels, were worried by the subsidence of rock salt pits near Northwich Lock from the late 1750s. By 1790 there was marked subsidence along Witton Brook; this landslip was near, but not part of, the old rock pit holes. A few years later Witton Brook Lock, and Northwich Lock and weir had sunk and by 1800 the mill at Witton had sunk sixteen inches. There were problems at Anderton, too, which caused damage to the saltworks there.

An engineer for the Weaver Navigation, Samuel Fowls, discovered that a section of the land along the Witton Brook had sunk considerably by 1802. Nine years later, the Navigation Trustees received many complaints. The land at Witton Brook Lock had now sunk so much that water from the river was overflowing onto the meadows. Fowls was ordered to remove the lock, and lower the water level by four feet so that the meadows were dry again. The navigation channel was also deepened to ensure boats had sufficient depth of water for sailing in. Over the next thirty years, the land sank another twenty-four feet.

Ormerod was probably the first Cheshire historian to note the ever-growing problems at Northwich: '... large portions of land have subsided ... roads have been obstructed, and houses destroyed. Many buildings have been weakened and thrown out of the perpendicular ... others in the suburbs have been rendered completely uninhabitable.' At Winsford, there was evidence of subsidence at the Bottom Flash in 1820.

A disastrous rock salt mine collapse occurred just after our time period. In October 1838, Ashton's mine at Northwich swallowed up several buildings, including the engine house, and twelve workers, seven of whom died. It was a dire warning of much worse to come.

But in the meantime, business boomed. At the turn of the century, production from the salt fields was 150,000 tons per annum. By 1823, salt production had doubled to 300,000 tons. The repeal of salt duty, falling prices and increasing industrial demand helped boost the market for salt and production sky-rocketed. Rock salt was beginning to be mined out, but the vast reservoirs of brine in the old workings could be exploited.

Winsford in particular benefited from the lifting of the salt tax in 1825 and five years later, it was sending over 143,000 tons of white salt down the Weaver. From the 1840s onwards a combination of commercial factors and worsening subsidence problems led to Winsford toppling Northwich from its position as top salt producer in the county. Cheshire maintained its place as the chief salt-making centre, with sixty works in the mid-nineteenth century; by this time the Winsford works alone produced over 331,500 tons annually.

Salt's journey from humble foodstuff to major industrial chemical was complete – a real recipe for success.

14

Full Steam Ahead

On 1 October 1827, a vast crowd assembled in Chester along the banks of the Dee. The band played, people cheered, and a twelve-gun salute and volleys of ammunition were fired as Earl Grosvenor laid the foundation stone for Thomas Harrison's new bridge across the Dee. Harrison, now a tired old man in his eighties, was too infirm to attend the ceremony. His breathtakingly beautiful design was a daring leap of faith in sandstone. For over thirty years, this 200ft arch was the longest single-span stone bridge in the world.

This was the official stone-laying; the very first stone had actually been put in place a couple of weeks earlier. The *Courant* (18 September 1827) had been dismayed by the lack of fanfare – very few people were present – and shocked because the men were working on Sundays. 'The first stone of the new bridge was most ingloriously laid, by candle-light, at eight o'clock on Saturday last, without the depositing of coins, the affixing of a plate of brass, to hand down to after ages, and admiring generations yet unborn, the name of the ingenious architect ...'

Controversy had surrounded the bridge's construction. It was needed because the old Dee bridge was choked with traffic from North Wales. The steep hill on the Handbridge side of the river culminated in a sharp, narrow turn and the lower part of Bridge St was also steep, and dangerous for carriages. (It was along this route that General Grosvenor's carriage cannoned into his opponents during election time.)

Competition from Telford's speedy new Holyhead road via Shrewsbury meant the city faced losing business. The corporation tinkered with the problem for a long time. An 1808 design by Welsh architect Thomas Penson for a new bridge was quietly dropped after his bridge over the Dee at Overton fell down five years later. Instead, the corporation spent money on widening and resurfacing the old Dee bridge.

Finally, the assembly conceded that the best solution to the perennial traffic problems was a brand new crossing linked to the city centre. A public meeting was held at the Exchange in 1818 to discuss a new bridge, but the scheme met with violent opposition. Landowners who owned properties in Lower Bridge St and Handbridge, which would lose trade if the new route was built, opposed it because they feared property values would fall. The plan fell by the wayside.

After 1819 work began to upgrade the coast road from Chester to Holyhead. The perilous Conway ferry crossing was to be replaced by Telford's beautiful bridge (1826) opposite the castle. The Dee bridge was clearly the weak point along this route. So a committee was formed at Chester to oversee plans for an extra crossing. In the summer of 1825, Parliament gave the assembly permission to construct the new bridge.

Thomas Harrison submitted plans for the crossing and buildings along the new route. His first design was for an iron bridge. After many discussions and more plans, Harrison put forward his pioneering stone design. The committee had qualms; although the concept of a stone arch wasn't new, such a wide span had never been attempted before with just one arch. A model of the new bridge was built by Staffordshire engineer James Trubshaw to try to convince the committee of the bridge's durability. (The model was displayed in the Grand Jury room of the Shire Hall for several years and it now has a home on Castle Drive.)

The committee still dithered and a brick bridge by engineer Marc Brunel was under consideration for a time. Harrison, fed up with the many delays, resigned his position as chief engineer early in 1826, citing his old age and ill health. One of his protégés, William Cole, and engineers Jesse Hartley and James Trubshaw took over the project. Thomas Telford was also consulted about the proposed site and costs. At last work began on this 'magnificent structure' in 1827, with minor adjustments to Harrison's design.[1] The bridge was under construction for six years. It was built mainly from Cheshire limestone; the voussoirs (wedge-shaped arch stones) were of Scottish granite. Sadly, Harrison didn't live to see his beautiful design completed.

The scheme was a harbinger of things to come. Nothing, not even a church, was allowed to get in the way of progress. St Bridget's Church, which dated back to at least the twelfth century (possibly even back to King Offa's time), was knocked down in 1827 to make room for the new road to the bridge. The church's graveyard was disturbed and gravestones and bodies were moved to the new church site. A new St Bridget's was erected – a simple classical design by Cole.

The citizens of Chester were very proud of their bridge and new road, which were named after the Grosvenor family. But the advent of steam trains was beginning to cast a shadow on the turnpikes' and canals' future prosperity.

Cheshire's waterway system was not yet fully complete. Anxiety about the threat from railways led to the construction of the Birmingham and Liverpool Junction Canal in 1828. The new canal's route went south through the county. It linked the Ellesmere & Chester Canal at Nantwich to Tettenhall on the Staffordshire & Worcestershire Canal. The idea was to speed up goods traffic between the Midlands and the River Mersey.

The long-awaited Middlewich junction (1831) linking the Chester Canal to the Midlands came too late to preserve the long-term future of Chester's canal traffic. On the plus side, the Weaver Navigation continued its success story and its trustees enjoyed increasing profits from coal and salt.

The earliest railed roads in the county, such as the one at Poynton in the 1790s, were for horse-drawn wagons doing the donkey work at quarries and collieries. During their infancy, railways weren't necessarily directly competing with canals. They were often designed to complement the existing canal network. As early as 1806, two horse-powered tram-roads were planned to link the Chester Canal with collieries at Apedale in Staffordshire and ironworks at Silverdale via the Newcastle-under-Lyme Canal. (The Apedale collieries carried coals to Newcastle along Sir Nigel Gresley's Canal.) These tram-roads would have converged near Audley but the plan never got off the ground.

A myriad of railway schemes to carve up the Cheshire countryside were floated as railway mania began to grip, but only a few came to fruition. The *Macclesfield Courier* (22 November) reported plans in 1828 for the Stockport Junction Railway. The idea was to connect the Liverpool & Manchester Railway with the Cromford High Peak Railway. But this plan hit the buffers two years later after encountering opposition from local landowners in the House of Commons. Stockport had to wait for more than a decade for its first railway station at Heaton Norris, on the Manchester & Birmingham Railway.

Three years later, a bill for a railway between Liverpool and Chorlton was presented to parliament. This plan was scuppered by the Weaver Navigation trustees and the owners of Mersey and Weaver flats, who had most to lose from the project.

Railway projects not only had to contend with opposition from other transport interests, but also from fears about the new hissing, snorting steam engines. Farmers were afraid that their cows would stop giving milk, horses would be startled, and birds would drop down dead in mid-flight. When George Stephenson surveyed the Nantwich area, which formed part of the projected Grand Junction Railway route in 1824, he discovered that canal company agents had got there before him. They had warned all the local farmers that the new locomotives were: 'most frightful' machines, with 'a breath as poisonous as the fabled dragon of old'.[2]

The first completed railway through Cheshire was the Grand Junction. However, it took years of campaigning to get the project successfully on track. A group of Birmingham businessmen first proposed a railway to join Liverpool and Birmingham via Chester in 1824, but the plan came off the rails when it encountered fierce opposition from canal proprietors. Another proposal with a slightly different route two years later met with a similar response. The runaway success of the Liverpool & Manchester Railway led to the idea's revival by some Liverpool businessmen. After more setbacks, it was decided to begin the route at Warrington Bank Quay, the terminus of the Warrington and Newton Railway. This recently opened railway, engineered by Robert Stephenson, linked Warrington to the Liverpool & Manchester Railway. The new route to Birmingham, now called the Grand Junction Railway, opened on 4 July 1837.

The rural village of Monks Coppenhall, near the old township of Crewe, had fewer than 150 inhabitants in 1831. Monks Coppenhall was earmarked as a suitable place for a junction for the various railways then in the planning stages and the village was transformed into the railway town of Crewe.

Plans to join Chester and Birkenhead by rail were bitterly contested by the Grand Junction Railway. A prospectus for the Chester & Liverpool Railway was published in the *Chronicle* on 26 November 1830. (Passengers went to Liverpool by ferry from Birkenhead.) The engineer for the line was George Stephenson and shares in the proposed line were for sale for £100. The railway's proposers hoped to cut travel time between Chester and Birkenhead by two-thirds. But Chester had to wait another decade to become part of the railway network. The Chester & Birkenhead Railway finally opened in September 1840. The Grand Junction Railway opened their branch from Chester to Crewe a month later. The county's landscape was changed forever as railway mania increased its grip.

New towns mushroomed into existence around important industries and transport hubs. The spread of Liverpool was mirrored by industrial growth on the opposite shore of the Mersey estuary, an example being Johnson's soap-works (1803) at Runcorn, which went on to become the vast soap and chemicals firm.

When Ormerod wrote his *History*, he praised the sea views from the Wirral coastline. But away from the main turnpike roads, communications were poor: its clayey lanes were cattle tracks. The houses were 'hovels' and the poorer people's appearance was 'extremely squalid'. Liverpool's success had the knock-on effect of transforming Birkenhead, Bebington and Wallasey into prosperous towns.

The village of Birkenhead was home to a few straggling houses and a population of just over a hundred souls in 1801. The hamlet was transformed after George La French began the first steam packet service between Birkenhead and Liverpool in 1821. Two years later, there were daily steam packets sailing to and from Runcorn, Birkenhead and Eastham. At the beginning of the 1830s, Rock Ferry boasted a smart new pier, improved roads, and steam packet services to Liverpool. Now Liverpool was just a short hop from rural Cheshire and its merchants moved out to the Wirral to enjoy the seaside and country air. The population of the hundred of Wirral was 10,444 in 1801; three decades later it had almost doubled to 19,014.

Although the steam packets were a success, the change in Birkenhead's fortunes really date from the arrival of Mr William Laird. Laird, originally from Greenock, owned boiler-making and ship-repairing businesses in Liverpool. In 1824, Laird bought a large tract of land bordering the shore at Wallasey Pool from the lord of the manor, Francis Price. A shrewd Liverpool merchant, Sir John Tobin, bought up the rest of the land along the shoreline. The following year, Laird founded a ship-building and boiler-making yard at Wallasey. Laird saw iron's potential as a ship-building material and his foresight was to have a huge impact on the Wirral's future prosperity.

Liverpool's runaway success meant that dockside accommodation there was at a premium and ships queued for days waiting to unload their cargoes. Laird and Tobin planned to create a new harbour and docks at Wallasey Pool to exploit Liverpool's embarrassment of riches. Some Liverpool ship-builders who had a rocky relationship with their journeymen shipwrights also set up business at Wallasey Pool. A slip was constructed so vessels needing repair could be hauled out.

Once William Laird's ship-building business was under way, he realized he needed a town to provide services for the works and for his planned docks. So Laird purchased a large quantity of land (in the centre of modern-day Birkenhead). He hoped to build his new town: 'in a style of magnificence unsurpassed in this part of the kingdom'.[3] Architect James Gillespie Graham planned out Hamilton Square and the adjoining streets. Progress with the new town was much slower than originally planned, but by 1831 Birkenhead's population had increased to over 2,500.

In the meantime, engineers Thomas Telford, his protégé Nimmo (an Irishman), and Robert Stephenson were called in during 1827 to survey the area and draw up plans for the docks. A startlingly bold plan to build a ship canal was under serious consideration. The canal would slice across the Wirral to link up Wallasey with another new harbour on the Dee at Hilbre. The idea was to avoid the perilous voyage threading through the sandbanks of the Mersey estuary and provide safe harbour for vessels while loading and unloading.

This eye-wateringly expensive scheme for docks and canal (over £1.4 million) soon ran into trouble, however. Liverpool Corporation caught wind of the plans in 1828. Rumours of a new joint-stock company to fund a new port to rival Liverpool spurred its mayor and councillors into action. The corporation borrowed money to buy up the land at Wallasey earmarked for docks. It seems they gave some vague assurances to Price, the chief landowner, that some kind of dock scheme would definitely go ahead. William Laird, who may have been discouraged by the cost of the Telford scheme, sold his land at a profit to the corporation. Of course, Tobin and other landowners were left with little option but to sell the remaining land involved. Strangely enough, once the corporation had bought up all the requisite land, it decided Liverpool didn't really need any more docks for some time to come. The Birkenhead dock scheme was over.

Although his dock scheme had failed, Laird's ship-building works prospered. His first iron ship for the American market, the *John Randolph*, was finished in 1834. But the Laird family had the last laugh. The land at Wallasey and the debt incurred by Liverpool Corporation for its purchase became a millstone around its collective neck. Later in the century they sold off the land to William Laird's son John and a firm of dock developers. The Birkenhead Dock Bill passed through Parliament in 1844.

Over the county as a whole, the 1831 census figures showed the population was still rising: from 270,100 in 1821 to 334,400 a decade later. Chester's population (21,300) was only growing modestly.

But in the manufacturing towns, industrial sprawl proceeded unchecked. Textile towns such as Dukinfield and Hyde were in the throes of a population explosion. Hyde's population leapt from 1,800 in 1810 to 7,100 twenty years later. The population of the Dukinfield and Stalybridge area (they were lumped together until 1836 for statistical purposes) rocketed from 1,730 in 1801 to 14,700 in 1831. The population of Stockport had risen to 25,469 (over 36,000 if we include Heaton Norris).

Macclesfield's population total was now over 23,000: almost triple the 1801 figure. Although the trade depression of the late 1820s had slowed the rate of increase, the town was beginning to gobble up the countryside and Macclesfield Hunt was forced to disband in 1825 because it was running out of fox country.

Diseases such as typhus, scarlet fever and smallpox were unwelcome and frequent visitors in the crowded slums. Britain's first cholera outbreak in 1831 caused much hand-wringing. Cholera terrified people – it didn't distinguish between rich and poor. New hospitals were clearly needed, as some of the existing ones were unable to cope with epidemics. At Chester, some temporary hospitals were constructed after the infirmary, presumably worried by the threat of cross-infection, refused to admit cholera patients. Stockport's infirmary was already overflowing with patients, so a new cholera hospital was built at Daw Bank during the following year. Work also began on a new Stockport Infirmary, built in the neoclassical style and opened in 1833.

But little was done by the authorities to tackle the underlying causes which provided breeding grounds for diseases: inadequate water supplies, poor housing and lack of sanitation. Macclesfield in particular suffered terribly from the cholera outbreak. Stockport recorded a comparatively small number of deaths, just thirty. Congleton was lucky – a public thanksgiving was held in November 1832 for the town's escape from the terrible disease.

Another problem associated with population growth was its effect on the poor rates. Cheshire had over 450 distinct poor law districts. A combination of population growth and the trade slump after the end of the wars meant there was an ever-growing burden on the poor rates. In 1801, total expenditure for Cheshire poor was £66,627 and the average amount spent on each person was 6s 11d. (This is about a third less than the national average of 9s 1d per head.) By 1831, the total county expenditure had reached £103,572, but the average amount spent per head was 6s 2d (still way below the national average of 9s 9d that year). So although far more people were being given parish relief, on average less was being spent on each person. However, because prices had fallen in the intervening three decades, it is nevertheless the case that more was being spent on the poor in real terms.[4]

Hemingway had written of the kindly regime at the Chester poorhouse for the aged and infirm. The inmates of individual workhouses usually varied according to the needs of the district. In the Macclesfield area, workhouses co-operated so that the Rainow workhouse took in elderly paupers, the Sutton workhouse looked after child paupers, and the Macclesfield institution housed adults.

Under the 'out-door' system of relief, in which the poor were given help while still living in their own home, the overseers in towns like Stockport distributed food and clothes, or provided medical care for those in dire need. Pauper children were apprenticed out and odd jobs were found for unemployed labourers. Sometimes the overseers might provide a poor family with the means to earn some money by purchasing a loom or spinning wheel. In the poorhouse, for those unable to work, the overseers provided a basic if boring diet: tea, potatoes, beef, bread and milk.

But the system became increasingly unable to cope as the population grew, particularly in the industrial towns. If trade was slack, hundreds of people might be thrown out of work at once. And if people lost their homes through unemployment, the large numbers of homeless meant the workhouses became ever more overcrowded and squalid. At Macclesfield, old and young, sick and well were huddled together in disgraceful conditions.

As the poor rates mounted, government intervened with an overhaul of the poor laws. The Poor Law Amendment Act of 1834 was a cost-cutting exercise. It abolished the system of out-door relief. Able-bodied paupers would only receive help if they and their families went into the workhouse. New workhouses were built but conditions were deliberately made so forbidding that only those in direst need would enter the 'Bastilles', as they were dubbed by the workers. The sexes were segregated, which meant that families were broken up.

The new Poor Law met huge resistance in the northern manufacturing districts of Lancashire and Cheshire and the system of out-door relief continued for some time in the north west. Opposition was based not only on a belief that the new system was uncaring and brutal, but also on anger that the government was interfering in local affairs. Towns like Macclesfield believed that the old system, however imperfect, worked after a fashion. So Macclesfield dragged its heels for several years and its corporation refused to build a new workhouse.

If trade was good, the workers found jobs, and the burden on the poor rates eased. After the 1820s slump, the cotton industry recovered early in the next decade. Stockport enjoyed a brief boom and several new mills were built in the town centre and further out, including Ralph Orrell's mill at Heaton Norris.

The Greg family concern at Styal had continued to expand, founding mills at Lancaster, Bollington and Bury. But the firm suffered in the aftermath of the banking crash of 1825–6 when yarn prices plummeted. Powerlooms were only installed after Samuel Greg's death, perhaps because the patriarch didn't want the expense of further capital outlay after the firm's meteoric expansion. The late introduction of power weaving adversely affected the firm's profitability. Greg's sons Robert, John, William and Samuel were already partners in the business, so in theory the firm should have been set fair for a prosperous future after its founder's death.

Robert Hyde Greg's introduction of powerlooms turned around Quarry Bank Mill's fortunes. But William and Samuel lacked business acumen; they weren't temperamentally suited to be mill-owners. Just a few years after Samuel senior's death in 1834, the firm of Samuel Greg & Co. was broken up and the brothers took one mill each as their own business.

The Greg family maintained a paternal interest in their employees. Robert Hyde Greg constructed more housing at Styal and Samuel Greg Jr worked hard to provide good living conditions for his Lowerhouse Mill workers at Bollington. He modernized the workers' cottages, founded a Sunday school, and looked after their general well-being. But his mill failed to make a profit. Samuel was bitterly hurt when his workers struck after he introduced new machinery. Heartbroken and in debt, he retired from the cotton business. William also struggled to make a profit with his mill and he left the industry. Robert and John remained to ensure the Greg name lived on in the Cheshire cotton industry.

Mills and factories continued to be a dangerous place to work. Stockport Infirmary recorded 120 admissions from factory accidents in just one year (1837–8). Many injuries (especially the loss of fingers) were caused because the operatives were expected to clean the machinery while it was in motion. A Select Committee in 1841 reported the case of one little girl in Stockport who was crippled for life after her clothing was caught up in unguarded machinery. She was carried round an upright shaft and both her thighs were broken and her ankles dislocated.

The silk trade continued to suffer ups and downs after the reduction of silk tariffs. By 1835, Cheshire had eighty-eight factories employing over 10,700 workers (around 2,500 of these were children aged eight to twelve years; over 6,100 were women).[5] Silk weaving technology continued to improve until 'it was clear to unprejudiced eyes that the

English silks had become superior to the French,' and France became an importer of English silk.[6] The Brocklehursts and other Macclesfield firms won prizes for their beautiful silks later in the century at the Great Exhibition of 1851.

We have seen how agitation for parliamentary reform, both peaceful and violent, was met by the authorities in the un-enfranchised towns of Stockport and Macclesfield. During the 1820s, Lord John Russell made several attempts to push electoral reforms through parliament.

In the summer of 1830, the country was in a state of crisis and workers were starving and desperate. A succession of bad harvests sparked the 'Swing' riots over a vast area of southern England. (The cry for reform wasn't confined to the industrial north west.)

Another revolution in France this year terrified the ruling classes. The Whigs finally grasped the nettle and made reform the keystone of their policies. The middle classes, equally alarmed by events on the Continent, believed reform was the only way to stop a revolution happening here. Radical William Cobbett summed up the situation: 'The country was full of discontent, which was at last concentrated in a cry for parliamentary reform.'

The country's pressing affairs were momentarily arrested by the death of George IV on 26 June 1830, after a long illness. The flags at Chester Castle were displayed at half mast and the Great Bell of the cathedral tolled a dirge. The Cheshire newspaper editors added black edging to their columns to show their respect. Both papers printed a potted biography of the King, with a retrospective look at his reign: 'George the Fourth is no more – the Sovereign who, in the capacity of the Regent and King swayed the sceptre during the most eventful period of her history – the period of her greatest perils and her greatest glory – has passed from this scene ...'[7]

The *Chronicle* paid tribute to George IV's liberal support of the arts: 'The highest in the land has fallen before the relentless dart of Death ... never did a liberal patron, by refined taste and liberality, stimulate personal genius to noblest enterprise so efficiently as the generous and accomplished Monarch, King George the Fourth.'[8] The editors only briefly alluded to more controversial events such as the Queen's trial.

They seemed content to attribute the late King's faults to his over-strict upbringing and the bad influence of his early friends. It was perhaps time to bury his mistakes with him.

The late monarch was mourned by few. When George IV was buried on 15 July with due pomp and ceremony, it was alleged that the chief mourner at the service, his brother William, could barely conceal his joy at becoming King. The London shops closed, but otherwise the capital showed little disposition to mourn their sovereign lord. Cobbett commented that the day of the funeral, a beautiful summer's day, was treated almost as an unofficial holiday. Carriages and wagonloads of people went out for the day and enjoyed themselves.

The King's death was followed by the dissolution of Parliament. The pressure for reform continued. All seemed lost when the Tories were returned to government yet again, and the Duke of Wellington became Prime Minister. But the Duke's opposition to reform meant that he was quickly forced to retreat to another billet. When the Whigs finally gained control of Westminster in 1831, after many years of Tory government, the lower and middle classes held their breath. Surely reform must come at last?

A Reform Committee was set up early in 1831 and its proposals were announced on 1 March. The extent of the planned reforms, which were top secret until the last minute, stunned even Whig supporters like the Grosvenors. Sixty rotten boroughs were weeded out and over forty boroughs with few voters but several seats had their number of MPs curtailed. Unrepresented towns such as Manchester, Leeds and Stockport were enfranchised.

The planned Reform Bill caused uproar among supporters and critics alike. But the country had set its heart on it and the middle and working classes united to demand the Bill's passage. In Cheshire, petitions in favour of reform were sent to the House of Commons, and addresses sent to the King. Chester citizens showed their displeasure with the independent Sir Philip Egerton of Oulton in the 1831 election. Sir Philip, a Tory, had been a great favourite with the public when elected MP the previous year. But he 'greatly exasperated his constituents' by repeatedly voting against the Reform Bill.[9] The tide of public opinion against him became so strong that his friends advised him not to stand for re-election. Sir Philip's seat was won by Foster Cunliffe Offley, no doubt aided by his purchase of the freedom of the city for over one hundred young men.

It took three attempts to get the Reform Bill through a reluctant House of Lords. Amid massive rioting and popular tumult, and in spite of desperate Tory opposition and the fury of William IV, the new Bill became law on 7 June 1832.

The Act promised a fresh dawn for politics and a widening of parliamentary representation. Cheshire's parliamentary seats were increased from four to ten. The county was divided into two constituencies, north and south Cheshire; each constituency had two seats. The north Cheshire constituency was formed from the hundreds of Macclesfield and Bucklow. The south Cheshire constituency was composed of the Northwich, Eddisbury, Nantwich, Broxton and the Wirral hundreds. Chester city retained its two seats and in addition, Stockport and Macclesfield boroughs were given two seats each.

The momentous 1832 elections went ahead with the usual allegations of bribery and vote-rigging. The Chester papers were up to all their old tricks. The Whig *Chronicle* rallied support for the Grosvenors and their friends while the *Courant* supported the Tories. Each editor used scurrilous invective against his rival, while supporting his favourite candidates with stomach-churning partiality. (The *Chronicle*, in a special election supplement, said Lord Richard Grosvenor was like 'a lion roused from his lair that rises in his might' while addressing the voters.)[10] The issue of reform was of course a major campaigning point. To their eternal credit, the Whig Grosvenor family supported reform up to the hilt, even though the demise of pocket boroughs greatly reduced their political influence.

The campaign was hard fought and it went on for weeks. After tremendous efforts (which included the traditional treating of the voters by both sides) Robert Grosvenor (later Baron Ebury, the third son of Earl Grosvenor) and John Jervis, both Whigs, were elected for Chester. Richard Grosvenor (now Lord Grosvenor) and the Whig George Wilbraham of Delamere House won Cheshire South, trouncing the opposition, Sir Philip Egerton. Cheshire North was won by Whigs Edward Stanley of Alderley, a supporter of the abolition of slavery, and William Tatton Egerton of Tatton Hall.

In the manufacturing towns, the new Act proved to be a bitter disappointment for the working classes. They had watched the vicissitudes of the Reform Bill with huge interest, and with dismay each time it seemed doomed to failure. When the second Reform Bill failed to pass the House of Lords in October 1831, a noisy public meeting was held at the Macclesfield Guildhall in protest.

There wasn't a general consensus in favour of the Bill, however. Not only was it opposed by the Tories, but some angry Radicals felt the government's proposals didn't go far enough. Henry Hunt visited Stockport and Macclesfield in 1831 to campaign against the Bill.

The workers' wish for universal male suffrage had fallen on stony ground. Although the Great Reform Act gave an extra half a million people the right to vote, the voting qualification was restricted to men with property worth at least £10. The Whigs had been anxious for reform because they hoped the enfranchisement of the middle classes would help to end the endemic cronyism and influence of the Crown. But the Whigs were resolutely against allowing workers to have a vote, believing that revolution would inevitably follow. The new House of Commons was still an upper-class hunting ground, albeit with rather more Whigs than previously and a sprinkling of new Radical faces such as the redoubtable William Cobbett, the new MP for Oldham.

The workers felt cheated. The property qualification meant that in Stockport, only just over 930 men out of 36,600 were entitled to vote. The polls took place amid window smashing and vandalism. A pitched battle broke out in the marketplace and several people were badly hurt. The candidates were the mill-owner Major Thomas Marsland of Daw Bank (Tory), the ostensibly radical John Horatio Lloyd (son of the Radicals' implacable foe) and the Whig Henry Marsland, son of mill-owner Peter Marsland of Park Mills. Lloyd and Major Thomas Marsland won the election.

At Macclesfield, the situation was very similar: around 1,000 men now had the vote. The election was fought between two silk manufacturers, the Whig John Brocklehurst and the Tory John Ryle, and the solicitor Thomas Grimsditch, a Tory. Amid huge clamour in the town, Brocklehurst and Ryle were elected and the Brocklehurst family went on to represent Macclesfield in Parliament for many years to come.

Unsurprisingly the Reform Act, with its limited franchise, didn't bring any respite from industrial unrest and violence. In the late 1830s,

Stockport, Macclesfield and Hyde became fertile breeding grounds for the growing Chartist movement. Congleton silk workers, too, took part in Chartist agitation even though there was an upturn in the economy. The workers struck, mills closed down, and houses were left tenantless.

Everything had changed, but nothing had changed. Although the county's MPs now included businessmen and mill-owners, the voting system was still highly exclusive and open to abuse. Several decades were to pass before a secret ballot was introduced and the lower classes had to wait until the twentieth century before they were allowed to vote.

The death of George IV marked more than just the death of the monarch, it was the end of an era. It was as if the inimitable style of the Regency was buried with its chief gentleman. Sir Walter Scott died in the same year and Jane Austen, John Keats, Percy Bysshe Shelley and Lord Byron had already passed away. The age of the Romantics was over; novelists such as Mrs Gaskell, the Brontë sisters, George Eliot and Charles Dickens ushered in a new interest in social realism.

A new moral imperative had taken root. The Evangelical movement, which had flourished during the Georgian period in towns like Macclesfield and Stockport, helped to change social attitudes. The excesses of the Regency, with its drinking, gambling, corruption and loose women, were frowned on. Reformers like William Wilberforce and Hannah More waged war on vice and slavery was abolished. The Sunday schools which taught the lower classes how to read and write also reminded them of their duties and proper place in society. The pragmatic Christian morality of the middle classes spread onwards and upwards, even breaching the bastions of high society. The Victorian age was already under way before George IV breathed his last.

The future arrived in the form of a fresh-faced princess. In October 1832 the people of Cheshire – high and low, young and old, Whig and Tory, farmers and labourers – forgot their differences for a day. They united to give young Princess Victoria a real hearty Cheshire welcome. Chester was jammed solid with wellwishers as the Princess, accompanied by her mother, the Duchess of Kent, was driven in her carriage through the city streets. The sun shone, flags fluttered in the breeze, and the Rows of Chester were decked with flowers and laurel leaves.

On 17 October, Princess Victoria officially opened the new Grosvenor Bridge across the Dee. Lord Robert Grosvenor, mounted on horseback, led the royal cortege across the bridge, which was adorned with a triumphal arch. As the Princess's carriage reached the arch, the royal standard was hoisted to its summit. The Mayor of Chester requested his eminent visitors to name the bridge. The Princess replied: 'I seize the occasion of our being the first persons to pass over this magnificent Bridge … to name it Grosvenor Bridge.'[11]

It was a symbolic moment. The 13-year-old Princess already knew how to please the crowds and she offered a fresh start for Britain. For the crowds who cheered, 'Long live the Princess Victoria!', those racy Regency days had faded into history. A new age with its own distinct values, fashions and follies had begun.

Notes

CHAPTER 1

1. John Britton and Edward W. Brayley, *The Beauties of England and Wales* (Vernor & Hood, 1803)
2. John Corry, *The History of Macclesfield* (unknown, 1817)
3. Charles Knight, *Popular History of England* (Bradbury and Evans, 1856)
4. *Chester Chronicle*, 5 January 1821
5. Corry, *History of Macclesfield*
6. Corry, *History of Macclesfield*
7. Corry, *History of Macclesfield*
8. Corry, *History of Macclesfield*
9. *Chester Guardian*, 10 February 1820
10. *Chester Guardian*, 3 February 1820
11. Venetia Murray, *High Society: Social History of the Regency Period, 1788–1830* (Viking, 1998)

CHAPTER 2

1. Britton and Brayley, *Beauties of England and Wales*
2. Henry Smithers, *Liverpool, Its Commerce, Statistics, and Institutions; with a History of the Cotton Trade* (Thomas Kaye, 1825)
3. G. Batenham, *A Stranger's Companion in Chester* (G. Batenham, 1828)
4. George Alexander Cooke, *Topographical and Statistical Description of the County of Chester* (c.1803)
5. Cooke, *Topographical and Statistical Description*
6. Corry, *History of Macclesfield*
7. George Slater, *Chronicles of Lives and Religion in Cheshire and Elsewhere* (Andrew Crombie, 1891)
8. Thomas Percival Bunting, *The Life of Jabez Bunting, D.D: With notices of contemporary persons and events* (A. & C. Black, 1859)
9. Slater, *Chronicles*
10. Corry, *History of Macclesfield*
11. Corry, *History of Macclesfield*
12. Joseph Hemingway, *History of the City of Chester, from its foundation to the present time* (unknown, 1831)
13. Cooke, *Topographical and Statistical Description*
14. W. Cowdroy, *Directory and Guide to the City and County of Chester* (Cowdroy, 1789)
15. A letter to the *Christian Observer* (1848), pp. 658–9, from S. Higginbotham cited evidence that Simpson gave Sunday school classes as early as 1778

16. Hemingway, *History of the City of Chester*
17. *Cheshire Courant*, 22 September 1818
18. *Cheshire Courant*, 5 April 1796
19. *Cheshire Courant*, 2 June 1818
20. Cowdroy, *Directory and Guide*
21. Cowdroy, *Directory and Guide*
22. Hemingway, *History of the City of Chester*
23. Cooke, *Topographical and Statistical Description*
24. *Chester Guardian*, 20 and 27 January 1820
25. *Chester Courant*, 5 April 1796
26. Cowdroy, *Directory and Guide*
27. *Chester Chronicle*, 6 March 1818
28. *Chester Chronicle*, 12 May 1826
29. *Chester Guardian*, 13 January 1820
30. *Chester Guardian*, 20 January 1820

CHAPTER 3

1. Thomas Pennant, *Tours in Wales* (H. Humphreys, 1883)
2. Pennant, *Tours in Wales*
3. *Chester Courant*, 7 July 1794
4. Hemingway, *History of the City of Chester*
5. Thomas Pennant, *The Journey from Chester to London* (Wilkie and Robinson et al., 1811)
6. Thomas Hughes, *Stranger's Handbook to Chester and its Environs* (E.J. Morten Publishers; reprint of 1856 edition, 1972)
7. Batenham, *Stranger's Companion*
8. Pennant, *Tours in Wales*
9. Hemingway, *History of the City of Chester*
10. Batenham, *Stranger's Companion*
11. G. Batenham, *A Visit to the Cathedral Church of Chester* (unknown, 1823)
12. Corry, *History of Macclesfield*
13. George Ormerod, *History of the County Palatine and City of Chester* (G. Routledge, 1882)
14. Britton and Brayley, *Beauties of England and Wales*
15. *Chester Chronicle*, 24 April 1812
16. Cooke, *Topographical and Statistical Description*
17. Corry, *History of Macclesfield*
18. Cooke, *Topographical and Statistical Description*
19. *Chester Chronicle*, 24 April 1812
20. *Chester Courant*, 21 April 1812

CHAPTER 4

1. Cowdroy, *Directory and Guide*
2. Batenham, *Stranger's Companion*
3. Corry, *History of Macclesfield*
4. Batenham, *Stranger's Companion*
5. Cowdroy, *Directory and Guide*
6. *Chester Chronicle*, 9 October 1795

7. *Chester Chronicle*, 15 May 1812
8. *Chester Courant*, 7 December 1819
9. *Chester Courant*, 8 July 1794
10. *Chester Chronicle*, 1 May 1812
11. *Chester Chronicle*, 9 December 1796
12. Charles James Apperley ('Nimrod'), *Memoirs of the Life of the Late John Mytton, Esq.* (Methuen & Co. Ltd, 1949)
13. Cowdroy, *Directory and Guide*
14. *Chester Courant*, 22 March 1803
15. Cowdroy, *Directory and Guide*
16. *Chester Courant*, 25 August 1818
17. Cooke, *Topographical and Statistical Description*
18. *Chester Chronicle*, 28 April 1826
19. *Chester Courant*, 17 August 1819
20. *Chester Courant*, 9 June 1818
21. *Chester Chronicle*, 15 May 1829
22. Corry, *History of Macclesfield*
23. *Chester Chronicle*, 10 April 1829
24. *Chester Chronicle*, 4 September 1818
25. *Chester Courant*, 28 July 1818

CHAPTER 5

1. Hemingway, *History of the City of Chester*
2. *Chester Chronicle*, 27 March 1829
3. Hemingway, *History of the City of Chester*
4. Hemingway, *History of the City of Chester*
5. Hemingway, *History of the City of Chester*
6. Hemingway, *History of the City of Chester*
7. *Chester Courant*, 14 April 1812
8. Hemingway, *History of the City of Chester*
9. *Chester Courant*, 2 June 1818
10. *Chester Chronicle*, 12 June 1818
11. *Chester Chronicle*, 3 July 1818
12. *Chester Courant*, 30 June 1818
13. *Chester Chronicle*, 3 July 1818
14. *The Times*, 29 October 1818
15. *Chester Chronicle*, 29 October 1819
16. *Chester Guardian*, 9 March 1820
17. *Chester Guardian*, 24 August 1820
18. Hemingway, *History of the City of Chester*
19. Hemingway, *History of the City of Chester*
20. Hemingway, *History of the City of Chester*

CHAPTER 6

1. *Chester Guardian*, 7 September 1820
2. *Chester Guardian*, 14 September 1820
3. *Chester Guardian*, 16 November 1820
4. Britton and Brayley, *Beauties of England and Wales*

5. *Macclesfield Courier*, 12 April 1823
6. *Macclesfield Courier*, 18 April 1812
7. *Chester Courant*, 14 and 21 April 1812
8. *Chester Courant*, 5 May 1812
9. *Edinburgh Annual Register*, 1812
10. *Macclesfield Courier*, 19 April 1823
11. *Chester Chronicle*, 10 April 1818
12. *Chester Chronicle*, 4 September 1818
13. William Hone, *The Every Day Book and Table Book* (unknown, 1827)
14. *Chester Chronicle*, 24 April 1812
15. J.P. Earwaker, *East Cheshire: Past and Present* (printed for the author, 1877)
16. *Edinburgh Annual Register*, 1826
17. *Annual Register*, 1827
18. *Chester Chronicle*, 30 March 1827

CHAPTER 7

1. *Chester Chronicle*, 30 December 1796
2. Corry, *History of Macclesfield*
3. *Chester Chronicle*, 25 November 1796
4. *Chester Chronicle*, 9 December 1803
5. *Chester Chronicle*, 14 March 1817
6. Leicester Warren Papers: 'Letters and Papers relative to HRH the Prince Regent's Regiment of Cheshire Yeomanry commanded by Col. Sir J.F. Leicester', DLT/D463/6–7, Cheshire County Council, Archives and Local Studies
7. *Chester Guardian*, 23 March 1820
8. Leicester Warren Papers
9. Knight, *Popular History of England*
10. Leicester Warren Papers
11. *Chester Chronicle*, 1 October 1819
12. Knight, *Popular History of England*

CHAPTER 8

1. Corry, *History of Macclesfield*
2. Henry Heginbotham, *Stockport Ancient and Modern* (2 vols) (Sampson Low, Marston, Searle and Rivington, 1882)
3. Robert Southey, *Letters from England* (Cresset Press, 1951)
4. Thomas de Quincey, *The English Mail Coach and other Writings* (Adam and Charles Black, 1862)
5. Hemingway, *History of the City of Chester*
6. Samuel Smiles, *Lives of the Engineers* (John Murray, 1874)
7. Charles James Apperley ('Nimrod'), *The Chace, the Turf and the Road* (John Murray, 1843)
8. William Barker Daniels, *Rural Sports* (2 vols) (no publisher, 1813)
9. *Chester Chronicle*, 6 May 1796
10. *Chester Chronicle*, 24 April 1818
11. *Chester Courant*, 11 May 1819
12. *The Times*, 11 February 1799

13. *Chester Chronicle*, 24 April 1812
14. *Macclesfield Courier*, 8 June 1822
15. Thomas Baldwin, *Airopaidia* (unknown, 1786)
16. *Chester Courant*, 14 July 1812
17. *Chester Chronicle*, 11 June 1824

CHAPTER 9

1. Smiles, *Lives of the Engineers* (John Murray, 1874)
2. Britton and Brayley, *Beauties of England and Wales*
3. Hemingway, *History of the City of Chester*
4. Stephen Glover, *The History, Gazetteer and Directory of the County of Derby* (Henry Mozley and Son, 1829)
5. Cowdroy, *Directory and Guide*
6. Cowdroy, *Directory and Guide*
7. *Chester Chronicle*, 9 December 1796
8. Batenham, *Stranger's Companion*
9. Hemingway, *History of the City of Chester*

CHAPTER 10

1. Britton and Brayley, *Beauties of England and Wales*
2. *Chester Courant*, 8 July 1794
3. *Chester Courant*, 5 September 1809
4. Henry Holland, *General View of the Agriculture of Cheshire* (unknown, 1808)
5. Britton and Brayley, *Beauties of England and Wales*
6. Britton and Brayley, *Beauties of England and Wales*
7. *Chester Chronicle*, 20 March 1818
8. Cowdroy, *Directory and Guide*
9. Holland, *General View of Agriculture*
10. *Chester Courant*, 19 May 1829
11. *Chester Chronicle*, 26 October 1798 and 20 March 1818
12. *Chester Chronicle*, 25 July 1828
13. *Macclesfield Courier*, 25 April 1829
14. *Chester Chronicle*, 24 April 1829
15. *Chester Chronicle*, 18 July 1828
16. Ormerod, *History of the County Palatine*
17. John Brand, *Observations on the Popular Antiquities of Great Britain* (Henry G. Bohn, 1849)
18. Ormerod, *History of the County Palatine*
19. *Chester Guardian*, 27 April 1820

CHAPTER 11

1. Britton and Brayley, *Beauties of England and Wales*
2. Britton and Brayley, *Beauties of England and Wales*
3. Britton and Brayley, *Beauties of England and Wales*
4. Corry, *History of Macclesfield*
5. Corry, *History of Macclesfield*

6. Peter Gaskell, *The Manufacturing Population of England* (Baldwin and Craddock, 1833)
7. Adam Rushton, *My Life, as Farmer's Boy, Factory Lad, Teacher and Preacher 1821–1909* (unknown, 1909)
8. *Macclesfield Courier*, 18 April 1812
9. *Chester Chronicle*, 10 April 1818
10. *Macclesfield Courier*, 10 April 1824
11. *Macclesfield Courier*, 23 April 1825
12. *Macclesfield Courier*, 9 April 1825
13. *Macclesfield Courier*, 4 March 1826
14. *Macclesfield Courier*, 9 May 1829
15. *The Times*, 4 May 1829
16. *Macclesfield Courier*, 25 April 1829

CHAPTER 12

1. Gaskell, *Manufacturing Population*
2. *Chester Courant*, 16 September 1806
3. Corry, *History of Macclesfield*
4. Britton and Brayley, *Beauties of England and Wales*
5. *Chester Courant*, 25 October 1798
6. *Macclesfield Courier*, 9 February 1822
7. Andrew Ure, *Cotton Manufacture of Great Britain* (Charles Knight, 1836)
8. Edward Baines, *History of the Cotton Manufacture in Great Britain* (H. Fisher, R. Fisher and P. Jackson, 1835)
9. *Chester Chronicle*, 17 April 1812
10. *Chester Chronicle*, 1 May 1812
11. *Chester Courant*, 2 June 1812
12. Richard Guest, *A Compendious History of the Cotton Manufacture* (unknown, 1823)
13. *Chester Chronicle*, 3 April 1818
14. Heginbotham, *Stockport Ancient and Modern*
15. Leicester Warren Papers

CHAPTER 13

1. 'Account of a Visit to the Rock-Salt Mines at Northwich, Cheshire', *Ackermann's Repository of Arts, Literature, Commerce, Manufacturers, Fashion and Politics*, June 1814
2. Britton and Brayley, *Beauties of England and Wales*
3. Pennant, *Journey from Chester to London*
4. Thomas Mortimer, *A General Commercial Dictionary* (unknown, 1819)
5. Cowdroy, *Directory and Guide*
6. Joshua Gilpin, journal entry (in Science Museum, London)
7. Britton and Brayley, *Beauties of England and Wales*
8. Holland, *General View*
9. *Ackermann's Repository*
10. Britton and Brayley, *Beauties of England and Wales*
11. Britton and Brayley, *Beauties of England and Wales*
12. *Gentleman's Magazine*, September 1799

13. D.A. Iredale, 'The Rise and Fall of the Marshalls of Northwich', *Transactions of the Historical Society of Lancashire and Cheshire*, Vol. 117 (1965) 59–82
14. *Chester Courant*, 9 May 1809
15. Smithers, *Liverpool, Its Commerce*
16. Mortimer, *General Commercial Dictionary*
17. Cuthbert William Johnson, *Observations on the Employment of Salt in Agriculture and Horticulture* (unknown, 1828)

CHAPTER 14

1. Hemingway, *History of the City of Chester*
2. Smiles, *Lives of the Engineers*
3. William Williams Mortimer, *History of the Hundred of Wirral* (Whittaker & Co., 1847)
4. George Richardson Porter, *Progress of the Nation* (John Murray, 1851)
5. Porter, *Progress of Nation*
6. Harriet Martineau, *History of the Peace, Vol. II* (Walker, Wise and Company, 1865)
7. *Chester Courant*, 29 June 1830
8. *Chester Chronicle*, 2 July 1830
9. Hemingway, *History of the City of Chester*
10. *Chester Chronicle: Supplement*, 14 December 1832
11. *Chester Chronicle*, 19 October 1832; *Chester Courant*, 23 October 1832

Select Bibliography

CONTEMPORARY WORKS

Contemporary newspaper accounts
Barclay, Rev. James, *Dictionary* (Bungay Edition, 1813)
Batenham, G., *A Stranger's Companion in Chester*, 4th edition (Chester, c.1829)
Batenham, G., *A Visit to the Cathedral Church of Chester* (Chester, c.1829)
Britton, John, and Brayley, Edward W., *The Beauties of England and Wales, Vol. II* (London, 1801)
Byng, John, *Torrington Diaries* (4 vols) (Methuen Library Reprints, 1970)
Cobbett, William, *History of the Regency and Reign of King George IV, Vol. II* (London, 1834)
Cooke, George Alexander, *Topographical and Statistical Description of the County of Chester* (London, no date, c.1803)
Cowdroy, W., *Directory and Guide to the City and County of Chester* (Chester, 1789)
Gilchrist, James P., *Brief Display of the Origin and History of Ordeals, Trials by Battle*, etc. (1823)
Hanshall, J.H., *History of the County Palatine of Chester* (Chester, 1823)
Hemingway, Joseph, *History of Chester* (Chester, 1831)
Holland, Henry, *General View of the Agriculture of Cheshire* (1808)
Ormerod, George, *History of the County Palatine and City of Chester*, 2nd edition (ed. Thomas Helsby) (1882)
Pennant, Thomas, *The Journey from Chester to London* (London, 1811)
Pennant, Thomas, *Tours in Wales* (ed. John Rhys) (Caernarvon, 1883)
Pigot & Co., *Commercial Directory* 1822–3.
Simond, Louis, *Journal of a Tour* (2 vols) (Edinburgh, 1815)
Smithers, Henry, *Liverpool, Its Commerce, Statistics and Institutions* (Liverpool, 1825)
Southey, Robert, *Letters from England* (Cresset Press, 1951)
Wedge, Thomas, *General View of the Agriculture of the County Palatine of Chester* (1794)

GENERAL WORKS

Handbook of Shropshire & Cheshire (John Murray, 1879)
Baines, Edward, *History of the Cotton Manufacture in Great Britain* (Cass reprint, London, 1966)
Bryant, Arthur, *Years of Victory 1802-1812* (Collins, 1975)
Bryant, Arthur, *The Age of Elegance 1812-1822* (Collins, 1950)

Butler, E.M. (ed.), *A Regency Visitor: The English Tour of Prince Pückler-Muskau* (Collins, 1957)
Chadwick, Edwin, *The Sanitary Population of the Labouring Population of Britain, 1842* (ed. M.W. Flinn) (Edinburgh University Press, 1965)
Chaloner, W.H., *Palatinate Studies: Chapters in the Social and Industrial History of Lancashire and Cheshire* (Chetham Society, 1992)
Coward, T.A., *Picturesque Cheshire* (Sherratt & Hughes, 1903)
Crosby, Alan, *A History of Cheshire* (Phillimore, 1996)
Crossley, Fred, *Cheshire* (Robert Hale, 1949)
Earwaker, J.P., *East Cheshire Past & Present, Vol. II* (London, 1880)
Edgcumbe, R. (ed.), *The Diary of Frances, Lady Shelley 1787-1817* (John Murray, 1912)
Green, Henry, *Knutsford: Its Traditions and History* (E.J. Morten, 1969)
Gregg, Pauline, *A Social and Economic History of Britain, 1760-1970* (G. Harrap, 6th edition, 1971)
Harris, B.E. (ed.), *Victoria History of the Counties of England: A History of the County of Chester, Vol. II* (Oxford University Press, 1979)
Harris, B.E. (ed.), *Victoria History of the Counties of England: A History of the County of Chester, Vol. III* (Oxford University Press, 1980)
Hammond, J.L. and Barbara, *The Skilled Labourer* (Allan Sutton, 1995)
Hammond, J.L. and Barbara. *The Town Labourer* (Longman, 1978)
Heginbotham, Henry, *Stockport Ancient and Modern* (2 vols) (Sampson Low, Marston, Searle and Rivington, 1882)
Hibbert, Christopher, *George IV: Prince of Wales* (Readers' Union, 1973)
Hibbert, Christopher, *George IV: Regent and King* (Readers' Union, 1975)
Hughes, Herbert, *Chronicle of Chester 1775/1975* (Macdonald and Jane's, 1975)
Hughes, Thomas, *Stranger's Handbook to Chester* (reprint of 1856 edition, E.J. Morten, 1972)
Ingham, Alfred, *Cheshire: Its Traditions and History* (Edinburgh, 1920)
Kennett, Annette M. (ed), *Georgian Chester* (Chester City Record Office Historical Publications, 1987)
Knight, Charles, *Pictorial Gallery of Arts, Vol. I* (London, c.1860)
Knight, Charles, *Popular History of England* (London, c.1868)
Leach, Joan, *Knutsford: A History* (Phillimore, 2007)
Lewis, C.P. and Thacker, A.T., (eds) *Victoria History of the Counties of England: A History of the County of Chester, vol. V, Part 1* (Boydell & Brewer, 2003)
Lewis, C.P. and Thacker, A.T., (eds), *Victoria History of the Counties of England: A History of the County of Chester, vol. V, Part 2* (Boydell & Brewer, 2005)
Mitchell, S.I., *Food Shortages and Public Order in Cheshire 1757-1812, TLCAS*, Vol. 81, 1982, pp. 42–66.
Morris, William O'Connor, *Napoleon: Warrior and Ruler* (G.P. Putnam's Sons, 1893)
Murray, Venetia, *High Society: A Social History of the Regency Period, 1788-1830* (Viking, 1998)
Phillips, C.B. and Smith, J.H., *Lancashire and Cheshire from AD 1540* (Longman, 1994)
Priestley, J.B., *The Prince of Pleasure* (Sphere Books Ltd, 1971)
Richardson, Joanna, *George IV: A Portrait* (Sidgwick & Jackson, 1966)

Rimmer, Alfred, *Summer Rambles Around Manchester* (John Heywood, c.1890)
Rushton, Adam, *My Life, as Farmer's Boy, Factory Lad, Teacher and Preacher 1821-1909* (Manchester, 1909)
Schama, Simon, *A History of Britain: The Fate of Empire 1776-2000* (BBC Worldwide, 2002)
Smiles, Samuel, *Lives of the Engineers: Brindley and the Early Engineers* (John Murray, 1874)
Sylvester, Dorothy, *A History of Cheshire* (Phillimore, 1980)
Sylvester, Dorothy, and Nulty, Geoffrey (eds), *Historical Atlas of Cheshire,* (Cheshire Community Council 1958)
White, R.J., *Life in Regency England* (B.T. Batsford, 1963)

CHAPTER 1: AN AGE OF CONTRASTS

Gronow, Captain, *The Reminiscences and Recollections of Captain Gronow 1810-1860* (ed. John Raymond) (Bodley Head, 1964)
Harris, R.W., *Romanticism and the Social Order* (Blandford Press, 1969)

CHAPTER 2: CHANGING TIMES

Bagley, J.J. and A.J., *The State of Education in England and Wales, 1833-1968* (Macmillan, 1969)
Bunting, Thomas Percival, *Life of Jabez Bunting* (Harper & Brothers, 1859)
Chaloner, W.H., *The Cheshire Activities of Matthew Boulton and James Watt, Palatinate Studies: Chapters in the Social and Industrial History of Lancashire and Cheshire* (Chetham Society, 1992)
Gérin, Winifred, *Elizabeth Gaskell* (Oxford University Press, 1977)
Slater, George, *Chronicles of Lives and Religion in Cheshire* (London, 1891)

CHAPTER 3: IN THE LATEST STYLE

Brown, A. (ed.), *The Rows of Chester: Chester Rows Research Project* (English Heritage, 1999)
Carrington, Peter (ed.), *English Heritage Book of Chester* (Batsford, 1994)
Champness, John, *Thomas Harrison, Georgian Architect of Chester and Lancaster 1744-1829* (University of Lancaster, 2005)
Cunnington, Phillis, *Costume of Household Servants* (A. & C. Black, 1974)
de Figueiredo, Peter and Treuherz, Julian, *Cheshire Country Houses* (Phillimore, 1988)
Mitchell, S.I., *Retailing in Eighteenth and Early Nineteenth Century Cheshire, THSLC,* Vol. 130, 1981, pp. 37–60
Pevsner, Nikolaus, and Hubbard, Edward, *The Buildings of England: Cheshire* (Penguin Books, 1990)

CHAPTER 4: HIGH LIFE AND LOW

Angus-Butterworth, Lionel M., *Old Cheshire Families and their Seats* (E.J. Morten, 1970)
Apperley, Charles James ('Nimrod'), *The Chace, the Turf and the Road* (John Murray, 1843)

Apperley, Charles James ('Nimrod'), *Memoirs of the Life of the Late John Mytton, Esq.* (Methuen, 1949)

Bevan, R.M., *The Roodee: 450 years of racing in Chester* (Cheshire Country Publishing, 1989)

Burrows, G T., *The Cheshire Hunt* (Chester, no date)

Egerton-Warburton, Rowland E., *Hunting Songs, Ballads, etc.* (Chester, 1834)

Fergusson, Gordon, *The Green Collars: The Tarporley Hunt Club & Cheshire Hunting History* (Quiller Press, 1993)

Huxley, Gervas, *Lady Elizabeth and the Grosvenors* (Oxford University Press, 1955)

Latham, F. (ed.), *Cuddington and Sandiway* (Local History Group, 1975)

Payne, Rev. G.A., *Mrs Gaskell and Knutsford* (Clarkson & Griffiths, 1905)

Yarwood, Derek, *Cheshire's Execution Files* (Breedon Books Publishing, 2007)

CHAPTER 5: A VESTED INTEREST

Huxley, Gervas, *Lady Elizabeth and the Grosvenors* (Oxford University Press, 1955)

Summerson, John, *Georgian London* (Pelican Books, 1962)

CHAPTER 6: SCHOOL FOR SCANDAL

Atkinson, Kate M., *Abduction: The Story of Ellen Turner* (Blenkins Press, 2002)

Blanch, Lesley (ed.), *Harriette Wilson's Memoirs* (Century Publishing, 1985)

Combermere, Rt. Hon. Viscountess Mary and Knollys, Capt. W.W., *Memoirs and Correspondence of Field Marshal Viscount Combermere, Vol. I* (Hurst and Blackett, 1866)

Hone, William, *The Every Day Book and Table Book* (London, 1827)

Lofts, Norah, *Emma Hamilton* (Michael Joseph, 1978)

Neild, Maureen, *Rope Dance* (Cheshire County Council, 1993)

Southey, Robert, *Life of Nelson* (Oxford University Press, 1911)

CHAPTER 7: THE KING'S PEACE

Letters and papers relative to HRH the Prince Regent's Regiment of Cheshire Yeomanry commanded by Col. Sir J.F. Leicester, Bart.: Leicester Warren papers: DLT/D463/6, DLT/D463/7, Cheshire County Council, Archives and Local Studies

Earl of Chester's Regiment Gentry & Yeomanry Casualty Accounts 1803-1815: Leicester Warren papers: DLT/D169/1. Cheshire County Council, Archives and Local Studies

Armstrong, A.B., *The Regiment 1797-1897* (supplementary chapter in Verdin, Lt. Col. Sir Richard, *The Cheshire (Earl of Chester's) Yeomanry 1898-1967* (Birkenhead, 1971))

Bamford, Samuel, *Passages in the Life of a Radical* (Macgibbon & Kee, 1967)

Darvall, Frank O., *Popular Disturbances and Public Order in Regency England* (Oxford University Press, 1969)

Holmes, Richard, *Redcoat* (HarperCollins Publishers, 2001)

Holmes, Richard, *Wellington: The Iron Duke* (HarperCollins Publishers, 2003)
Leary, Frederick, *The Earl of Chester's Regiment of Yeomanry Cavalry 1797-1897* (Edinburgh, 1898)
Marlow, Joyce, *The Peterloo Massacre* (Readers' Union, 1969)
Rigby, Bernard, *Ever Glorious: The History of the 22nd Cheshire Regiment* (Chester, 1982)
Shipp, John, *Memoirs of the Extraordinary Military Career of John Shipp* (ed. H. Manners Chichester) (T. Fisher Unwin, 1890)
Simpson, Frank, *The Chester Volunteers* (Chester, c.1920)
Walmsley, Robert, *Peterloo: The Case Reopened* (Manchester University Press, 1969)

CHAPTER 8: THE GOLDEN AGE OF COACHING

Burke, Thomas, *Travel in England* (B.T. Batsford, 1942)
Daniels, William Barker, *Rural Sports* (1813)
De Quincey, Thomas, *The English Mail-Coach and other Writings* (Adam and Charles Black, 1862)
Gore, John, *Creevey* (John Murray, 1948)
Harper, Charles G., *The Holyhead Road* (Chapman & Hall, 1902)
Harrison, William, *Development of the Turnpike System in Lancashire and Cheshire, TLCAS*, Vol. 4, 1886, pp. 80–92
Hazlitt, William, 'The Letter-Bell', *The Mirror of Literature, Amusement and Instruction* (J. Limbird, 1831)
Reader, W.J., *Macadam* (William Heinemann, 1980)
Smiles, Samuel, *Lives of the Engineers: History of Roads, Metcalfe & Telford* (John Murray, 1874)
Tristram, W. Outram, *Coaching Days and Coaching Ways* (Macmillan, 1910)
Watney, Marylian, *The Elegant Carriage* (J. Allen, 1973)

CHAPTER 9: MAKING A PACKET

Glover, Stephen, *History, Gazetteer and Directory of the County of Derby* (H. Mozley & Son, 1829)
Hadfield, Charles, *The Canal Age* (David & Charles, 1968)
Hadfield, C. and Biddle, G., *The Canals of North West England* (2 vols) (David & Charles, 1970)
Head, Sir George, *A Home Tour through the Manufacturing Districts of England* (Frank Cass, 1968)
Phillips, J., *General History of England Navigation* (1803)
Place, Geoffrey W., *The Rise and Fall of Parkgate, Passenger Port for Ireland 1686-1815* (Chetham Society, 1994)
Priestley, Joseph, *Historical Account of the Navigable Rivers, Canals and Railways of Great Britain* (London, 1831)
Smiles, Samuel, *Brindley and the Early Engineers* (John Murray, 1874)
Willan, T.S., *The Navigation of the River Weaver in the Eighteenth Century* (Chetham Society, 1951)

CHAPTER 10: COUNTRY LIVING

CCALS: DDX 106. James Higginson's Diary 1817–1819
Boyd, Arnold W., *A Country Parish* (Collins, 1951)
Boyd, Arnold W., *The Comberbach (Cheshire) Version of the Soul-Caking Play, TLCAS*, Vol. 44, 1929, pp. 41–55.
Brand, John, *Observations on the Popular Antiquities of Great Britain* (Henry G. Bohn, 1849)
Chambers, J.D. and Mingay, G.E., *The Agricultural Revolution 1750-1880* (B.T. Batsford, 1970)
Davies, C.S, *Agricultural History of Cheshire 1750-1850* (Chetham Society, 1960)
Hammond, J.L. and Hammond, Barbara, *The Village Labourer* (2 vols) (Guild Books, 1948)
Hole, Christina, *Traditions and Customs of Cheshire* (S.R. Publishers, 1970)
Marshall, William, *Review of the Reports to the Board of Agriculture* (London, 1810)
Scard, Geoffrey, *Squire and Tenant: Life in Rural Cheshire 1760-1900* (Cheshire Community Council, 1981)
Wilkes, Sue, 'Soul mates appease the spirits', *The Countryman*, October, 2000

CHAPTER 11: SMOOTH AS SILK

Select Committee on the State of Children Employed in Manufactories. 1816
CCALS DSW/2116/73/5 Apprenticeship indenture of Joseph Bowker, 25 September 1827
Ashton, T.S., *The Industrial Revolution 1760–1830* (Oxford University Press, 1968)
Calladine, A. and Fricker, J., *East Cheshire Textile Mills* (RCHME, 1993)
Chaloner, W.H., *People and Industries* (Frank Cass, 1963)
Corry, John, *History of Macclesfield* (1817)
Davies, C.S. (ed.), *A History of Macclesfield* (Macclesfield Borough Council, 1961)
Earles, John, *Streets and Houses of Old Macclesfield* (M.T.D. Rigg Publications, 1990)
Head, Robert, *Congleton Past and Present* (Congleton, 1887)
Malmgreen, Gail, *Silk Town: Industry and Culture in Macclesfield 1750-1835* (Hull University Press, 1985)
Scott, Sir Walter, *Journal of Sir Walter Scott, Vol. I* (Burt Franklin, 1890)

CHAPTER 12: SPINNING A YARN

Reports of Commissioners, Factories Inquiries Commission: First Report, 1833, XX
Arrowsmith, Peter, *Stockport: A History* (Stockport Metropolitan Borough Council, 1999)
Aspin, Chris, *The Cotton Industry* (Shire Publications, 1995)
Chapman S.D., *The Cotton Industry in the Industrial Revolution* (Macmillan, 2nd edition, 1987)
Collier, Frances, *The Family Economy of the Working Classes in the Cotton Industry 1784-1833* (Manchester University Press, 1964)
Gaskell, P., *Artisans and Machinery* (1835)

Gaskell, P., *The Manufacturing Population of England* (Baldwin and Craddock, 1833)
Gaskell, P., *Prospects of Industry* (Smith, Elder, 1835)
Guest, Richard, *A Compendious History of the Cotton Manufacture* (1823)
Howe, Anthony, *The Cotton Masters 1830-1860* (Oxford Historical Monographs, 1984)
Hutchins, B.L. and Harrison, A., *A History of Factory Legislation* (Frank Cass, 1966)
Kay-Shuttleworth, Dr James, *Moral and Physical Condition of the Working Classes* (1832)
Middleton, Thomas, *Annals of Hyde and District* (Longden Publications, 1973)
Murray, Robert, 'Peter Holland: A pioneer of occupational medicine', *British Journal of Industrial Medicine*, Vol. 49, 1992, pp. 377–386
Rose, Mary B., *The Gregs of Quarry Bank Mill* (Cambridge University Press, 1986)
Turnbull, Geoffrey, *A History of the Calico Printing Industry of Great Britain* (John Sherratt & Son, 1951)
Uglow, Jenny, *Elizabeth Gaskell* (Faber and Faber, 1994)
Unwin, George, *Samuel Oldknow and the Arkwrights* (Manchester University Press, 1924)
Ure, Andrew, *Cotton Manufacture of Great Britain* (Charles Knight, 1836)
Wilkes, Sue, *Narrow Windows, Narrow Lives* (History Press, 2008)

CHAPTER 13: SALT OF THE EARTH

'Account of a Visit to the Rock-Salt Mines at Northwich, Cheshire', *Ackermann's Repository of Arts, Literature, Commerce, Manufacturers, Fashions and Politics*, June 1814, Vol. XI, No. 67, pp. 322–7 (B/NOR.338.2, Northwich Library)
Atkinson, Glen, *The Canal Duke's Collieries* (2nd edition, Neil Richardson, 1998)
Barker, T.C. and Harris, J.R., *A Merseyside Town in the Industrial Revolution: St. Helens 1750-1900* (Liverpool University Press, 1954)
Calvert, Albert F., *Salt in Cheshire* (E. and F. N. Spon, 1915)
Dickinson, Joseph, *Report on the Subject of Landslips in the Salt Districts* (HMSO, 1873)
Furnival, William, *A Statement of Facts ... submitted to ... His Majesty, His Majesty's Ministers and both Houses of Parliament* (1833)
Furnival, William, *Brief Statement of Facts in respect to the Wharton and Marston Saltwork and of the Proceedings taken by Mr Furnival* (London, 1838)
Gilpin, Joshua, Journal entry for 28 October 1796. Transcription by G.D. Twigg from copy in Science Museum, London
Hancock, Harold B. and Wilkinson, Norman B., 'Joshua Gilpin', *Trans. Newcomen Society XXXIII*, 1960–1, pp. 61–2
Iredale, D.A., 'John and Thomas Marshall and the Society for Improving the Salt Trade', *Economic History Review*, Vol. 20, No. 1, April 1967, pp. 79–83
Iredale, D. A., 'The Rise and Fall of the Marshalls of Northwich', *THSLC*, Vol. 117 1965, pp. 59–82
Johnson, Cuthbert William, *Observations on the Employment of Salt in Agriculture and Horticulture* (London, 1828)

Mortimer, Thomas, *A General Commercial Dictionary* (2nd edition, London, 1819)

Rochester, Mary, *Rock Salt Mining in Cheshire* (Salt Museum, Cheshire Libraries and Museums)

Rochester, Mary, *Trade Associations in the Salt Industry* (Salt Museum, Cheshire Libraries and Museums)

Rochester, Mary, *Working Conditions in the Cheshire Salt Industry* (Salt Museum, Cheshire Libraries and Museums)

Samuel, Raphael (ed.), *Miners, Quarrymen and Saltworkers* (History Workshop Series, Routledge & Kegan Paul, 1977)

Squire, Mary, *Social and Environmental Conditions in the Salt Industry* (Salt Museum, Cheshire Libraries and Museums)

Stammers, Michael, *Mersey Flats and Flatmen* (National Museums and Galleries, Liverpool, 1993)

Stonehouse, James, 'Salt and its Manufacture in Cheshire', *THSLC*, Vol. V, 1852–53, pp. 100–17

Twigg, George, *Salt and the Chemical Revolution*, www.saltsense.co.uk

Twigg, George, *Open Pan Salt Making* (Cheshire Museums Service, 1993)

CHAPTER 14: FULL STEAM AHEAD

Report from the Select Committee on the Act for Regulation of Mills and Factories 1841

Butterworth, Edwin, *An Historical Account of the Towns of Ashton-under-Lyne, Stalybridge and Dukinfield* (Ashton, 1842)

Chaloner, W.H., *Social and Economic Development of Crewe* (Manchester University Press, 1973)

Freeling, Arthur, *Freeling's Grand Junction Railway Companion* (Whittaker, 1838)

Kaye, T., *The Stranger in Liverpool* (7th edition, Liverpool, 1823)

McCulloch, J.R., *Statistical Account of the British Empire* (Charles Knight, 1839)

Mcintyre, W.R.S. 'The First Scheme for Docks at Birkenhead and the Proposed Canal across Wirral', *THSLC*, Vol. 124, 1973, pp. 108–27

Martineau, Harriet, *History of the Peace, Vol. II* (Walker, Wise and Company, 1865)

Mortimer, William Williams, *History of the Hundred of Wirral* (Whittaker & Co., 1847)

Porter, George Richardson, *Progress of the Nation* (John Murray, 1851)

Roscoe, Thomas, *Book of the Grand Junction Railway* (Orr, 1839)

Smiles, Samuel, *Lives of the Engineers: George & Robert Stephenson* (John Murray, 1879)

Williams, E.N., *Life in Georgian England* (B.T. Batsford Ltd, 1962)

Abbreviations used:

CCALS: Cheshire and Chester Archives Services.
THSLC: *Transactions of the Historic Society of Lancashire and Cheshire.*
TLCAS: *Transactions of the Lancashire and Cheshire Antiquarian Society.*

Index